THE TRAINER

CSM (R) Mark Gerecht

EDITED BY PRESTON FITZGERALD

6TH EDITION

Published by:

7910 Memorial Parkway Suite F-1

Huntsville, Alabama 35802

256-885-3535

Fax: 256-885-3531

Email: info@mentorenterpisesinc.com

WARNING - DISCLAIMER

This product is designed to provide a source of information concerning the subject matter. It is sold with the understanding that the Corporation (Mentor Publications) and its employees, agents, authors, distributors, officers, publishers, attorneys, assigns, successor parent companies, members, or any other associated entity with Mentor Publications and/or its affiliates are not providing any legal or any other type of professional service. If legal services/opinions or any other type of professional service is required, the reader should seek guidance from a competent professional. It is also understood that the above mentioned individuals and entities shall in no way be held liable (including, without limitation, any and all compensatory, special, general, punitive, and/or statutory damages of any kind), fees, penalties, cost or expenses arising out of the use or the inability to use the product. Furthermore it is understood that the individuals or entities previously mentioned cannot be held liable for any compensatory, special, direct, indirect, incidental, consequential damages, exemplary damages however caused, whether for negligence, breach of contract, warranty, or otherwise. No individual or entity mentioned above previously assumes or can be held legally liable or responsible for the accuracy or completeness of this product. It is further understood and agreed that the terms and conditions set here in supersede any other agreement or understanding concerning access to any product of Mentor Publications through direct or indirect access.

The content of this product is a compilation of information from public domain information (the formatting of which is copyrighted), and the personal (copyrighted) experience of the numerous contributors, and editors. The samples in this product are suggestions, not exact models. Readers should consult regulatory guides for specifics and staff agencies as required. <u>This product is a guide</u>. It does not in any way take precedence over military regulation or local policies and procedures. In all cases, for the purpose of this product, military regulations, local policies, and orders, are considered the governing sources concerning the subject matter. Readers are encouraged to read all relevant material covering the subject involved.

Every effort was made to ensure that this product was complete and accurate at the time of printing. It is possible that mistakes may be found both in content and typography. This product should be used only as a <u>guide</u> and not as the source or ultimate authority.

The purpose of the product is to educate and entertain only. The authors, agents, editors, or publisher shall have no liability or responsibility to any person or entity concerning loss/damage alleged, to be caused or caused by any means directly or indirectly by the information in this product.

By utilizing and purchasing this product the customer agrees and is in strict understanding and agreement that this product is provided without any expressed or implied warranties as to the product's completeness and/or correctness, legal effect or validity.

<u>This product should and can only be used as a guide</u>. It should be modified to fit the situation that exists by seeking guidance from competent professionals including military lawyers, Inspector Generals, Equal Opportunity, proper staff agencies or other competent staff professionals.

No warranty is made or implied with regard the completeness, and/or correctness, legal effect, or validity, of this product in any state or jurisdiction. It is further understood that any person or entity that utilizes this product does so at their own risk with full knowledge that they have a legal obligation, duty and responsibility to ensure the information they provide is in accordance with up to date military law, procedure, regulation, policy, or order. No part of this product shall in anyway substitute for professional guidance or expertise on a subject.

TERMS OF USE

NOTE

In this product the term "commander" refers to commanders at all levels. Some commanders have different levels of authority. The local policy on the authority of a commander should be checked in your area. In addition, any reference to the term "he" should be understood to include both genders.

We trust you will find this book useful. If you have any ideas, suggestions, or comments; please contact the writer directly at: **MENTORPUBS@bellsouth.net**

Dedicated to:

My Lovely Wife Patty,

Our Daughter Shania Ann,

My Loving Parents,

All the Soldiers With Whom I Have Had the Honor to Serve

Contents

PROLOGUE

My goal in developing this book is to provide ideas, invoke thought, and assist leaders in developing training tools that assist in realistic outcome-based training that challenges the Warrior to excel. As we enter the 6th printing of The Trainer I find myself reflecting on the Global War on Terrorism and the impact this war has had with regard to training our Warriors. While it is important to utilize and train on technology, we cannot allow our Warriors to become dependent on technology. We must continue to teach basic methods of navigation, communication, and other perishable combat skills so that our Warriors can adapt to their environment should technology fail.

We used unconventional and asymmetrical tactics against the British during the revolutionary war, the Vietnamese used the same tactics against the us. Guerilla warfare has consistently proven to be a tactic that can be exploited to great advantage against a conventional force. As Leaders it is our responsibility to train the next generation of Leaders and teach them how to adapt, think, be flexible, and fight with high tech equipment while being able to utilize unconventional tactics when appropriate.

The keys to a successful training program are organization, leadership, proper utilization of limited resources, and thinking outside the box. The methods and tools discussed in this book are time tested building blocks used to achieve a successful and challenging training program. A training program must motivate Warriors and inspire their creativity. Here are some suggestions for obtaining training ideas: read the lessons learned from history and current operations, view your current situation or future mission from the eyes of the enemy. Most importantly remember that typically an Army always trains for the last war it fought not the new war. While asymmetric warfare will no doubt have a place in future battles, the new battlegrounds may include rogue nations with weapons of mass destruction, terrorist organizations that have the capability to invoke panic through use of chemical or dirty bombs, economic warfare, and operations aimed at destabilizing governments. At this point, large Cold War-style battles do not seem highly probable, but our armed forces must be prepared to deal with these threats as well. Given the broad spectrum of threats; a focused training program that encourages innovation, and thought is imperative to the success of our Army Forces.

Train your Warriors to operate in the absence of leadership. The true measure of your worth as a Leader is not what happens when you are there, but what happens when you *are not* there!

The Warriors of today are the leaders of tomorrow and the training they receive now will form the foundation of how they will train the next generation of Warriors and will also reflect how they will act as citizens should they choose to exit the service. Incorporate elements of infantry, armor, signal, NBC, engineer, etc into your training. Utilize units that have resources and capabilities you need to complete your mission. Develop a sense of teamwork with other units. Build relationships with other units you may not normally be involved with during day to day operations. This will stimulate friendship/thought and you will learn from the leaders in the unit. You can learn from their training methods, ideas, concepts, and perhaps even be able to build a partnership with a unit that has capabilities you may need in the future. Each type of unit can learn from the other. Competition is good but teamwork makes us successful on the battlefield.

A powerful lesson was learned during the Korean War. Task Force Smith was poorly trained and equipped. They were thrown into battle with devastating consequences. We cannot allow another Task Force Smith. We as leaders can do our part by providing innovative training that challenges the Warrior. Train the Warrior as if their life depended upon it.....because it does and so does yours! There are resource limitations when it comes to training, but rather then focus on limited resources, seize the opportunity to be innovative and still provide quality training.

Chapter One
CONDUCTING A TRAINING ASSESSMENT

Introduction

Before you begin any training program, you must assess your current level of proficiency and establish your goals or end state. In the military, some leaders provide the following advice with regard to invoking organizational change; "Sit back, observe, listen, and wait before you make any changes." For the most part this is sound advice. However, I must state that some changes need to be made immediately. Changes that require immediate action are usually obvious and tend to fall into one of the following categories: immoral, unethical, illegal, or unsafe (life, limb, or potential to cause severe injury). I like to refer to these as the four unforgivable sins of leadership.

How to Implement Change

If you observe a violation that is immoral, unethical, illegal, or unsafe fix it immediately. It should not take seven to 30 days of observation to make a correction for something that is obliviously wrong. Correct known discrepancies upon discovery.

With regard to daily operations, take your time evaluating policies and procedures that seem to be working but may appear to be inefficient in their use of resources or you just don't like the process. If you do not like a policy or procedure, consider the following actions:

1. Ask questions of the individuals responsible for the area or process
2. Talk to the leaders within the organization
3. Talk with the Warriors the policy/procedure effects
4. Make a list of your observations with notes that include the Pros/Cons of the issue.

How Change Occurs

Before making any changes, consider that the changes you want to implement may have already been tried and may have been changed for a specific reason. Understanding why an original decision was made usually enhances your ability to make a sound judgement.

Example - Poor Reason for Change
A procedure was put in place because one person upset someone in a position of authority who was ultimately embarrassed. As a result, a new policy was implemented that affected the entire organization.

Why Nothing Happens

Typically a process or procedure remains in effect for one of three reasons:

1. No one sees a problem or the ability to enhance the efficiency of the operation
2. Individuals see the need for change but are apathetic
3. Individuals see the need for change but believe their ideas, thoughts, suggestions, will not be heard by senior personnel.

The following example can easily illustrate all three of these points.

> **Example - Maintaining the Status Quo**
> When I asked why we processed training schedules in a certain manner I was told "That's how we have always done it since CPT Jones was here." By the way, CPT Jones left 3 years ago. No one saw the need to change the process because they did not see a problem.

The idea is to encourage your Warriors to improve the standard and efficiency of their areas of responsibility. As you observe your element (squad, section, platoon, or company), make note of items you believe need to be changed and be prepared to discuss these issues and allow the team to provide alternatives before you provide your suggestions or changes. You will most likely be surprised at the suggestions and solutions your team comes up with.

Realize your way may not always be the only way. If a leader has an effective method that is legal, moral, ethical, and safe be prepared to examine the results it produces with an objective eye. Keep in mind that we are creatures of habit and change is something that we tend to resist.

Keys to Implementing Change

1. Never implement change for the sake of change
2. Encourage initiative
3. Make sure your Warriors know you care and their ideas, thoughts, and suggestions are valued
4. Understand that the individual who usually performs the work often finds the most efficient way to accomplish the task. Your job is to evaluate the method for safety and seek out opportunities to improve upon their procedure .
5. Be inclusive (solicit suggestions and comments)
6. Let people own their areas of responsibility
7. Make suggestions rather than dictate solutions

Beginning Your Assessment

You should begin your assessment by reviewing FM 7-0 and FM 7-1. You also need to become familiar with the FM's and other manuals that cover collective, individual, and Mission Essential Task List (METL). Once you have reviewed these manuals you should extensively review and understand the unit and next higher unit's METL. Pay particular attention to the relationship between METL, Collective, and Individual tasks. Read and understand the Commander's Annual and Quarterly Training Guidance. Add to this your personal lessons learned and develop a course of action that fosters teamwork.

How to Assess Training Effectiveness

The following questions and statements should assist in providing insight into your element's (squad, section, platoon, company) training effectiveness. Use these items to help stimulate your thought process.

1. Is the training schedule posted in the element area?
2. How far out is the training scheduled posted? 4-6 weeks should be required.
3. Are next day training events reviewed with key leaders during daily key leaders meeting?
4. Are Warriors kept informed by unit leaders?
5. Do Warriors know what items to bring to the next training session?
6. Ask an individual identified on the training schedule to review their training plan with you. Is there a training outline?

7. Have resources been identified? (training aids/training areas)
8. Have discrepancies been addressed with the key leader?
9. Has an alternative method of instruction been identified?
10. Has the key leader (PSG/1SG) conducted pre-execution checks with the trainer at least two weeks prior to the training event?
11. Has the location of the training been properly identified by eight-digit grid coordinate (or GPS coordinates) and strip map?
12. Does the training support the METL?
13. Have transportation needs been addressed?
14. Have all external coordination requirements been completed?
15. Ask trainers how much notification they were given to prepare their training.
16. Ask Warriors who attended training to discuss positive and negative aspects of the session. If Warriors don't speak up, look for non-verbal signs that they may fear commenting or are otherwise uncomfortable.
17. Discuss with the Warriors their view of the training program as conducted to date (at the squad, platoon, and company level).
18. Solicit ideas for improving training.
19. What type of training would the Warriors/leaders like to see in the future?
20. Do not take any comments personal! Ensure your Warriors and Leaders understand this.

Processing the Information you Gather

Once you have considered all the information listed above and organized your notes and observations, you should have a solid foundation to adequately assess your element's training program from an external point of view.

The next step in the process is to gather information from your key leaders. You should notify your key leaders that you will conduct a meeting to discuss the training program. Encourage them to bring ideas and suggestions to the meeting. Ask them to actively seek opinions from the Warriors in the unit. Ensure that you give the key leaders adequate time to prepare for the meeting (at least three to five days).

When conducting this meeting you have at least two options. The first choice and recommended course of action is to allow the team to speak first. This way, they begin to say what's on their mind with no bias from your point of view. The second option is that you begin by discussing your observations and assessment from an external view. In my opinion this could prevent or obstruct the free flow of information.

Regardless of the approach you choose, solicit comments and suggestions from the key leaders. Ensure that they understand you are requesting their input in order to develop a more effective training plan; after all, the key leaders are the individuals that must execute the training guidance. Encourage innovation and new ideas, but do not allow the meeting to turn into a complaint session. Ensure they understand this is a team effort and that good leaders share ideas. Typically a leader who stands above his peers is not sharing. They are trying to make themselves look good at the expense of others.

The goal of this meeting is to get all leaders to share ideas. In this way you develop a plan that everyone owns. In addition, you need to identify the leaders that are not pulling their weight and put them in charge of leading a project so that the others see they are being held accountable. Responsibility and accountability are a two way street.

A quote I heard from a leader in my career:

"The Mission of a Leader: HOG THE BLAME! SHARE THE GLORY!"

In the ideal situation you should be able to hammer out the major points of your training plan with the key leaders present. Most likely this will be a positive learning experience for all involved. An informal setting might be a good idea, pizza at lunch, an informal get together after work, a BBQ, etc. Choose an enjoyable location where you can brainstorm and get to know each other.

After the meeting is complete, review your observations with the suggestions and comments of the key leaders. Formulate your final plan and present it to your key leaders. Ideally, your plan should be presented in the form of a draft training SOP and draft training plan. These documents will standardize the procedures across the element and ensure that everyone understands the standard. Get feedback from your key leaders and then go final with the documents.

These actions should ensure that all members of your element understand the expectations and know that you will hold them accountable for the standards set forth in the SOP. You can view a sample of an SOP in: Tools of the Trade Volume 1.

Summary of Actions

1. Review FM 7-0 and FM 7-1
2. Review Commander's Training Guidance.
3. Review METL, Collective, and Individual Tasks, Battlefield Operating System (BOS) matrix.
4. Make changes to items that require immediate attention.
5. Conduct your own assessment of unit training.
6. Schedule a meeting with key leaders to discuss training.
7. Discuss your thoughts and observations.
8. Encourage comments and suggestions.
9. Hammer out the basics of your training plan.
10. Develop a draft training SOP.
11. Submit the SOP to the key leaders for comments and review.
12. Finalize the SOP and make it the standard for unit training.

Resources

Publications for Review

1. AR 350-1   Army Training and Leader Development
2. FM 7-0   Training for Full Spectrum Operations
3. FM 7-1   Battle Focused Training
4. Applicable Mission Training Plans (MTPs)
5. Applicable Soldier Training Plans (STPs)

Local Information for Review

1. Local Training Policies/Procedures
2. Commander's annual and quarterly training guidance
3. AARs from previous training events
4. AARs from previous deployments
5. Unit METL
6. Next higher HQ's METL
7. IG/CIP inspection results
8. CTT results
9. APFT results
10. Weapon qualification results

Chapter Two
CONDUCTING A TRAINING MEETING

Introduction

The success of training depends upon the amount of emphasis training receives from the chain of command. One way to provide that emphasis is to ensure that your training meetings are conducted in an organized and efficient manner. The training meeting is the function that guides, refines, and shapes a unit training program. A lack of emphasis and organization is detrimental to a successful training event. The First Sergeant (1SG), Commander, Training NCO, Operations Sergeant, and other key leaders are critical to the success of this meeting.

Preparation for the Training Meeting

Prior to the training meeting the Commander, 1SG, and key leaders should review the AARs from the previous week's training and any past AARs that pertain to upcoming training. It is essential that the unit incorporate lessons learned and suggestions gathered during the AAR process.

Incorporating lessons learned serves two purposes. First, it improves the quality and effectiveness of the training. Second, it shows the Warriors that you truly care about their ideas. Let the Warriors know you are reading the AARs. Give a shout out in formation to Warriors who come up with good ideas or observations! When Warriors know you care and that their suggestions make a difference, they tend to be become more involved in the AAR process. The end result is a win for everyone.

Note: Consider posting the suggestions and ideas from recent AARs that have been approved for future training on your unit bulletin board. This provides feedback to the Warriors and lets them know that the chain of command is proactive in accepting new methodologies or approaches to training.

Once AARs have been reviewed, use the "Training Meeting Agenda Worksheet" (see blank form in this chapter) to compile your notes from the AARs and your observations of the previous week's training. The left side of the form is for notes made prior to the training meeting and the right side is for notes made during the training meeting. This form is also used to hammer out any questions the Commander may have for the next three training weeks (See completed example in this chapter). It may be necessary to have one sheet per platoon or section, depending upon how your unit is structured.

The individuals listed below should consider the following suggestions in preparing for a training meeting:

1. Commander:
    a. Update training calendars.
    b. Make sure platoon leaders are prepared for training meeting.
    c. Discuss training plans with the Executive Officer (XO) and 1SG to make training more effective.
    d. Fill out left side of the training meeting agenda worksheet.
2. XO:
    a. Ensure that the motor sergeant and supply sergeant are prepared for training meeting.
    b. Ensure all service schedules are coordinated with the battalion motor officer.
    c. Work closely with the S4 and support agencies concerning all classes of supply required for training.
    d. Coordinate and incorporate CBRN, Commo, DFAC, and Weapons maintenance into the unit training schedule.

e. Place scheduled maintenance requirements on the training schedule and go over it during the training meeting. This provides command emphasis for the maintenance program. Also consider that spot checking maintenance lets leaders and Warriors know you are serious and will hold them accountable for their equipment.

Note: Lead by example. When Warriors see senior leaders cleaning their weapons, pulling maintenance on their vehicles, radios, etc... the respect gained is immense. Nothing but good comes from troops realizing they have Officers and NCOs who don't mind getting dirty once in awhile and taking care of their own equipment. This is called Service Leadership.

3. 1SG:
   a. Ensure that platoon sergeants and other NCOs are prepared for training meeting.
   b. Review leader books on a random basis.
   c. Coordinate with the Operations Sergeant on current battalion taskings.
   d. Determine if the unit or a specific section is overtasked.
   e. What taskings are projected in the next 6-8 weeks?
   f. What quarterly events are expected to take place and could interfere with unit operations or training?
   g. Make sure the leaders (to include the officers, along with the Operations Sergeant) are prepared to have a huddle.
   h. Verify the meeting area is set up and ready.
   i. What task have you selected?
   j. Why have you selected these tasks?
   k. How do these tasks tie in with the shortfalls and assessments of the Company CDR , BN CDR and BDE CDR?
   l. If these tasks do not directly support the assessment, how can you support your assessment for training so that the CDR can fight your fight and support your training when he briefs the next higher CDR?
   m. Has your training request been submitted?
   n. Have instructors and assistant instructors been identified?
   o. What measures have been taken to reduce risk?
   p. When was the last time you trained on these tasks? If recent why are you training on it again? Support your rationale.
   q. What actions have you taken to junior leaders and Warriors in this training?

4. Platoon Leader/Sergeant:
   a. Coordinate all details that support training.
   b. Ensure lesson plans are developed.
   c. Keep training books up to date.
   d. Understand events may conflict with training (examples include: key personnel going on leave, and key equipment being down).
   e. Attempt to minimize training resource conflicts.
   f. Develop a program that trains junior Warriors to teach and lead. For example: In the middle of a class on convoy procedures the instructor is taken out by an IED. Can a junior Warrior (assistant instructor) take over? What would happen if this was combat and he was next in charge?

g. Develop training challenges into a training event. These challenges provide a great learning experience. When utilizing this technique capitalize on what was done well. Discuss mistakes but also let Warriors learn from their mistakes. Warriors need to understand that learning from mistakes during training is accepted. It helps them grow as leaders and teaches them to make better decisions.

Note: If platoon sergeants and leaders do not complete their tasks and coordinate properly, the proposed training will most-likely be shot down at the training meeting. Do your homework. Plan, organize, prepare, and coordinate the training. Be able to explain the purpose of your training and how it supports the mission. Describe how, upon completion of this training, the unit will be better prepared to execute its mission.

How to be Successful at a Training Meeting

1. Schedule a training rehearsal well in advance.
2. Rehearse at the actual training site if possible.
3. Leaders should:
   a. Observe trainers to improve weak areas and highlight strengths.
   b. Coach the trainer until the trainer is comfortable with the tasks.
   c. Ask questions of the trainer to check technical/tactical proficiency.
4. The trainer should demonstrate or review the evaluation portion of the training during the training meeting (if applicable).
5. Submit training aid requirements at least six weeks out.
6. Pick up training aids two weeks prior to training to allow for rehearsal.

Training Meetings: Who Attends & Their Roles

Attendees will vary depending on the structure of your unit but on average the following personnel should attend the training meeting:

1. <u>Commander</u>: Responsible for all training events. Conducts the meeting.
2. <u>Executive Officer</u>: Must be prepared to assume duties of the commander and run the meeting. Therefore it is extremely important that the commander and XO communicate effectively on all issues that affect training.
3. <u>Platoon Leaders/Platoon Sergeants</u>: Responsible for conducting training assessment and identifying tasks that need training. They must be able to:
   a. Plan training
   b. Rehearse the trainers
   c. Evaluate the squad/section leaders
   d. Select opportunity training
   e. Conduct pre-execution checks
   f. Assure that Warriors are prepared for and attend training
   g. Conduct platoon training meetings
   h. Brief the collective task proficiency of their element
4. <u>First Sergeant</u>: Responsible for:
   a. Keeping his finger on the pulse of unit training
   b. Monitoring all facets of Warrior training and battle tasks
   c. Ensuring substandard training is corrected
   d. Reviewing training plans

e. Checking training execution
f. Providing feedback to subordinate leaders
g. Mentoring NCOs and Officers in different training methods
h. Encouraging an environment that helps leaders to share innovative ways to coach, teach, and train Warriors
i. Ensuring unit leaders are enforcing Army standards fairly
j. Encouraging the use of training books
k. Balancing training between technical and tactical skills
l. Ensuring the Warrior ethos is instilled in the unit
m. Ensuring pre-execution checks are completed
n. Spot checking platoons and squads
o. Taking a critical look at all facets of safety operations and pushing this responsibility down to the lowest level
p. Encouraging leaders to learn by doing
q. Allowing forgivable mistakes
r. Mentoring Warriors to improve without degrading them
s. Being hands on and out front
t. Ensuring that platoon sergeants and leaders are competent in the training they are instructing so that Warriors have confidence in their leaders.

5. <u>Motor Sergeant/Motor Officer</u>:
   a. Brings out maintenance-related problems that could conflict with or prevent training.
   b. Scheduling of all maintenance service should be listed on the training schedule (maintenance means all equipment CBRN, Commo, Weapons, Vehicles, etc).
   c. Identifies maintenance related trends or problems that could indicate areas that require maintenance training at the operator or leader level.

6. <u>CBRN NCO</u>:
   a. Brings out training shortfalls that may exist in the area of CBRN or related problems that could conflict with or prevent training.
   b. All CBRN maintenance requirements should be identified on the training schedule.
   c. Identify any issues that may indicate that soldiers or leaders are not properly trained in a specific area relating to CBRN.

7. <u>Training NCO or Operations NCO</u>: Holds a critical position in the unit training program. He can make or break the unit.
   a. Must be forward-looking and proactive not only in terms of training, but in terms of coordination with the BN S-3 as to what taskers are outstanding and what quarterly events are on the horizon.
   b. The Company Commander and 1SG depend upon this individual to ensure accuracy of training schedules, coordination with both internal and external elements, and accuracy of records.
   c. The training NCO must inform the chain of command of issues that may affect training.
   d. During the training meeting, the training NCO should be able to tell the Commander what elements of training have been completed and what elements are required to ensure a future successful training event (i.e., identify the roadblocks to training).
   e. Should be able to identify what elements of the unit have not submitted required documents per the unit training SOP. The training NCO should first try to resolve this problem with the platoon sergeant and leader. When this fails, he must raise the flag to the command level for action.

8. <u>Supply NCO</u>: Brings out any shortfalls from the supply arena that may interfere with or prevent a successful training event. In addition, all 10% inventories and other major supply activities that require coordination with other elements should be placed on the training schedule. Status of food rations, water, blanks, and other training equipment should also be brought up at this time.

9. <u>Others as designated by the Commander</u>: May include section sergeants, dining facility NCO, driver's training NCO, Commo NCO, etc.

Time and Place

Training meetings should be held at the same time and place each week. They should follow the battalion training meetings within two days, so that any information gathered during the battalion meeting may be incorporated into the company training meeting. Try to pick a time that does not conflict with other unit requirements and does not delay the normal release of Warriors. The meeting location should be determined by considering the following factors:

1. Is the site easily accessible to all?
2. How many people will attend?
3. Is the environment comfortable?
4. As a general rule, a training meeting should not exceed one hour.
5. Sometimes a standing environment may be preferred as it tends to keep the meeting short (if you have your stuff together)!

Items to Bring to the Training Meeting

1. Company battle rosters
2. Training meeting worksheet
3. METL with current assessment
4. Long- and short-range training calendars
5. Training schedules (previous week's and future approved)
6. Maintenance schedule (motor pool, NBC, dining facility)
7. Inspection schedule
8. Supply inventory schedule
9. Status of resources requested for training
10. Leader books
11. Battalion/company duty rosters
12. Taskings
13. School schedules
14. Platoon assessment work sheets
15. Pre-execution checklists
16. Leave Rosters

Example Agenda

An agenda for the training meeting may include the following items:

1. Completed training
2. Next week's training
3. Near-term training (four-six weeks out)

4. Future training (seven weeks and out)
5. Comments from members of the meeting
6. Comments from Commander/1SG

Conducting the Training Meeting

The training meeting should be conducted in three phases; the assessment phase (completed training), the coordination phase, and the future planning phase. By following this pattern all areas should be covered.

Assessment Phase

The assessment phase seeks to discover the effectiveness of all training conducted since the last training meeting. The Commander gathers information from key leaders and combines it with his personal observations and his review of past AARs, and comes up with an assessment. Based upon the commander's assessment, the unit may be considered trained, untrained, or in need of practice. If the element is not trained in the task, the event should be rescheduled. Some questions that you may consider asking are:

1. Why was this element's training so successful or productive?
2. Why was this training not productive?
3. Why were the trainers unprepared?
4. Why was coordination for _____ not properly conducted?
5. How can we do these things better next time?
6. Why was the AAR worksheet not properly filled out?
7. Before you determine that your element is untrained, consider the following:
    a. Is it because you are new to the unit or element?
    b. Remember each Warrior comes to the unit with a level of experience and a set of skills. When you say they are untrained you are making a bold statement. Basically, you are saying they are unfamiliar with the skills or that they lack the experience and proper training to do the job or task effectively.
    c. Make sure you balance this decision against the training days you submit in your USR reporting.
    d. Rarely is a unit, section, squad untrained in an area. They may need practice in an area or need to develop teamwork in an area. If you are sure an element is untrained, ensure you have a solution and be prepared to defend your decision.

Coordination Phase

After the commander's assessment, the meeting will proceed to the coordination phase. The purpose of this phase is to ensure that all requirements for future training have been coordinated. These coordination requirements may include:

1. Reservation of training areas
2. Range certification
3. Ammunition pickup
4. External vehicle transportation
5. Dining facility considerations
6. Medical support
7. Engineer support
8. Trainer rehearsal

9. External equipment considerations

Attempt to hammer out all coordination activities at this phase. In-depth coordination requirements may need to be handled off-line. Some questions that you may consider asking during this phase are:

1. Have training areas been reserved?
2. Have ammunition requirements been identified and submitted?
3. Have ammunition pickup and return dates been coordinated?
4. Have meal requirements been identified?
5. Have any external support requirements been identified?
6. Have transportation arrangements been made?
7. Have combat lifesaver bags been inventoried?
8. Are combat lifesaver certifications up to date?
9. Are range certifications up to date?
10. Have lessons learned (AARs) been incorporated into the training?
11. Is the training outline prepared?
12. Is the training book up to date?
13. Have fuel requirements been identified?
14. Is the required amount of fuel available for training?
15. Can you coordinate with a sister unit to gain added benefits from the training?

Future Planning Phase

During the future planning phase, subordinate leaders work with the commander to develop future training activities based on the Commander's assessment, platoon assessment, and quarterly training guidance. Some questions to consider are:

1. Does this training support the METL?
2. Does this training track with the quarterly training guidance?
3. Should the entire unit participate in this training (rather than just one platoon)?

The Commander should allow everyone at the meeting to offer input in each of the three meeting phases. Soliciting ideas, suggestions, and observations from these individuals may reveal different points of view. Leaders, Warriors, and the training usually benefit from the exchange of information and improved communications.

Certifying Leaders and Trainers

To ensure quality training, key leaders should conduct rehearsals and have the trainers present training outlines, risk assessments, training books, and other required materials for review. During this process the leaders correct shortcomings and ensure that all elements are in place for a successful training event. The following chart displays who should conduct these events.

Size of Element	Trainer	Certifier	Validation
Individual	Squad Leader	Platoon Sergeant	First Sergeant
Section	Platoon LDR/SGT	CDR/1SG	BN CDR/CSM
Company	BN CDR	BDE CDR	ADC

Thoughts to Consider

The following is a list I used to minimize my time on repetitive training tasks. These items saved time and added to the quality of the training.

1. Develop a Training SOP. The SOP should contain information regarding:
    a. Timeline requirements for submitting training
    b. How to submit for training aids
    c. The format for submitting proposed training
    d. Who is responsible for picking up/signing for training aids
    e. Certification requirements for ranges and training areas
    f. Certification requirements for combat lifesavers
    g. Uniform required for training events
    h. What the training book must contain

It should also contain examples of the forms and how to properly fill them out. A proposed training sheet should include all information necessary to make entries on the training schedule and procedures for submitting changes to the training schedule, etc.

2. Develop a proposed training worksheet: This worksheet will help the training NCO input information for the training schedule and should identify all areas that require coordination. (See example at the end of this chapter.)
3. Establish a training library: While manuals are important, I would suggest that you concentrate on establishing files on lesson outlines. These outlines will save valuable time. There is no sense in doing the work twice if it already exists and is of professional quality. This was a big hit in previous units. The idea is to make sure that every outline meets the standards. Have all leaders turn in a copy of their outlines to the 1SG, Ops Sgt, or Commander during the company training meeting. Then the outlines can be filed in the training library. It is also a good idea to save the files in digital format. Leaders may sign out copies of the lesson plans or you may email them digital copies of the lesson.
4. Establish a standardized lesson plan or outline for your unit: By doing this all lesson outlines in your library will be consistent with each other. Be sure to incorporate items such as task, condition, standard, safety considerations, risk assessments, etc.
5. Develop a training book: Each element in your unit that conducts training should be required to have a training book. This book should contain:
    a. All current and future (approved) training schedules
    b. Training outlines for the day's training
    c. Risk assessment for the training being conducted
    d. Unit METL matrix tasks
    e. A training status report
    f. Standardized AAR format
    g. Pre-execution checks for conducting training
    h. Training exemption approvals for individuals not attending training.

Each element is responsible for updating its book and must bring the book to rehearsals and training meetings.

6. Establish an AAR review file: Maintain copies of all AARs in the training office. Organize them in one filing system by type of training, or in some other way that allows you to quickly review them and incorporate them into future training. One method may be to group AARs by the type of training and then consolidate all changes onto a single piece of paper. These changes will then be incorporated into future training.

7. Satisfying other training requirements: Depending upon the structure of your unit, you may be tasked with other mandatory training. One way I handled this in the past was to incorporate these events into weekly training. For example:

    a. Warrior Tasks and Battle Drills: Since Warrior Tasks and Battle Drills are mandatory requirements, each week I would have two testable tasks on the training schedule. Each platoon has to conduct opportunity training during the week. The platoon sergeant or 1SG would certify all testers in each platoon. During Sergeants Time Training these two tasks were tested. The appropriate documentation was submitted to the training office each week. This avoided an end-of-year rush to complete the training, and meant that we did not have to close the unit down for a round of CTT testing. This method requires close supervision from unit leadership. It worked because it had command emphasis; the leaders and Warriors knew we were serious and would retrain/retest for substandard performance. This included testing officials and Warriors being tested. The Commander and I checked the training and if we caught someone not testing to standard we dealt with the tester and their supervisor The Warrior was retested. Needless to say, word traveled fast that substandard performance and lack of integrity was unacceptable. In addition we set the example by ensuring we were tested on the skills.

    b. First Aid and NBC Tasks: These were also incorporated into our weekly training day following the same procedures as above.

By implementing these training plans, the unit was able to accomplish multiple requirements and sustain proficiency. In addition, each training book had the required documentation for each training task evaluated. These documents would be turned into the training room at the conclusion of training and then transcribed to unit records. The training was conducted and documented.

Company Huddles

Huddles are quick meetings to put out last-minute changes. These meetings should include key leaders and should be conducted before the first formation of the day. Huddles are an excellent means for addressing last-minute issues such as changes to training, pre-execution checks, special or new command guidance, maintenance, and personnel status changes. Yes, this happens before formation. That means leaders have to show up early. That's part of being a leader! The goal is to not keep the Warriors late. You want to get them out as soon as the daily mission is done. When this becomes the norm, Warriors don't mind as much when they have to work late. Morale is kept high because they know their leaders care and that they keep the unnecessary time-wasters to a minimum.

Platoon Meetings

These meetings closely model the training meeting, but they have three main objectives: gather information from junior leaders concerning training, discuss preparation for upcoming training, and solicit training ideas for future training. The following individuals should attend: platoon leader, platoon sergeant, squad leaders, and section sergeants. These meetings should also keep a close eye on Warrior issues and family issues. This is especially important if the issues need to be raised to the chain of command. You may not need to address the issue in the meeting, but shortly after inform platoon leadership of issues requiring their attention. Warrior and family care is vital to our success.

To help ensure a successful meeting, try having a standing meeting (this should help keep the meeting short). Make meetings mandatory and conduct them at the same time and place each week. Enforce the use of leader and training books, and focus on training issues-- not administrative issues. The only admin issues that should surface during these meetings should be hot Warrior issues. Even those should normally be taken offline after the meeting.

Consider adding the following items to the remarks block of your training schedules: (It will help to remind leaders of these sensitive issues)

1. Vehicle service schedule
2. All inventories
3. AOAP schedule
4. TMDE schedule
5. Counseling due dates (when monthly's and quarterly's are due)

Comments on Training

These are some favorite comments concerning training and leadership:

1. "If you are the shining star and everyone else is substandard or below you, you are not a team player!" You are not sharing your knowledge; you are not working or helping others! Therefore, I do not need you. Those are hard words, but think about it. No one needs someone who is out to make himself look good.

2. "THIS is NCO Business": Here are my thoughts on this comment:
   a. If it was NCO business we would not need Officers!
   b. Either the NCO who said this is not squared away or is insecure when he is being checked.
   c. The Officer that states this tends to be lazy not wanting to work or check on his/her Warriors.
   d. My answer to both the Officer and the NCO: It Is Leader Business we work together as a team!

3. Checking vs Micromanagement:
   a. "I don't care who you told, who did you check? CHECK the CHECKER!"
   b. Someone has got to be checking and rechecking. There is a level of trust each of us must have in each other, but checking is not a breach of trust. It is a duty and a responsibility we have to each other.
   c. There is a fine line between checking and micromanagement. Remember we are not perfect and we all miss things.

4. We have strong points and weak points. We complement each other. Focus on each other's strengths.

5. Share your knowledge. Your leaders will pick up on the fact that you are sharing and you will shine! You will hover slightly above the rest, but they will be closer to you, respect you, look up to you, and the team will be tight! This all makes a more combat effective element.

Sample Documents

The following worksheets and matrixes may assist you in developing your own tools. I have also included an AAR format. I used these tools in each of my units. It was part of the training SOP and assisted trainers in completing the training worksheet required for each training event. These documents were valuable and helped ensure all areas of training had been reviewed prior to being approved.

METL TO COLLECTIVE TASK TRAINING MATRIX AS OF4/3/2008

COLLECTIVE TASKS	METL TASKS					BATTLE FIELD OPERATING SYSTEM					
	Alert & Marshal	Deploy	Occupy Area of Operation	Defend Assigned Area	Preserve the Force	INTEL	FIRE SUPPORT	MOBILITY COUNTER MOBILITY & SURVIVABILITY	AIR DEFENSE	CSS	COMMAND & CONTROL
Conduct Unit Recall	X										X
Coordinate SRP	X							X			
Implement Family Support Plan	X				X						
Move to APOE, RPOE, or SPOE Marshaling Area	X										X
Deploy Elements By Air		X									
Deploy Elements By Land		X									
Deploy Elements By Sea		X									
Perform Risk Management Procedures		X			X			X			X
Defend assigned area			X				X	X	X		
Establish Command & Control			X								X
Establish Communication			X	X				X			X
Combat Battlefield Stress					X			X			X
Employ Crew Serve Weapons				X				X			
Establish & Perform TOC Operations			X	X							X
Conduct Split Base Operatons	X				X			X			X
Conduct Family Support Meetings					X						X
Maintain Equipment & Personnel Readiness					X			X			
Conduct Operations in an NBC Environment					X			X			
Perform Field Sanitations					X			X			
Perform Unit Level Intelligence Functions				X	X	X					
Execute Movement Plan		X	X					X			X
Operate Unit Supply					X			X		X	
Perform Administrative Functions					X			X			
Perform Grave Registration Functions					X						X

COLLECTIVE TO INDIVIDUAL TASK TRAINING MATRIX AS OF 3/10/2009

COLLECTIVE TASKS (columns) vs **INDIVIDUAL TASKS** (rows)

INDIVIDUAL TASKS	Conduct Unit Recall	Coordinate SRP	Implement Family Support Plan	Move to APOE, RPOE, or SPOE, Marshaling Area	Deploy Elements by Air	Deploy Elements by Land	Deploy Elements by Sea	Perform Risk Management Procedures	Defend Assigned Areas	Establish Command & Control	Establish Communication	Combat Battlefield Stress	Employ Crew Sreve Weapons	Establish & Perform TOC Operations	Conduct Split Base Operations	Conduct Family Support Meetings	Maintain Equip & Personnel Readiness	Conduct Operations in NBC	Perform Field Sanitation Functions	Perform Unit Level Intel Functions	Execute Movement Plan	Operate Unit Supply	Perform Administrative Functions	Perform grave Registration Functions
Prepare For Movement																								
Alert & Assemble the Force	X	X																						
Brief Family Members on Situation			X													X								
Issue Combat Equip.										X							X							
Outload & Deploy Force				X	X	X	X																	
Issue a Warning Order	X									X														
Issue an Operations Order										X														
Issue a Frago Order										X														
Conduct Route Recon										X														
Coordinate Supply Requirements																								
Develop/Implement load plans																								
Organize Convoy @ Staging Area					X	X	X																	
Inspect Personnel,Equip & Loads				X																				
Assemble, Brief, & Dispatch Adv Party																	X							
Depart Staging Area				X	X	X	X														X			
Report SP, CP, & Closure Reports										X				X										
Operate Vehicles in Blackout Drive																	X				X	X		
Maintain Driver's License On Unit Vehicles																	X				X			
FIGHT																								
Recognize Friendly/ Threat Vehicles									X												X			
Estimate Range									X															
Send Salute Report									X															
React to Sniper Fire									X															
Defend Against Unblocked Ambush									X															
Defend Against Blocke Ambush									X															

COLLECTIVE TO INDIVIDUAL TASK TRAINING MATRIX AS OF 3/10/2009

COLLECTIVE TASKS

INDIVIDUAL TASKS	Conduct Unit Recall	Coordinate SRP	Implement Family Support Plan	Move to APOE, RPOE, or SPOE Marshaling Area	Deploy Elements by Air	Deploy Elements by Land	Deploy Elements by Sea	Perform Risk Management Procedures	Defend Assigned Areas	Establish Command & Control	Establish Communication	Combat Battlefield Stress	Employ Crew Sreve Weapons	Establish & Perform TOC Operations	Conduct Split Base Operations	Conduct Family Support Meetings	Maintain Equip & Personnel Readiness	Conduct Operations in NBC	Perform Field Sanitation Functions	Perform Unit Level Intel Functions	Execute Movement Plan	Operate Unit Supply	Perform Administrative Functions	Perform grave Registration functions
Call for Indirect Fire									X															
Use Close Air Support									X															
Evacuate Wounded									X															
Prepare Casualty Witness Statement																							X	
Perform Maint on Assigned Weapon									X															
Perform Maint on Crew Served WPNS									X															
Load, Reduce Stoppage on Unit WPNS									X															
Prepare a Range Card									X															
Employ Hand Grenades									X															
Install, Fire, & Recover M18 Claymore Mine									X															
Move Under Direct Fire									X															
Prepare Casualty Feeder Card																							X	
AIR DEFENSE																								
Reorganize After Air Attack									X															
Implement Passive Air Defense Measures									X															
Engage Hostile Aircraft with Small Arms									X															
Implement Active Air Defense Measures									X															
DEFEND																								
React to Indirect Fire									X															
React to Flares									X															
Construct Unit Defense Plan									X															
Practice Noise & Light Discipline									X															
Collect & Report Information									X											X				
Use Night Vision Goggles									X															

COLLECTIVE TO INDIVIDUAL TASK TRAINING MATRIX AS OF 3/10/2009

COLLECTIVE TASKS

INDIVIDUAL TASKS	Conduct Unit Recall	Coordinate SRP	Implement Family Support Plan	Move to APOE, RPOE, or SPOE Marshalling Area	Deploy Elements by Air	Deploy Elements by Land	Deploy Elements by Sea	Perform Risk Management Procedures	Defend Assigned Areas	Establish Command & Control	Establish Communication	Combat Battlefield Stress	Employ Crew Sreve Weapons	Establish & Perform TOC Operations	Conduct Split Base Operations	Conduct Family Support Meetings	Maintain Equip & Personnel Readiness	Conduct Operations in NBC	Perform Field Sanitation Functions	Perform Unit Level Intel Functions	Execute Movement Plan	Operate Unit Supply	Perform Administrative functions	Perform grave Registration functions
Employ Night Sights									X															
Employ Physical Security Measures									X															
Employ OPSEC Measures																				X				
Process Captured Documents																								
Evacuate EPW																				X				
Construct Indv. Fighting Postions									X											X				
Establish Observation Post									X															
COMMUNICATE																								
Send a Radio Message											X													
Operate FM Radio											X													
Install/Operate TA312											X													
Use SOI											X													
Erect OE 254											X													
MAINTAIN																								
Repair Inoperable Equipment																								
Perform Org. Maint. on Equipment																	X							
Request Supplies																						X		
Order Supplies																						X		
Request Basic Load																						X		
Provide Mail Service																							X	
Evacuate Remains												X					X							X
Request GRREG Team																	X							
Conduct Transactions with an SSA																						X		
NAVIGATE																								
Identify Terrain Features																					X			
Determine Grid Coordinates																					X			

COLLECTIVE TO INDIVIDUAL TASK TRAINING MATRIX AS OF 3/10/2009

COLLECTIVE TASKS

INDIVIDUAL TASKS	Conduct Unit Recall	Coordinate SRP	Implement Family Support Plan	Move to APOE, RPOE, or SPOE Marshaling Area	Deploy Elements by Air	Deploy Elements by Land	Deploy Elements by Sea	Perform Risk Management Procedures	Defend Assigned Areas	Establish Command & Control	Establish Communication	Combat Battlefield Stress	Employ Crew Sreve Weapons	Establish & Perform TOC Operations	Conduct Split Base Operations	Conduct Family Support Meetings	Maintain Equip & Personnel Readiness	Conduct Operations in NBC	Perform Field Sanitation functions	Perform Unit Level Intel Functions	Execute Movement Plan	Operate Unit Supply	Perform Administrative functions	Perform grave Registration functions
Determine Magnetic Azimuth Using a Compass																					X			
Determine Location By Terrain Association																								
Use a GPS																					X			
Measure Distance on a Map																					X			
Use Resection & Intersection																					X			
Determine Direction Using Field Expedient Methods																					X			
Use a Map Overlay																					X			
NBC																								
Prepare for Nuclear Attack																		X						
Cross Radiologically Contaminated Area																		X						
Conduct Radiological Recon																		X						
Prepare For Chemical Attack																		X						
React To Biological Attack																	X	X						
Conduct Decon Ops																		X						
Conduct MOPP Gear Exchange																	X	X						
Maintain M40 Mask																	X	X						
Decon Self & Equip																		X						
Replace Filter on Mask																	X	X						
Use m9/8 Paper																		X						
Mark Contaminated Area																	X	X						
Emplace M8 Alarm																	X	X						
FIRST AID																								
Administer First Aid																	X							
Care For Chemical Causaulties																	X	X						
Evacuate Causalties																	X							
Construct Field Expedient Litters																	X							
Inventory CBL Bag																	X							

COLLECTIVE TO INDIVIDUAL TASK TRAINING MATRIX AS OF 3/10/2009

COLLECTIVE TASKS

INDIVIDUAL TASKS	Conduct Unit Recall	Coordinate SRP	Implement Family Support Plan	Move to APOE, RPOE, or SPOE Marshaling Area	Deploy Elements by Air	Deploy Elements by Land	Deploy Elements by Sea	Perform Risk Management Procedures	Defend Assigned Areas	Establish Command & Control	Establish Communication	Combat Battlefield Stress	Employ Crew Sreve Weapons	Establish & Perform TOC Operations	Conduct Split Base Operations	Conduct Family Support Meetings	Maintain Equip & Personnel Readiness	Conduct Operations In NBC	Perform Field Sanitation Functions	Perform Unit Level Intel Functions	Execute Movement Plan	Operate Unit Supply	Perform Administrative functions	Perform grave Registration functions
Clear Object From Throat																								
Evaluate a Casualty																	X							
Give First Aid for Burns																	X							
Apply a Tourniquet																	X							
Treat Chest Wound																	X							
Treat Abdominal Injury																								
Treat Head Injury																	X							
Splint a Fracture																	X							
Administer Nerve Agent Antidote to Self/Buddy Aid																		X						
Perfrom CPR																	X							
Perform Mouth-Mouth																	X							
STABILITY OPS																								
Conduct Patrols									X															
Establish/Operate a Check Point																								
React to Media									X															
Escort a Convoy									X															
Secure a Route									X															
React to Minefield									X															
Conduct Negotiations With Local Nationals									X															
Conduct MOUT Operations									X															

A Company 1st Platoon
TRAINING MEETING AGENDA

DEVELOPMENT CYCLE	TRAINER'S NOTES
Assess Training Since Last Meeting	

• Discuss AARs
• Discuss recommended actions from AARs
• What actions will be implemented to improve future training?
	• Conduct NBC operations
	   • Evaluators were weak (why?)
	   • OPFOR (excellent)
	   • Evacuation of casualties needs work
	   • Do we reschedule training?

(Next Week)	
• Has the proposed training worksheet been reviewed? • Are risk assessments, training outlines, & training aids prepared? • Has the 1SG/PSG certified and reviewed the training? • Have all actions that require coordination been confirmed?	Establish Area of Operations • Maint platoon owes me risk assessment • Supply needs to coordinate refill of combat lifesaver bag before training • 1st Platoon Sgt/LDR did not review training (Why? Discuss with 1SG)
(Week 2)	
• Has the proposed training worksheet been reviewed? • Have road clearances been granted? • Has a recon of the site been conducted? • Have meals been coordinated?	Conduct Night Road March • Need to check coordination of training site. • Road clearances are good 'til midnight. • Meals need to be laid on.
(Week 3)	
• Has the proposed training worksheet been reviewed? • Have individuals been certified in MILES gear? • What are the plans for issuing/zeroing MILES? • Do we have enough batteries for MILES gear?	Conduct Ambush • SSG Possible and SSG Alpha will attend MILES certification on Friday • Supply has requested batteries but they have not arrived (alternate plan?) • Zeroing & issue will begin 1 hour prior to formation (arms room will be open by PFC Lifer)

TRAINING MEETING AGENDA

DEVELOPMENT CYCLE	TRAINER'S NOTES
Assess Training Since Last Meeting	
(Next Week)	
(Week 2)	
(Week 3)	

PROPOSED TRAINING WORKSHEET

Date submitted: _____

Squad, Section, Platoon submitting training: _____

Date training is to be conducted: _____

Training Week T8 T7 T6 T5 T4 T3 T2 T1   (Circle one)

Primary trainer/ (duty phone): _____   Secondary trainer/ (duty phone): _____

Primary training location (bldg #, strip map/ grid coordinates required): _____

Alternate training location (bldg#, strip map/grid coordinates required): _____

References for proposed training (List all that are applicable):   _____

METL task(s) to be trained:
  1. _____
  2. _____
  3. _____

Collective task(s) to be trained:
  1. _____
  2. _____
  3. _____

Individual task(s) to be trained:

  1. _____   4. _____
  2. _____   5. _____
  3 _____   6. _____

CTT tasks to be trained: 1. _____   2. _____

First Aid task   1. _____

NBC Task   1. _____

Training Support Requirements

1. Training location is _____and has been verified?   Y   N
    Alternate location has been verified?   Y   N
2. Transportation requirements have been laid on and verified?   Y   N
3. Training aids have been requested and are available for training?   Y   N
4. Is live or training ammunition/pyro required?   Y   N
        a. Has the required ammunition/pyro been requested?   Y   N
        b. Has the appropriate paperwork been submitted?   Y   N
        c. Has coordination been made for pick up and residue return?   Y   N

5. Does this training require special equipment or uniform modification?   Y   N
6. Has all external and internal coordination been conducted?   Y   N
7. Review date: You are required to conduct a review of training with the 1SG/PSG on_____
        You must have a completed training outline, risk assessment, and all other items prepared at this time.

Signature of 1st Line Supervisor: _____
First sergeant's recommendation concerning proposed training: Approval, Disapproval, Recommend approval with the following changes:

Commander' Signature: _____   Training is APPROVED/ DISAPPROVED
*Pre-execution checks will be conducted by the first-line leader two weeks prior to the training event.

After Action Review

Date: _____

Primary Instructor: _____

Alternate Instructor: _____

Topic of Training (Tasks) _____

_____

1. What was done correctly?

_____

_____

_____

_____

2. What actions/portions of the training were done wrong?

_____

_____

_____

_____

3. What could be done to improve the training?

_____

_____

_____

_____

Additional Comments:

_____

_____

_____

Resources

Publications for Review

1. AR 350-1   Army Training and Leader Development
2. FM 7-0   Training for Full Spectrum Operations
3. FM 7-1   Battle Focused Training
4. TC 25-30   A Leader's Guide to Company Training Meetings

Local Information for Review

1. Previous week's training
2. Long range training calendar
3. Short range training calendar
4. Near term training
5. Commander's training guidance
6. After Action Reviews (AARs) from previous training
7. GTA catalog from the local training resource center

On the Web

1. http://call.army.mil
2. Search by training subject or AAR

Chapter Three
TRAINING SCENARIOS

Introduction

The following chapter will introduce you to several training scenarios designed to test an element's ability to react to a given situation. These scenarios can be used during field exercises or during unit scheduled training at home station. These scenarios may assist leaders in determining what type of training should be conducted in the future.

Goals

1. Train and teach Warriors and their leaders how to think and react to scenarios with minimal thought
2. Encourage Warriors to use innovative methods to deal with situations
3. Introduce a personal training principle that I call 'train to failure'

Principles of training

The most current training manual lists seven principles of training. For the in-depth explanation of these principles, please refer to FM 7-0.

1. Commanders and other leaders are responsible for training
2. Noncommissioned officers train individuals, crews, and small teams
3. Train as you will fight
4. Train to standard
5. Train to sustain
6. Conduct multi-echelon and concurrent training
7. Train to develop agile leaders and organizations

I sincerely believe that all of these principles are important and should be incorporated into the training program. I particularly found my Warriors enjoyed a good challenge, especially when the purpose of the training was clearly understood.

In addition, I would like to add a principle that I have seen utilized during my career. I call this principle "Train to Failure." So what exactly does that mean?

Train to failure means that Warriors must overcome adversity and understand that the good side does not always win the fight. The Warriors should be informed by the chain of command that the Train to Failure principle is not designed to break their will to fight, but to give them an understanding of what failure can do to the morale and effectiveness of a unit. In addition this principle is useful in helping Warriors identify and utilize resourceful methods in order to accomplish a mission.

I must emphasize that Warriors should be told that failure is likely but that they are encouraged to be innovative in order to accomplish the mission. Leaders must also be extremely conscious of safety and ensure that Warriors do not involve themselves in unacceptable hazardous behavior. The Train to Failure principle can be tied directly to Train to Develop Agile Leaders and Organizations.

Here are some examples of what I would consider to be Train to Failure scenarios.

Scenario 1

A squad size element is directed to move by foot march to an area approximately 10 miles away and secure a bridge. The squad leader is told that failure to secure the bridge will most certainly result in loss of life and failure of another element's mission. In addition, the squad leader is informed that it will take at least 10 Warriors to properly execute the mission; however, only nine personnel are available. The squad is allowed minimal time to prepare and execute the mission. While en route to the bridge, a member of the squad trips a booby trap. One member of the squad is killed and two are severely wounded. In addition the radio is now unserviceable. If the leader continues the mission, the bridge will be found occupied by enemy forces that must be cleared.

Actions

The squad leader is now faced with several issues (both moral and ethical dilemmas). The leader was probably initially frustrated about being undermanned and not given adequate time for mission preparation. However, the leader must now make several decisions:

1. What action will the leader take concerning the wounded personnel?
2. Will the leader abandon the wounded, or choose to evacuate them?
3. Will the leader take the wounded on the mission?
4. Will the leader leave the wounded in place for later recovery?
5. Will the leader continue the mission?
6. How will the leader deal with contact at the bridge?
7. Can the leader hold the team together?

Scenario 2

A convoy commander has been informed that their convoy is carrying supplies critical to mission success of a unit currently in contact with the enemy. You provide the convoy commander with the details of the mission and allow only minimal preparation time. As the convoy prepares to depart, two vehicles become inoperable. These vehicles are carrying ammunition (class V). All vehicles are required to reach the destination in order to achieve mission success. If the convoy commander is successful getting the vehicles moving, the convoy will encounter a mined road, Improvised Explosive Device (IED), ambush, or other obstacles that would require a detour.

Actions

1. Does the convoy commander leave the vehicles?
2. Attempt a transload operation?
3. Will they attempt to tow the vehicle with other vehicles in the convoy?
4. Try to reconfigure loads?
5. Search for alternate vehicles to haul the supplies?

Leaders and Warriors participating in these missions will learn valuable lessons about themselves and each other. You can also observe how innovative your Soldiers become. What is their level of commitment to the mission and each other? This type of training scenario can be applied to any type of unit or any type of mission.

The key to this type of training is to ensure that the Warriors understand the purpose of the training, the consequences of failure, and that they are being placed in situations they could face in the real world. It is critical that observers be with Warriors during these events and that the observers watch closely for poor decisions that could affect safety (risking life, limb, or injury). The observer must intervene and stop any unsafe actions. In addition, it is critical that the observer be a vital part of the After Action Review.

There are several other types of scenarios that can be used to increase training value. I cannot stress the importance of safety and risk assessment. Make sure that your scenarios are safe and do not jeopardize assets or resources.

Reaction Training

This type of training can be used as a unit is preparing for Sergeant's Time Training or other activity in which the unit is not necessarily in a field environment. Your Warriors should be advised that they should be vigilant in observing their surroundings and to immediately take appropriate action upon observation of activity.

The purpose of this type of training is not to teach the Warrior but to assess the Warrior's level of proficiency. How will the Warrior react if caught off guard? If the Warriors react poorly perhaps the unit should conduct refresher training to ensure proficiency.

In addition, these scenarios can develop innovation and critical thinking skills. It's not always the leader who solves the problem. Sometimes a young private will have the key to success. A good leader needs to know when to follow. These situations help to encourage teamwork. Perhaps one of the best leadership lessons I have learned is this: It is not what you see in a person on a daily basis that determines how a person will react in a hostile or critical situation. A person you consider substandard may in fact be the hero who saves the lives of many Warriors because they rise to the challenge.

A person you consider high speed and a self starter may in fact crumble under pressure and be incapable of leading or completing the mission. This is why this type of training is important. The more you can stress your Warriors mentally and physically so that they react on instinct rather than thought, the better the team will be. This dramatically increases the success and survivability of the Warrior and the team on the battlefield while improving the odds of mission success.

Technology and machines are great force multipliers, but remember that it is the common everyday Warrior that will defeat the enemy on the battlefield. That is why unconventional warfare is so effective against an unprepared conventional force. Use technology, but be certain that you are able to function without it.

Train your Warriors to think asymmetrically (outside the box). Teach them to be unconventional, using all legal and moral methods at their disposal to stay ahead of the enemy. You must think like the enemy to exploit their weaknesses.

Scenario 1

As a leader you are forming your element (squad, section, platoon, or company) for the morning formation. Sergeant's Time Training is scheduled to begin immediately following the formation. Upon being released from the accountability formation someone gives the alarm for an NBC attack (either verbally, visually, or unit signal).

Preparatory Actions

1. Prior to the activity, designate an individual to start a stop watch when the NBC alarm is given.
2. Prior to activity designate personnel to observe the element for critical mistakes.
3. When 15 seconds have passed (standard for donning and clearing a mask with hood), command the element to freeze.
4. At this time any individual who did not properly don their protective mask will be considered a casualty (either injured or killed).
5. Each casualty should be given a card describing the type and severity of their injury.
6. The element must now deal with this situation and attempt to complete its mission that was already planned for that morning's training.

Actions

1. Have the remaining uninjured Warriors conduct first aid procedures IAW with the casualty cards that were distributed.
2. Have the element transport casualties to its training location using the transportation scheduled for the morning's training. This may require constructing field-expedient litters or carrying personnel.
3. Warriors will be allowed to continue with scheduled training upon arrival at the planned training site.

Evaluation

1. Does the element
   a. fill out casualty feeder reports?
   b. send a NBC 1 report?
   c. conduct a NBC survey?
2. Did the element
   a. treat the wounds correctly?
   b. attempt to contact higher headquarters to evacuate casualties?
   c. make plans for the remains of dead Warriors?
   d. function as a team?
   e. use critical and innovative skills in dealing with the problem?
3. Conduct
   a. an After Action Review (AAR) with each individual element (squad, section, platoon).
   b. an AAR with overall element (platoon or company).

Note: The training possibilities are endless. Other scenarios in this setting could include:

1. React to indirect fire
2. React to sniper
3. React to air attack
4. Field Training Exercise Scenarios

Scenario 2

Advance party encounters gunshots during the occupation of new area of operations.

Setting the Stage

The element is the first element occupying a new piece of terrain. The element has been sent in to establish an area of operation in support of peacekeeping operations. As the advance party conducts its search of the area gunshots are heard. The main body is due to arrive in 30 minutes.

Note: The gunshots were fired by the property owner; he is hunting on his land. No shots have been fired in the direction of the advance party. The advance party is not in a position to directly observe the property owner, they can only hear gunshots.

Options for the Event

1. If the element does not investigate the gunshots, have the property owner approach the element and tell the Warriors to get off his land.
2. If a soldier kills or assaults the property owner have the local authorities arrive and try to arrest the soldier.
3. Have news media arrive stating they are doing a story on the death or assault of the property owner and want to speak with the Commander.

Evaluation

1. How does the element react to the gunshots?
2. Does the element engage the non-hostile property owner, who is simply hunting on his own property?
3. How do the leaders of the element interact with the land owner?
4. Do they attempt to win the land owner over or simply subdue him?
5. If the element engages the land owner in gunfire what are the consequences of their actions?
6. If the land owner is killed or injured what are the possible repercussions?
7. How did the element handle the local authorities arriving to arrest the Warrior who assaulted/killed the property owner.
8. How did the element handle the news media arriving stating they are doing a story on the death or assault of the property owner?
9. Were the rules of engagement followed?
10. Did the element inform the main body?
11. Was a spot report sent to higher headquarters?
12. Conduct AAR.

Scenario 3

Drive-by shooting

Setting the Stage

The unit has successfully occupied a new area of operations. A vehicle approaches one of the observation posts close to an avenue of approach. As the vehicle nears the observation post gunfire and grenades erupt from the vehicle.

Options for the Event

1. Post an observer close by the event and have the observer hand out casualty cards.
2. You may also pass a situation report to the element's leadership stating that other units have been hit by drive-by shootings. Describe the vehicle or method of attack, and state the time of attacks. See if the leaders of the element pass this information to the Warriors in an effective manner. This aspect of the scenario not only tests the Warriors' reaction to the incident but also evaluates the leadership's ability to pass on communication in a timely manner.

Evaluation

1. How did the individuals at the OP handle the incident?
2. Were the Warriors manning the OP alert to their surroundings?
3. Did the command element pass along the possibility of an attack, the description of the vehicle, etc?
4. Did the Warriors engage the vehicle?
5. Did the Warriors send a spot report?
6. Did the unit immediately react to the situation?
7. Were combat lifesavers utilized to aid the wounded?
8. Did Warriors take immediate first aid action?
9. Did the reaction force assemble?
10. Did unit leadership focus all its attention on the drive-by shooting incident, or did leaders ensure that unit personnel focused on their areas of responsibility and maintained security on the entire perimeter?
11. Conduct AAR.

Scenario 4

Local civilian leaders arrive to protest occupation of land.

Note: While this scenario relates to a law enforcement officer it could be changed to read: mayor, chief of police, governor, religious leaders or any other civilian officials with influence in the community.

Setting the Stage

A guard post calls to inform the command post that the local law enforcement officer is at the checkpoint with the land owner. The law enforcement officer demands to speak with the commanding officer. In addition, he states that the occupation of the land is unlawful and directs your unit to displace immediately.

Evaluation

1. How does the unit leadership handle this situation?
2. Does the incident monopolize the time of key leaders in the unit?
3. Could the action have been an attempt to identify the commanding officer for later activity?
4. Does the leadership provide alternative channels for resolution of the problem (JAG/PAO)?
5. Does the leadership inform higher headquarters of the problems they are experiencing?
6. How did the Warrior at the checkpoint interact with the law enforcement officer?
    a. Was a weapon pointed at the officer?
    b. Was the officer treated with dignity and respect?
    c. Was the officer properly identified as a law enforcement officer?
    d. Was the law enforcement officer allowed to enter the perimeter?
7. Conduct AAR.

Scenario 5

TV news crew arrives

Setting the Stage

A major TV news anchor of the country appears and begins filming the occupation of the assembly area. The crew is conducting a live broadcast to the local nationals. As the reporter attempts to conduct an interview with one of the Warriors at the checkpoint, there is a negligent weapons discharge from a Warrior close to the news reporter. The news crew runs for cover, believing they have been fired upon intentionally.

Evaluation

1. Does the chain of command attempt to gain control of the situation?
2. What actions are taken by the chain of command concerning the Warrior?
3. Does the command element inform higher headquarters of the incident and request that PAO and JAG be informed?
4. Does the situation monopolize the time of the command element and detract from the command's ability to execute its mission?
5. Are junior level leaders utilized to their fullest potential?
6. Conduct AAR.

Scenario 6

Demonstrators begin to rally outside the perimeter

Setting the Stage

Due to the recent occupation of private property and the way in which the civilian population has been treated, demonstrators begin to rally outside the perimeter, shouting slogans that are anti-American. These are the people your operation was designed to protect. Most of the demonstrators do not speak English.

Evaluation

1. Are signs posted along the perimeter in English and the host nation language?
2. Do the signs include language explaining the use of deadly force?
3. Does the incident monopolize the command element's time?
4. Are junior leaders utilized to the fullest extent possible?
5. Did the command element notify higher headquarters?
6. Did the command element attempt to resolve the problem at the lowest level?
7. Did the command involve local law enforcement or civilian authorities to try and resolve the matter?
8. Did the command attempt to identify the leader of the demonstration?
9. Conduct AAR.

Scenario 7

A local vendor arrives

Setting the Stage

A local vendor begins to sell food items to Warriors on the edge of the perimeter. The items include sodas, candy, tobacco products, and hot dogs. The vendor speaks some English and is very friendly.

Evaluation

1. Has the vendor been approved/certified by the command to sell items to the Warriors?
2. What type of questions is the vendor asking?
3. Is he probing for information?
4. Did the Warriors closest to the vendor remain focused on the mission?
5. Did the Warriors on duty report the incident to the command element?
6. Did the command element notify higher headquarters?
7. Did the command take action to remove the vendor if he was not authorized?
8. How was the situation handled?
9. Conduct AAR.

Scenario 8

Hostage standoff

Setting the Stage

Your daily supply truck left in the morning to acquire rations for the element. When it returns, four armed men exit the vehicle approximately 500 meters from the dismount point; they hijacked the truck on its return trip. These men are pointing weapons at the driver and assistant driver of the supply truck. They demand to speak to the commander. The commander must come out unarmed and meet the men outside the unit perimeter. The men use the hostages as protective cover. The men state they will kill the Warriors if the commander does not comply. As time passes the gunmen become impatient and shoot a service member in the leg to demonstrate they are serious.

Evaluation

1. Does the commander respond to the situation?
2. Does the command quietly mobilize its reaction force?
3. Does the command place proficient marksman at key vantage points?
4. Does the unit analyze the situation prior to taking action?
5. Does the command element notify higher headquarters or local authorities?
6. Does the command attempt to surround the gunmen without their knowledge?
7. Conduct AAR.

Scenario 9

Beating of civilian outside of perimeter

Setting the Stage

In view of a guard post several individuals begin to harass and beat another individual. It appears that the group is displaying acts of racial, ethnic, or religious violence.

Evaluation

1. What are the actions of the guard?
2. Does the element attempt to stop the beating?
3. Does the guard report the incident to the command post?
4. Is the subject that was beaten brought into the safety of the perimeter?
5. Does the individual attempt to explain what happened?
6. Does the command attempt to utilize information provided by the subject?
7. Do members of the unit search the individual prior to allowing access to other personnel or the area of operations?
8. Does the command inform higher headquarters or civilian authorities?
9. Conduct AAR.

Scenario 10

Unit receives indirect fire

Setting the Stage

The unit receives indirect fire from an unknown position. Two Warriors are wounded and three Warriors are killed. The commander is killed and the first sergeant is seriously wounded and requires an IV.

This is an excellent training tool. It tests the combat lifesaver's ability to administer an IV under stressful conditions and provides a level of confidence. Ensure that you check with your chain of command for approval of this training. Make sure that there are enough IV bags on hand in the event of an actual incident. Remember the fact that your Combat Lifesavers are giving a real IV to a Commander or 1SG. This is a significant emotional event. It means something to them, they will be nervous! Play the part. Be wounded, in pain, and suffering. Perhaps they will require assistance to hold you down to give you the IV.

I have used this during every exercise possible and each Combat Lifesaver loved it in the end. They were not thrilled to start with, however they realized that it gave them confidence in their abilities to administer an IV. On the downside, I did come home with some pretty bruised up arms on occasion.

I would encourage leaders to receive training on how to properly receive and give an IV so that you can make sure it is being administered properly. Case in point: I have had Warriors become so worried they were sticking the 1SG or CSM that they dropped the IV needle on the ground in the mud and then tried to stick me with it. This is obviously a NO GO. Maybe it would be acceptable in a dire combat situation. It's definitely not acceptable during training.

Some made critical errors that resulted in improper IV insertion and, more importantly, possible injury to the Warriors as a result of poor hygiene practices. Big Lesson Learned: Make sure your CBLs wear gloves because the blood does fly, eye protection would be a good idea as well

My recommendation is to have another Combat Lifesaver nearby. They will not be involved in a hands-on sense, but their presence offers a safety check. It is hard to play the role and act as the primary safety checker. Use a video camera during the process. It is a great tool for the AAR process and the Warriors will get a kick out of it.

Evaluation

1. Does the unit treat and move casualties to the casualty collection point?
2. Is the casualty collection point located in a safe area?
3. Does the unit send a situation report to higher headquarters?
4. Does the chain of command transition smoothly?
5. Does the combat lifesaver administer the IV to the first sergeant successfully?
6. Does the unit fill out casualty feeder reports?
7. Do the members of the unit seek cover in a timely manner?
8. Does the unit prepare the remains of the dead for movement?
9. Does each Warrior have a prepared position in which to seek cover?
10. Does the unit conduct crater analysis if projectiles were ground-bursting?
11. Conduct AAR.

Scenario 11

Element takes sniper fire

Setting the Stage

While conducting normal operations the element comes under sniper fire. Two Warriors are severely wounded. One of the casualties is on open terrain and it is possible that the sniper could observe any effort to aid the Warrior.

Evaluation

1. Did members of the element observe the flash or report of the weapon?
2. Did the element immediately react to the situation by seeking cover or returning fire if possible?
3. Was first aid rendered to the casualties?
4. Did members of the element attempt to bring the casualties to a safe area?
5. Did the element organize itself to recover the casualty from the open area?
6. Was the incident reported to higher headquarters?
7. Were casualty feeder cards filled out?
8. Conduct AAR.

Scenario 12

Humanitarian assistance

Setting the Stage

A woman approaches the gate with a young child that has been wounded by either enemy forces, a mine strike--- or is seriously ill. The woman begs for assistance from the guard.

Evaluation

1. Does the guard report the incident?
2. How does the guard handle the incident?
3. How does the guard treat the woman and child?
4. Is a weapon pointed at the woman and child?
5. Are the woman and child under constant surveillance while the Warrior reports the incident?
6. Does the guard leave his post or exit the perimeter to provide assistance?
7. Does the element provide assistance?
8. Conduct AAR.

Scenario 13

Guard post does not report in for a scheduled communications check

Setting the Stage

The element CP does not receive a scheduled radio check from an observation/listening post.

Evaluation

1. How does the element respond?
2. Is a lone individual sent to check the situation?
3. If the guard was found asleep what action was taken?
4. If the guard was found missing what action was taken?
5. Was higher headquarters alerted if the Warrior was missing?
6. Was the unit alert level heightened?
7. Was a patrol established to look for the missing Warrior?
8. Conduct AAR

Scenario 14

Squad-size probe

Setting the Stage

During hours of darkness the element is probed by a squad-size force.

Evaluation

1. Did the OP/LP report the probe?
2. Did the OP/LP check with unit command post to determine if friendly units were in their area?
3. Did the position open fire?
4. If they opened fire did they expose their position by failing to use grenades first?
5. Did the reaction force mobilize?
6. Did the unit go to full manning?
7. Did the unit focus attention on the portion of the perimeter being probed?
8. Was the next higher element informed?
9. Conduct AAR.

Scenario 15

Request for Fire Support

Setting the Stage

While on a random patrol an element receives heavy weapons fire and becomes surrounded and requires fire support.

Evaluation

1. Does the leader of the element request fire support?
2. Does the individual know how to properly call for fire support?
3. Did the fire support element have to use untrained observer techniques to direct fire?
4. Was the leader able to accurately determine his location and report it?
5. Conduct AAR.

Scenario 16

Patrol ambushed

Setting the Stage

The patrol is pinned down and members of the unit (within the perimeter) can hear and see the engagement.

Evaluation

1. Does the element in contact report their situation?
2. Does the element request assistance?
3. Does the leadership at the CP organize a plan to engage the enemy?
4. Do members of the unit on the perimeter direct fire to assist the element in contact, coordinating with the unit CP?
5. Is the reaction force assembled?
6. Are casualties evacuated and treated using first aid procedures?
7. Conduct AAR.

Scenario 17

Patrolling mine strike

Setting the Stage

A patrol inadvertently enters a minefield and takes casualties.

Evaluation

1. Does the leader of the element maintain control of the patrol?
2. Are casualties treated?
3. Are Warriors instructed to probe their way out?
4. Can Warriors return from the direction of entry with a high probability of success?
5. Do the Warriors check for boundary markers of the minefield?
6. Does the element cease radio operations? (in the event the mines may be triggered by frequency)
7. Is the minefield being over-watched? If so, does the element receive enemy fire?
8. Are casualties evacuated?
9. Conduct AAR.

Scenario 18

Demand for payment of damages

Setting the Stage

The landowner returns and is demanding payment for damage to his property by your element.

Evaluation

1. Was the landowner allowed inside the perimeter?
2. Should the landowner be allowed inside the perimeter?
3. If so did the landowner appear to be observing the locations of key pieces of equipment or other items?
4. Did the problem monopolize the time of the command element?
5. Did lower level leadership attempt to solve the problem?
6. Was the land owner referred to JAG?
7. Was higher HQ informed?
8. Conduct AAR.

Scenario 19

Capture of enemy Warrior or hostile civilian

Setting the Stage

During a random patrol the element captures an enemy Warrior or civilian apparently observing the actions and movements of the unit.

Evaluation

1. Is higher HQ notified?
2. Was proper security pulled on the individual and the area during the apprehension and the search?
3. Is the individual processed using the "Five S" system (search, segregate, speed, silence, safeguard)?
4. Is the individual completely searched for information?
5. Is all equipment picked up?
6. Is the individual's protective mask returned to him?
7. Is the individual protected from other Warriors/civilians?
8. Is the S-2 notified?
9. What methods are implemented when bringing the individual into the perimeter?
10. Conduct AAR.

Scenario 20

Roadside Checkpoint

Setting the Stage

While conducting a random search of a vehicle at a roadside checkpoint, the guard notices a package that is out of place or seems suspicious in nature.

Evaluation

1. How do the Warriors at the checkpoint react to the situation?
2. Do they attempt to remove the item?
3. Do they remove the individuals from the vehicle?
4. Do they search the vehicle?
5. Do they report the incident to higher HQ?
6. Is EOD notified?
7. Do the Warriors continue to observe the occupants of the car carefully?
8. Are radios, cell phones, or other electronic devices banned from use close to the vehicle? (possible denotation due to frequency)
9. Are all electronic devices removed from detainees?
10. Conduct ARR.

Scenario 21

Unit receives a chemical attack

Setting the Stage

A slow-moving civilian utility vehicle drives close to the unit perimeter. A fog is being sprayed from the vehicle. Unit perimeter guards report the drivers are wearing chemical suits. Several Warriors begin to show signs of nerve agent poisoning.

Evaluation

1. Does the unit go to MOPP 4?
2. Are NBC detection teams activated?
3. Does the unit attempt to engage the vehicle?
4. Are decontamination procedures followed?
5. Are unmasking procedures followed?
6. Are reporting procedures followed?
7. Are casualties treated correctly?
8. Is the medical facility informed they will be receiving NBC casualties?
9. Did the unit properly employ NBC alarms?
10. Conduct AAR.

Scenario 22

Unexploded ordnance

Setting the Stage

After being in place for approximately 48 hours a member of the element stumbles upon a piece of unexploded ordnance.

Evaluation

1. Is the chain of command notified?
2. Is higher HQ notified?
3. Is EOD contacted?
4. Is the area marked off to prevent individuals from entering the area?
5. Were the proper reporting procedures followed for reporting UXO?
6. Was a barrier erected?

Scenario 23

Assassination or attempted assassination of key unit leader

Setting the Stage

An individual posing as a high-ranking civilian official, local vendor, local civilian requesting assistance, or homeless person begging for food, approaches the perimeter and requests to speak with a key leader. As the leader arrives, the individual shoots the unit leader.

Evaluation

1. Did the unit plan for such an event?
2. Was proper security maintained on the individual requesting to speak with the leader?
3. Was the individual searched?
4. Did the unit engage according to the rules of engagement?
5. Did the unit provide first aid to the leader and individual if required?
6. Conduct AAR.

Scenario 24

News media

Setting the Stage

A local news crew observes the capture of a civilian who has been monitoring unit movements and conducting himself in a suspicious manner. The news crew has rallied to the aid of the civilian. They are calling for the public to rally at the unit location and are demanding a meeting with the commander.

Evaluation

1. What actions did the leadership take toward the media?
2. Was the civilian treated with the minimum force necessary?
3. Was higher HQ notified?
4. Was PAO notified?
5. Did the unit increase the readiness posture?
6. Was the reaction force placed on standby?
7. Was there a requirement to increase manning on the perimeter?
8. Conduct AAR.

Scenario 25

Suicide bombing

Setting the Stage

Intelligence reports seem to indicate the possibility of a terrorist attack. Suicide bombers have been used in the past. A large amount of explosives has been stolen from a nearby warehouse and a large utility vehicle was reported stolen within the past 24 hours.

Evaluation

1. Does leadership communicate increased threat to personnel?
2. Are personnel told what actions they should take in the event of a suspicious vehicle?
3. When the vehicle approached and displayed a hostile intent what actions were taken?
4. Was the incident reported immediately?
5. Was manpower increased on the guard points?
6. If available, were obstacles employed to slow the vehicle?
7. What capabilities did the element have available that they did not use?
8. Conduct AAR.

Moral and Ethical Dilemmas

Another method in which to evaluate Warriors is to place them in moral and ethical dilemmas. This can be done during field training exercises, classroom discussions, or as opportunity training. The idea is to challenge the Warrior by placing them in scenarios in which they must make a choice. Once the Warrior has made a choice, review the alternative solutions with him. At times there may be no right answer but these scenarios provide the Warrior insight into themselves and how their decisions can affect others.

Training Scenarios & The Real World

Our goal is to throw as much at our Warriors as possible. Stretching them, their resources, capabilities, and their leaders to the maximum extent possible in training. This will ensure they are challenged. They will learn from their mistakes and each other! This is not a new principle. Here is a list of suggestions you might want to consider as you prepare other training scenarios:

1. Every situation will be different and specifically governed by the rules of engagement for that conflict. What may work today, may not work tomorrow. The key is to build flexibility into the thinking of our Warriors and junior leaders as much as possible. Teach them to think in terms of "What if" scenarios rather than, structured thinking like: " We do A, B, C, etc."
2. GOOD IDEA Award: Some of you may be familiar with a 35mm report or a Class 3, 5, Maintenance, Medical Report. Meaning: Once you break contact you immediately begin to send information to your higher with the status of the elements listed above. The format is quick, simple, and easy to remember. In fact, as the story was recounted to me a young Lieutenant was writing on his Hummer windshield in grease pencil after contact! Now that's innovative...it's in your face, fast, quick, and close!
3. Some of you may have to work with military personnel of other countries. Perhaps they will provide support for your Warriors like: convoy security, perimeter security, etc. Here are some things to consider:
   a. It may be a good idea to get to know them on a personal level
   b. If they are not from an English speaking nation, do you have any native speakers?
   c. Can you establish a liaison with them?
4. What are their TTPs when encountering certain threats? For example: mines, IEDs, indirect fire, and ambush. Their TTPs may be counter to our own. If they are part of our mission we are a TEAM. We must function together. If we fail to discuss TTPs we will jeopardize the mission!

Typically in an unblocked ambush we have been taught to run the ambush. That concept is changing and depending on your unit procedures you will probably be encouraged to FIX and destroy the enemy. If you go loaded for bear and ready to fight, the enemy tends to look for softer targets. If he comes after you, give him what he wants. Circle the wagons (if you will) and focus your firepower outward. Utilize fire support and Tactical Air Support to crush his will to fight. Again, this tactic is situational and based on the unit's mission, ROE, political situation, etc. Think of several ways to work the situation. For example:

1. Running the ambush
2. Circling the wagons and calling in big guns and TAC Air
3. Blocking or fixing the enemy while you envelop his flanks
4. Plan for the worst

Risk Management Versus Risk Avoidance

Risk Assessment, Risk Management, and Risk Avoidance are all significant terms. To utilize a Risk Management process, the hazards must first be determined. This is the assessment phase. Once the hazards have been assessed, they must be managed in such a way that any negative impact on the element is minimized.

Risk, however, should never be out-right avoided. Risk Avoidance leads to a zero defect mentality. This means that even calculated risks are not taken because somebody may get in trouble or make a mistake. In our business, we cannot avoid risk. It is part of the job. However, it is our duty and responsibility as leaders to mitigate that risk and manage it as best as possible.

Once we have assessed, managed, and minimized the risk it is time to execute the plan aggressively and violently using surprise, shock, speed, and overwhelming force/firepower.

Modern Day Examples

We never know what the future holds. Here are some examples of things that are possibilities that you could use. Tweak them, use them, change them, and build upon them. Better your Warriors!

1. On patrol in an urban area, you are informed by a local national that there is an enemy safe house down the street. What are your actions? Are you being set up by someone that has a grudge against this person? Is it a real threat? Are you being sent into an ambush?
2. Your patrol is passing out candy and talking with local children. Shots ring out. An enemy sniper has taken out a child. One or two of your Warriors are down. What are your actions? How do you provide for the safety of the children? How do you take out the sniper? Do you take out the sniper? How do you care for your wounded? What is your casualty evacuation plan? Parents are starting to gather in the street and become hostile towards you for endangering their children.
3. Your unit has been on patrol for several days back to back. The day prior a squad member was killed by an enemy pretending to be dead. The next day, you perform an assault on the objective and become involved in a fire fight. There are wounded and dead enemy combatants. What actions should you take as leaders? What should your top priority be? How do you best ensure the safety of your men and the wounded combatants? What should you have done prior to the assault given the information of the previous day's events?
4. A vehicle pulls up some distance from a check point. A women and a man exist the vehicle and begin to have a physical altercation. What are your actions? Do you immediately approach to render assistance? Do you suspect the vehicle as a car bomb?
5. A local national comes to your check point one day and leaves a small box. She is shy, but kind. You put her through all the steps and motions. You suspect something is up. When you open the box it is a gift- food, and a note thanking you for freeing her country. The next day she returns and talks with a Warrior for a few moments before leaving another box. What are your actions? Are her intentions friendly? At what

point do you let your guard down? Could this be a bomb or some kind of monitoring device?

Summary

There are no textbook answers for these situations. Every situation is different. With modern communications the action/inaction of an individual Warrior or Junior leader could lead to an international incident within hours. Therefore, it is critical that we do our best to train for the unknown. One way to accomplish this is to be as unpredictable as possible in setting up training scenarios. Run low on food, water, ammo, etc. Why? Because it happens! Technology gives us the advantage, but it does not win the battle or the war. Leaders win battles and wars by instilling in their Warriors the will to fight, survive, and win on the battlefield. Leaders must provide a good example, discipline, tough/demanding training, and let their Warriors know they sincerely care about them and their families.

Notes to remember

The evaluation module of each scenario is not all-inclusive. It is designed to provoke thought and stimulate your own evaluation process. I strongly encourage you to review each scenario and its evaluation steps. Tailor the scenario to your needs.

Possibilities in these scenarios are endless and only limited to your imagination. Make them fit your mission and design them to challenge your Warriors.

Reaction training is a tool to gauge the level of proficiency of an element. It can provide a basis for assessing the readiness of an element in a given training scenario. Use it to benefit the element. Show the individuals their mistakes and provide other courses of actions in the AAR. Be sure to cover the strengths and encourage the Warriors to maintain the strengths and improve the weak areas.

Summary of Actions

1. Challenge your Warriors with quality scenarios and they will rise to meet the challenge.
2. Ensure the training is as safe and realistic as possible!
3. Use moral and ethical dilemmas

Resources

Publications for Review

1. FM 7-0   Training for Full Spectrum Operations
2. FM 7-1   Battle Focused Training
3. FM 21-75   Combat Skills of the Soldier
4. TC 25-30   A Leader's Guide to Company Training Meetings

Local Information for Review

Lessons Learned from previous training exercises (both internal and external to your unit)

Chapter Four
CHECKLISTS

The following checklists are guides to help you prepare and conduct efficient training sessions. Please keep in mind that local policies, procedures, and regulations take priority over any checklist or information in this book. The checklists should be used to stimulate thought and for planning purposes only.

After Action Review Checklist

SEQUENCE OF EVENTS	REMARKS
Planning Phase	
Establish objectives for the AAR	

Select qualified observers
 • Observers should not be involved in training
 • Must be
    • Able to perform tasks to be trained
    • Experienced in the duties they evaluate
    • Knowledgeable in current doctrine	

Review the training and evaluation plan	
Identify the participants • Commander identifies who will attend each AAR	
Plan stop points during the exercise for AARs • Plan time for the AAR in the training event ~1hr for Plt., ~1 ½-2 hrs for a company size element • Should be conducted as soon as possible after the event	
Make potential site selections • In the AAR plan, specify the proposed site for the AAR	
Select training aids • Training aids should be placed so that everyone can view them. Examples: models, terrain board, videos	
Draft an AAR Plan	
Review the unit's training objectives and plans	
Preparation Phase	
Review the training objectives, orders, and doctrine	
Observe the training	
Organize the selected AAR site	
Collect information from other observers	
Develop a discussion outline	
Organize and rehearse	
Conduct AAR Phase	
Restate the unit's mission and event's training objectives	

Generate discussions
 • Avoid critiques or lectures
 • Use questions like
    • Why did certain actions take place?
    • How did personnel react to the situation?
    • Have unit members describe what happened
    • Explore alternative courses of actions
    • What happened?
    • What was right/wrong with what happened?	

Focus on the training objective	
Seek maximum participation	
Continually summarize to emphasize key learning points	
Perform the task again as soon as possible to implement corrective action (if required)	

Administering the APFT Checklist

SEQUENCE OF EVENTS	REMARKS
Schedule APFT	
Notify personnel being tested	
Appoint OIC/NCOIC	
Brief OIC/NCOIC to administer APFT IAW FM 21-20 Chapter 14	
Ensure all personnel are properly trained	
Test Site should: (IAW FM 21-20 Chapter 14)	
• Be flat and free of debris	
• Provide a soft flat area for sit-ups & push-ups	
• Running track	
• Should have a solid surface	
• No more than a 3% grade	

• Free of significant hazards
       • Traffic
       • Slippery road surface
       • Heavy pollution	

Have at least two stopwatches on hand for timed events	
It would be a good idea to have communications capability between key leaders (walkie-talkies or vehicle mounted radios)	
Have sufficient quantities of numbered jerseys on hand for each running group	
The night prior to the test, have two vehicles (primary/alternate) with designated drivers dispatched as ambulances. Ensure that the vehicles can accommodate a stretcher.	
Have combat lifesavers at the test site with	
• A complete and inventoried combat lifesaver bag	
• A serviceable stretcher	
Have sufficient quantities of water and disposable cups on hand	
Read APFT instructions to individuals directly from FM 21-20	
• Ask if anyone is sick or has a reason in which they do not feel they cannot adequately take the APFT. (OIC/NCOIC should evaluate each on a case-by-case basis.)	
• Be sure to read the additional points concerning the push-up and sit-up events located in Figures 14-4 and 14-6.	
Have a demonstrator conduct both proper and improper movement of each event, to include items listed in Figures 14-4 and 14-6.	
If a turn-around point is required for the run have an individual stationed there.	
It may be a good idea to have one of the ambulances follow the last runner during the run. The other vehicle should remain at the designated location.	

Army School Checklist

SEQUENCE OF EVENTS	REMARKS
Has the Warrior been identified for school? • OML • ATRRS	
Does the Warrior meet the prerequisites for the course? • GT or other ASVAB scores • Vision requirements • Physical demand rating • TABE test • Security clearance • Passed an APFT within 30 days • Meets standards of AR 600-9	
Has appropriate approval been granted for any waiver to entry requirements?	
Does a temporary profile prevent entry into the course?	
Does the Warrior have a permanent profile?	
Does the Warrior have a copy of the profile on his/her person?	
Has the Warrior received • Read-ahead packets? • Course information packet?	
Does the Warrior have all required clothing and equipment?	
Has the clothing and equipment been inspected by a first-line leader?	
Have transportation arrangements been confirmed?	
Is the Warrior in receipt of travel tickets (if required)?	
Does the Warrior have adequate cash/Govt. credit card?	
Is the Warrior in possession of at least 10 copies of travel orders?	
Does the unit have emergency contact data on the Warrior?	
Has the family been provided an address and POC at the school?	
Does the family have POCs with unit leadership?	
Does the Warrior have valid ID card and tags?	

Range Preparation Checklist

SEQUENCE OF EVENTS	REMARKS
PREPARATION	
Schedule Range (and make-up range)	
Select Range OIC/NCOIC	
Is a Range SOP available? • Has it been picked up? • Are the range OIC/NCOIC familiar with the Range SOP?	
Does the Range require a certification? If so, is the OIC/NCOIC certified?	
Has the appropriate type of ammunition by type and quantity been ordered? (ball, tracer, smoke, blank, belt, drum, AP, WP, HE)	
Has a pickup date been established with the ASP? • What are the hours of operation for pickup? • What are the hours of operation for returning residue?	
Have the individuals firing on the range been notified? • Has a packing list for the range been included in the OPORD?	
Have the following range support personnel been identified? • Armorer • Medical support • Communication support • Ammo detail/Gate guards • Safety NCOs	
Has the following equipment been identified and inspected? • Range vehicles • Communication equipment • Armorer's tool kit • Combat lifesaver bag • Supply items (cups, toilet paper, nails for zero, etc.) • Range kit from range control	
Is the Combat Lifesaver's certification current?	
Have personnel attending the range received marksmanship refresher training? (use simulators, and other methods:dime/washer, shadow box)	
Is concurrent training required? If yes: • Have instructors been identified? • Are the proper training aids available? • Has the training been reviewed?	
Is a meal plan required?	
Have hot soup, juice, coffee been requested?	
Have all vehicles been dispatched?	
Publish Range Operation Order	

Range Checklist

SEQUENCE OF EVENTS	REMARKS
OCCUPATION/CONDUCT RANGE OPS	
Has permission been requested to occupy the range?	
Has the range flag been posted?	
Have two independent means of communication been established with range control?	
Designate ammunition storage area	
• Is the ammunition being stored correctly?	
• Is a fire extinguisher present?	
Designate a smoking area	
Designate a concurrent training area	
Designate Medical area	
Establish water/hot soup/coffee point	
Conduct a range safety briefing	
Review actions for a Misfire, Hang fire, and Malfunction	
Has permission been received to open the range for firing?	
Is a Warrior monitoring the radio with range control?	
Has an area been identified for MEDEVAC purposes?	
Conduct range operations	
Is every Warrior rodded off the range and asked for brass/ammo?	
Is the Warrior's scorecard properly filled out?	
RANGE CLOSURE	
Has the range been policed?	
Have all Warriors been requested to surrender any live ammo/residue?	
Has range control given you a closure time?	
Has the range flag been brought down?	
Have all personnel and equipment been accounted for?	
Complete ammunition paperwork	
Return residue to ammo holding area or ASP	
Ensure that live ammo is separated from residue	
Clean equipment/PMCS equipment	
Turn in scorecards to training NCO	
Ensure accountability of personnel/equipment	
Conduct AAR with Warriors and key leaders	
Out-brief chain of command	
Return range kit and SOP to range control	
Ensure live and blank rounds are not on the range at the same time	

Convoy Checklist

SEQUENCE OF EVENTS	REMARKS
Mission brief to all members of convoy/commander's intent	
Pre-combat inspection for movement completed	
OIC/NCOIC designated	
Listing of sensitive items/personnel/equipment by vehicle	
Order of March	
Convoy speeds: normal/catch-up and intervals	
Route (strip map)/grid to new location	
Lights (blackout drive/blackout markers (blackout areas)	
Ground guide requirements	
SP time	
Staging Area	
Seat belts mandatory	
Frequencies/call signs	
Challenge/Password	
MEDEVAC frequency	
Accident prevention <ul><li>Road conditions</li><li>Check operators for fatigue; replace if required</li><li>Are drivers licensed for vehicle?</li></ul>	
Contaminated areas (actions if encountered)	
Recovery Procedures	
Actions during a vehicle breakdown	
Rally points if lost/separated/attacked	
Check points	
Use of goggles/hearing protection	
Enemy situation	
Actions upon enemy contact: <ul><li>Ambush blocked</li><li>Ambush unblocked</li><li>Ambush (Far/Near)</li><li>Mine strike</li></ul>	
Have vehicles been hardened with sand bags?	
Air defense status <ul><li>Red or Yellow</li><li>Weapon control status is: Hold, Tight, or Free</li></ul>	
Warriors know convoy signals	
Warriors know to stagger at halts	
NOTE: Obtain a Copy of Tactical Convoy Ops (Call Handbook No 03-6)	

Pre-Combat Inspection for Movement Checklist

SEQUENCE OF EVENTS	REMARKS
Vehicle commander	
Vehicle bumper #'s in convoy	
Warriors in proper uniform	
Driver properly licensed	
Vehicle properly dispatched	
Equipment PMCS'd	
Assigned trailer hooked up	
Map or strip map (grid coordinates) to new location	
GPS if available	
Communications gear PMCS'd	
Weapons accounted for	
Weapons function check complete	
Weapons test fire	
Designate air guards	
NBC gear/equipment present/PMCS'd	
Camouflage loaded	
Vehicle basic issue items present/loaded	
Mechanics have assigned tool box	
Ammunition distributed	
NVGs PMCS'd	
Combat lifesaver bag present/inventoried for completeness	
Check blackout drive and lights	
Convoy flags or signals present/discussed in briefing	
Casualty feeder cards on each Warrior	
MREs distributed to each Warrior	
Water • Warrior's canteens full • Vehicle's potable water cans topped off	
Account for all sensitive items	
Account for all personnel	
Place NBC detection paper on hoods of vehicle	

Recovery Operations Checklist

SEQUENCE OF EVENTS	REMARKS
Recovery vehicle PMCS'd/dispatched	
Vehicle topped off	
Spare fuel cans topped off	
Tool box inventoried and present	
Tow bar with pins	
All vehicle basic issue items present	

MREs for:
   • Maintenance personnel
   • Warriors being recovered	

Water
   • Warriors canteens topped off
   • Vehicle's potable water cans topped off	

TA50
   • Rucksack
   • A & B bags
   • NBC gear	

Map (with location of down vehicle plotted)	
Review routes and alternate routes	
Escort requirements	

Sensitive items inventoried
   • NVGs
   • Weapon with ammo
   • Communications equipment	

Parts needed for repair of vehicle	

Check out with Command Post
   • Who, what, when, where, duration of mission
   • Route out and back
   • Call signs
   • Challenge and Password
   • Enemy threat/intelligence brief	

Debrief	
All personnel and equipment accounted for	

Deployment Checklist

Warrior's Printed Name:_____ Rank:_____

SSN:_____   Weapon type and serial number:_____

REQUIREMENT	DATE	REMARKS
Is Warrior's ETS within seven days of deployment?		
Does the Warrior have an approved family care plan on file?		
Has the SGLV been reviewed and updated?		
Has the DD Form 93 been reviewed and updated?		
Does the Warrior have two ID tags w/necklace?		
Has the Warrior received a Geneva convention card?		
Is Warrior a former Peace Corps member in deployed area?		
Has the Warrior been a former POW in the deployed area?		
Does the Warrior have dual citizenship?		
Is the Warrior a sole surviving family member?		
Has the Warrior completed Basic and AIT?		
Does the Warrior have a permanent profile? <ul><li>Does the profile allow for deployment?</li></ul>		
Is the Warrior pending an MMRB?		
Does the deployment require passports or visas? If yes, does the Warrior have the required documents?		
Is the Warrior pending discharge/separation/reassignment?		
Is the Warrior a conscientious objector?		
Has the Warrior's personnel file been reviewed (ORB/ERB)?		
Does the Warrior meet HIV screening requirements?		
Has the Warrior provided a DNA sample?		
Is the Warrior pregnant?		
Are immunizations up to date? <ul><li>Typhoid</li><li>TET/Diphtheria</li><li>MMR</li><li>Polio</li><li>Flu shot</li><li>Hepatitis A</li><li>Gamoglobin</li></ul>		
Does the Warrior require eyeglasses (two each)?		
Does the Warrior require NBC inserts?		
Does the Warrior require a hearing aid?		
Does the Warrior require a medical warning tag?		
Does the Warrior require prescription medication?		
Have the Warrior's medical records been reviewed?		
Are EFMP members enrolled?		
Has the Warrior passed a dental screening?		
Does the Warrior have all required clothing & equipment?		
Is the Warrior pending civilian charges?		
Does the Warrior require a power of attorney?		
Does the Warrior require a will?		

Deployment Checklist (Cont.)

Does the Warrior wish to change/stop/start allotments?		
Have entitlements been verified?		
Have all travel claims been settled?		
Preventative medical brief for deployed area?		
Pregnancy test administered?		
Brief on local laws in deployed area?		
Received terrorist briefing for deployed area?		
Have family members received a deployment brief?		
Have transportation arrangements been made if required?		
Have vehicle storage requirements been arranged?		
Have arrangements been made for storage of privately owned weapons?		
Have housing requirements been addressed (lease, termination of quarters)?		
Has the Warrior received a Geneva convention brief?		
Is the Warrior qualified on individual weapon within 12 months?		
Has the Warrior passed APFT within 12 months?		
Does the Warrior meet security clearance requirements?		
Does the Warrior have sure pay?		

Defensive Planning Checklist

SEQUENCE OF EVENTS	REMARKS
Conduct Recon	
Identify Key Avenues of Approach high speed and stealth	
Emplace most lethal weapons systems in most practical positions	
Ensure you provide 360 degree security including dead space	
Assign Primary/Secondary and Final Protective Fire Lines	
Ensure all avenues of approach are covered	
Identify Target Reference Points (TRPs); coordinate with Bn S-3	
Send out Recon and Security Teams to ensure area around you is secure upon their return	
Emplace Listening Post and Observation Post so that you have eyes around your sensitive areas while you improve your defensive position	
Designate primary and secondary fighting positions	
Designate primary position for NBC alarm System	
Organize and brief reaction force members	
Inspect the defensive position	
Exercise the reaction force	
Emplace barriers/obstacles/mines Cover these with observation and fields of fire	
Organize random patrols • Designate entry and exit points • Coordinate with all elements to include adjacent prior to sending out patrol	
Designate collection points for • Ammunition • POW • Contaminated casualty • Casualty • Maintenance	
Coordinate with all adjacent elements • Close the gaps • Attempt to cover deadspace • Interlock fields of fire	
Send sector sketch to higher S-3	
Plan indirect fire to cover • Dead space • Avenues of approach • Danger areas	
Use mines to cover deadspace	
Check and verify communications • FM radio • Land lines • Other as available	
Establish a dismount point	
Coordinate for use of UAV or other Intel assets	

Unexploded Ordnance (UXO) Checklist

LINE # AND SEQUENCE OF EVENTS	REMARKS
Line 1: Date/Time group discovered	
Line 2: Reporting activity (UIC) and location (Grid)	
Line 3: Contact method: • Radio Freq/Call Sign • Telephone #	
Line 4: Type of munitions: • Dropped = Bombs, sub-munitions, • Projected = Projectiles, Mortars, Rockets, Guided Missiles • Placed = Mines • Thrown = Hand Grenades	
Line 5: NBC contamination	
Line 6: Resources threatened	
Line 7: Impact on mission	
Line 8: Protective measures taken	
Line 9: Recommended priority (Immediate, Indirect, Minor, or no threat)	
PROTECTIVE MEASURES	
Build a barricade far enough away from UXO so it cannot fall on the UXO • 105mm and smaller = full circle barricade • 105mm up to 8 inch = semi circle barricade • Large missile and bombs = wall	
Always interlock sandbags	
Build tall enough to deflect fragmentation and blast effects	
Utilize the minimum number of personnel possible	
Utilize all personal protective equipment	
Clearly mark the UXO area	
SEE GTA 09-12-001 for graphic illustrations	

Mask Removal Checklist

SEQUENCE OF EVENTS	REMARKS
Mask Removal with M256 kit (~15 mins required)	
Check area using M256 kit if results are negative	
Senior person selects one or more Warriors	
Have the Warriors moved to a shady area	
Have the Warriors unmask for 5 minutes	
Clear and reseal the mask	
Observe the Warriors for 10 minutes (watch for symptoms)	
If no symptoms appear give the all-clear	
Watch for delayed symptoms	
Have first aid available	
Mask Removal without M256 kits (~35 minutes required)	
Senior person selects one or two Warriors	
Move the Warriors to a shady area	
Have the Warriors • Take a deep breath • Hold the breath • Break the seal on their mask • Open eyes for 15 seconds	
Clear and reseal the mask	
Observe the Warriors for 10 minutes	
If there are no symptoms have the Warriors • Break the seal on their mask • Take two or three deep breaths	
Clear and reseal the mask	
Observe the Warriors for 10 minutes	
If there are no symptoms have the Warriors • Unmask for 5 minutes • Then clear and reseal their mask	
If no symptoms appear after 10 minutes give the all-clear	
Watch for delayed symptoms	

Weapons Data Chart

WEAPON TYPE	EFFECTIVE RANGE	MAXIMUM RANGE	MINIMUM SAFE RANGE	ARMING RANGE	BACKBLAST AREA	BURST RADIUS
M9 Pistol	50 (P)	1,800	N/A	N/A	N/A	N/A
M16A2	800 (A) 580 (P) 200 (M)	3,600	N/A	N/A	N/A	N/A
M249 MG	800 (A) 600 (P)	3,600	N/A	N/A	N/A	N/A
M203	350 (A) 160 (P)	400	31	14	N/A	N/A
M60	1,100 (A) 600 (P)	3,750	N/A	N/A	N/A	N/A
M2	1830 (A) 1,200 (P)	6,765	N/A	N/A	N/A	N/A
M240	1100 (A tripod) 800 (A bipod) 800 (P tripod) 600 (P bipod) 1800 (suppression) 600 grazing	3,725	N/A	N/A	N/A	N/A
M72 Law	200 (S) 124 (M)	1,000	30	10	50	N/A
M136 (AT4)	300 (S) 300 (M)	2,100	30	30	60	N/A
Dragon	65 (min) 150 (top attack)	2000		65	25-100	
Javelin	2,000	2000	150	150	25-100	
Fragmentation Grenade	N/A	40	16	N/A	N/A	15
WP Grenade	N/A	30	18	N/A	N/A	17
M21 Mine (AT)	N/A	N/A	N/A	N/A	N/A	1TANK
M14 Mine (Antipersonnel)	N/A	N/A	N/A	N/A	N/A	1 Person
M16A1 mine (Antipersonnel)	30	30	31	N/A	N/A	30
M18A2 mine (Claymore)	50	250	N/A	N/A	16	16

All measurements are in meters: (A)= Area, (P)= Point, (S)= Stationary, (M)= Moving targets

NBC & MEDEVAC Request Format

SEQUENCE OF EVENTS	LINE DESIGNATION
NBC-1 (OBSERVER REPORT)	
Type of report • Nuclear • Biological • Chemical	
Position of the observer	Line B
Direction of attack	Line C
Date/Time of attack	Line D
Location of attack	Line F
Type of attack • Nuclear airburst or surface burst or unknown • Chemical (type of agent)	Line H
Flash to Bang time (Nuclear)	Line J

SEQUENCE OF EVENTS	LINE DESIGNATION
MEDEVAC REQUEST	
Wartime Frequency	
Unit Designation and Announce MEDEVAC	Line 1
Grid Location or Landing zone	Line 2
Number of Patients by precedence • 1- Urgent • 2- Priority • 3- Routine • Litter or Ambulatory	Line 3
Type of injury • Laceration, Burn • Fracture, Snake bite, Etc.	Line 4
Intended Manner of Marking LZ	Line 5
Security of LZ (Wartime), Terrain and LZ hazards • Wires, CS, Antennas, Etc.	Line 6
Method of marking pickup site	Line 7
Patient's Name, Rank, SSN & unit	Line 8
Person's Name, Rank, SSN, & unit of person making request	Line 9
Where did it happen, When did it happen, How did it happen	Line 10

* If secure communication is used, request can be transmitted in the clear. Maintain contact with MEDEVAC.

Chapter Five
PHYSICAL TRAINING

The APFT

Let's begin by discussing the requirements of the APFT, frequently asked questions, and areas that may be overlooked. Chapter 14 of FM 21-20 outlines the requirements for administering the APFT while AR 350-1 outlines the specifics of testing and how testing should be administered. Please refer to all applicable ARs, FMs, and local policies/procedures.

Planning and Preparation for Conducting the APFT

Provide notification of the test at least two weeks in advance. Schedule a make-up day approximately one to two weeks later to ensure that absent personnel (due to leaves, pass, TDY, etc.) are afforded the opportunity to test. I highly recommend that unit record tests be scheduled on the long-range training calendar to comply with the semi-annual testing requirement. My suggestion is to schedule these two record tests during the months of October and April.

In addition, I recommend that a monthly for record APFT test be established for new arrivals and other personnel such as Warriors who have fully recovered from profiles, or who do not have a valid APFT. This method can also be used as a proactive measure to ensure that individuals deploying or going TDY are kept within APFT tolerance.

Key Points to Remember

1. You should try to maintain a ratio of one scorer for every 15 Warriors.
2. Anything that gives the Warrior an unfair advantage is not permitted during the APFT.
3. "Weight belts or elastic bandages may or may not provide an advantage. However for standardization, such additional equipment is not authorized unless prescribed by medical personnel; gloves may be worn in cold weather." FM 21-20
4. Safety is the first consideration
5. Medical personnel are not required to be at the test site; however this is subject to local policy. The OIC/NCOIC should have a plan for emergencies and all Warriors involved in administering the APFT should know what that plan is and how to implement it. FM 21-20
6. Warriors who start an event incorrectly must be stopped by the scorer before they complete 10 repetitions and explained what their errors are. FM 21-20
7. Warriors resting in an unauthorized rest position will have their performance in that event terminated immediately. FM 21-20
8. Warriors should be allowed no less than 10 minutes but ideally no more than 20 minutes to recover between each event. FM 21-20.
9. An APFT is not considered valid if the "Warrior cannot begin and end all three events in two hours or less." FM 21-20.
10. The event supervisor will call out the time every 30 seconds and every second for the last 10 seconds of the event. FM 21-20.
11. "Scorers must allow for differences in body shape and structure of each Warrior. The scorer uses each Warrior's starting position as a guide to evaluate each repetition" FM 21-20.

12. If a mat is used the entire body must be on the mat. FM 21-20

13. Warriors may not take any part of the APFT in bare feet. FM 21-20.

14. Feet may not be braced during the pushup event. Ensure a non-slip surface is provided. FM 21-20

15. While doing the sit-up a Warrior "may not help themselves stay in the up position by using the elbows or any part of the arms to lock onto or brace against the legs...Warriors who use this technique will be warned once for the first violation and immediately terminated if it continues." FM 21-20.

16. When a run time falls between two point values on the run score table the lower value is used. FM 21-20

Messages Concerning PT Test

1. Change: Scoring above 300 on the DA form 705 is no long authorized as described in FM 210-20. See message dated 251800Z Jul 2001, Subject: Clarification and Reinforcement of Army Training Policies.... Subject APFT and Height/Weight Requirements.

2. Change: Deployed Warriors: MSG Date Time Group 17121Z DEC 03, Subject: Army Physical Fitness and PME for Warrior deployed in support of OIF and OEF and GWOT:

    a. Para 3B PME reads: The APFT requirement is waived for Warriors returning from combat operations/GWOT deployment, reporting directly to a PME course with 30 or fewer training days. School Commandants will ensure Warriors returning from combat operations/GWOT deployments, reporting directly to a MPE course for more than 30 training days meet the APFT standards prior to graduation

    b. Para 3 E Post deployment reads: Upon return from deployment Warriors will be administered a record APFT no earlier than 3 months for active component and 6 months for reserve component Warriors.

Warriors Should Not Be Tested When

1. Fatigued or ill

2. They have had tiring duties just before taking the APFT

3. Weather or environmental conditions may inhibit performance

Temporary Profiles

According to FM 21-20, Warriors with temporary profiles must take the regular APFT after their profile has expired and they have been provided adequate recovery time. Recovery time is twice the length of the profile, not to exceed 90 days.

Alternate Events

Alternate events are listed in FM 21-20 beginning on page 14-20. Each event contains a scoring chart. The chart lists the minimum standards required to receive a go in the alternate event. It is imperative that anyone administering these events read and become familiar with the requirements of the event being administered.

Several facts not commonly known concerning these events

1. 800 Yard Swim: Key point: Walking on the bottom of the pool to recuperate is authorized. FM 21-20 page 14-21.

2. 6.2 Stationary bike test: "There are many electrically operated stationary bikes in gymnasiums on Army installations. Most are designed for physical fitness training. Only a limited number are designed to accurately assess a person's energy expenditure during exercise (these are the type required for the 6.2

mile test)...are generally found in medical and scientific laboratories...very few are found in gymnasiums on Army installations. Because most of the more common training electrically operated stationary bikes were not designed to accurately assess energy expenditure, they should not be used for the alternate, cardio respiratory APFT event. For accuracy and ease of administration, Warriors. ...Should be tested using a moving bicycle. FM 21-20 page D-0. Note: please check the new FM when it comes out for further guidance on this issue.

3. 6.2 Moving bike test: Can be found on page 14-25.

4. 2.5 Mile Walk: One foot must remain in contact with the ground at all times. No running is permitted.

Frequently Asked Questions

Q: Can a lifecycle be used for the alternative APFT stationary bicycle event?
A: No, only stationary bicycles which can be calibrated and which have mechanically adjustable resistance may be used to test profiled Warriors.

Q: If a Warrior runs a two-mile course that is longer than two miles is the test valid?
A: The test is invalid. The Warrior can accept the score but if the Warrior does not accept the score the test must be given again

Q: If a Warrior does not complete all events on the APFT or is injured during the APFT, does the Warrior fail the APFT?
A: Yes, the Warrior fails the APFT. An injury should be annotated by the OIC/NCOIC in the comment section of the scorecard and the Warrior should go for a medical evaluation. If the Warrior receives a profile a retest will be scheduled after twice the length of the profile, not to exceed 90 days from profile expiration.

Q: If a Warrior is on a temporary profile, can the Warrior perform the push-up and sit-up event without completing an aerobic event and have the APFT count for record?
A: No. IAW AR 350-1, para 1-24 the two-mile run event or an alternate aerobic event (for temporary profiles exceeding 90 days) must be taken for the test to count as record. There must be an aerobic event, for it to count as a record PT test.

Q: Is action required to be initiated by a company commander for personnel who fail two consecutive record APFTs?
A: Yes. IAW AR 350-1, para 1-24, the Warrior will be barred from reenlistment or separated

Q: What exercises are not authorized due to an increase injury rate?
A: None. A message released by the physical fitness school states "exercises listed in FM 21-20 are safe for healthy and uninjured Warriors..." Some exercises are safer than others depending on fitness level. Common sense should always prevail. Go to the physical fitness school Web site and search for a message titled, "Guidance on Safe Execution of Exercises for Physical Training."

Q: Does pregnancy automatically mean no physical training?
A: No. Upon diagnosis of pregnancy, a Warrior is exempt from the regular physical training program of the unit and exempt from PT testing as outlined in AR 350-1 for the duration of the pregnancy and up to six months after pregnancy termination. However, see Army Physical fitness website for Pregnancy programs, and pregnancy is also covered in AR 350-1

Q: Can a unit administer an APFT to a Warrior who is within 30 days of ETS?
A: Yes. A commander may administer an APFT as often as he or she wishes. AR 350-1

Q: Is there a fitness program for pregnant Warriors?
A: Yes. The USAPFS has partnered with the Center for Army Health Promotion and preventive Medicine (CHPPM)

in the development and training for the special conditioning program entitled the Army Pregnancy/Postpartum Physical Training Program. See the Army Pregnancy/Postpartum Physical Training Program Brief

Q: What are the requirements for Warriors over the age of 55 on the APFT?
A: The APFT is mandatory. The 2-mile run event is optional. Warriors over age 55 may replace the 2-mile run with one of the alternate aerobic events. Reference memo # R251850Z (JUL 2001) APFTPOLICYCHANGE25JUL01.pdf. Also see AR 350-1

Q: Can a Warrior scoring 90 points or better in their testable events and passing the alternate aerobic event on the APFT be awarded the APFT Badge?
A: No. A Warrior must score 90 points or better in all events of the APFT to be awarded the badge. Push-ups, sit-ups, and 2-mile run. Reference Chapter 4-9 para. AR 350-1. Chapter 4- para 4-9

Q: What is the proper uniform for the 800m swim test as an alternate event on the APFT?
A: Swimsuit or PFU shorts & shirt

Ideas for Conducting Physical Fitness Training

Several activities can be developed to assist Warriors in achieving physical fitness standards. These activities can be geared toward the unit mission or teamwork. Let your imagination be your guide. You should also ensure that the activity is safe and that the area is free of hazardous objects. Be sure to incorporate combat lifesavers, emergency vehicles, straggler control, communications, and water points as needed. AR 350-1 has now incorporated combative training and other types of physical training. Here are a few examples of PT activities that may be useful in your unit program.

CBRN PT

Most units require mandatory training of some type to be conducted in MOPP4. It is also possible to conduct physical fitness training in MOPP4. It is very important that these events be properly supervised. I would suggest that a medical vehicle and a combat lifesaver with a complete aid bag be on station. In addition, an adequate supply of water should be available for the Warriors participating in the training. It is also important to understand that fields of vision are restricted and that dexterity and agility are also affected by the MOPP suit. Some examples of CBRN physical training might include:

1. NBC volleyball
2. NBC football
3. NBC soccer

Pre Deployment PT

Plan for your deployment, will the deployment be in a hot or cold weather area? If possible train in this type of environment. Get your Warriors use to training in the heat or cold. Use a gradual approach. See the army physical fitness website for more information. Check the Fort Benning website under tenant units and look for the physical fitness school

Post Deployment PT

When returning from deployment Warriors tend to be less physically fit. Physical training programs need to be slowly ramped up. PT test should be scheduled in accordance with guidance on the Army Physical Fitness website.

Team-building Events

Try to select activities that require significant activity. Avoid games that have prolonged periods of rest, such as softball, bowling or other such activities. While these do have team-building qualities they do not require sustained physical activity from all participants. Some good examples of teambuilding sports may include:

Two-Ball Soccer

This game is played just like regular soccer; only two balls are used at the same time. The length of the field and width of the goals can be determined based on the size of the element: a company would need more space than a platoon. Using two balls increases the level of activity in the game and keeps all Warriors involved. It is imperative that Warriors stay alert to their surroundings. This can be a motivating game.

Frisbee Football

The game is played somewhat like regular football but an individual cannot run with the Frisbee. The Frisbee must be thrown; the Warrior that catches the Frisbee may only take two steps and then must attempt to throw the Frisbee to another member of his team. The opposing team must remain at least one arm's length from the individual attempting to throw the Frisbee. The opposing side may attempt to block or intercept the throw. If at any time the Frisbee hits the ground, the opposing team gains possession of the Frisbee at the point of grounding. The objective of the game is to get the Frisbee from your end of the field to your opponent's end zone. The fields may vary in length depending on the size of the element.

Punishment PT

Punishment PT is an excellent workout. As the name implies you are punished for substandard performance. This is an outstanding tool for developing teamwork, adding variety, and getting a great workout. It usually includes push-ups or sit-ups as the punishment exercise. It can be utilized with any type of sports PT event. Here is an example using a game of basketball. Divide into teams. Then anytime a Warrior takes a shot and misses the Warrior must drop and do 5-10 push-ups. While the Warrior that missed the shot drops and executes the exercise the game continues and his/her team must play short. In the event the opposing team scores a basket the team that allowed the score must drop and do push-ups.

Running

You may be innovative in running by adding to the conditions of the run. For example, you may wish to run in a flak vest or in different levels of MOPP gear. However, when conducting these types of runs, take precautions to ensure that the event is as safe as possible. You may need to add combat lifesavers, emergency vehicles, or water points.

Circuit Training

Circuit training is an outstanding physical fitness tool. Circuits are only limited by your imagination. Circuits can be set up in a line or circle formation and can either be timed or require a certain number of repetitions. A whistle should be used to inform the Warriors when to start, stop, and run. Depending on the intensity of the circuit it may be wise to add rest (recovery) stations to the circuit. This allows the Warrior to recovery slightly before moving on. Some examples of rest (recovery) exercises may include: side-straddle hop or jog in place. Here are a few examples of circuit training:

Note: Sandbags may be used for exercises that require weight. The sandbags should be properly marked and weighed. Weights may include 5-, 10-, 15-, 20-, and 25-pound bags. Ensure they are available in sufficient quantity.

Upper Body Circuit

Emphasis is on exercises that targets the upper body. Some examples for this circuit might include: wide arm push-up, tricep extension, diamond push-up, dips, and the bicep curl.

A complete round (all stations) would consist of completing all exercises in the circuit one time. Each exercise should be timed and based upon the fitness level of the personnel participating. The first round could consist of 30 second stations, the second could consist of 20 second stations, and so on.

Upon completing the first station have the Warriors run around the entire circuit and stop at their next station. Once they arrive at their next station have them jog in place until you blow the whistle and they begin exercising. Continue this process until all stations have been completed.

Once a set has been accomplished, you may wish to have the Warriors run around the outside of the circuit for approximately five minutes at a moderate pace (Warriors should use caution during this run and keep their head above their heart when beginning the next exercise. Warriors should not overexert themselves.) Next begin the second set of exercises. Continue the process until you have conducted the number of required sets.

Lower Body Circuit

Conducted in the same manner as the upper body circuit only use exercises for the lower body. For example: sit-up, crunches, bicycle, leg raises, mule kick.

Mixed Circuit

Incorporates exercises from both the upper and lower body circuits.

Running Circuit or Running Route

Establish a running course with exercises along the route. This can be used on an individual or team level. Warriors can compete against each other or against other teams.

Use of Playing Cards

In this technique, each suit of the deck represents a different exercise. For example, diamonds may represent diamond push-ups, clubs may represent crunches, hearts may represent leg raises, and spades may represent rocky sit-ups. The number on the card determines the number of repetitions for the exercise. Jacks and above are assigned an equal value (possibly 10-15 repetitions). For example, a five of hearts would represent five repetitions of leg raises, a Jack of diamonds would equal 10-15 repetitions of diamond push-ups, and so forth.

Aerobics

Aerobics are an excellent tool and only require a space large enough to accommodate your element, music, and an instructor. You may be able to find an aerobics instructor willing to give the class for free. Better yet, one of your Warriors or a spouse may be a certified aerobics instructor. It is definitely a good workout.

Pyramid

This method of exercise is most often used in push-up/sit-up improvement. The idea is to start off with one repetition of the exercise and increase the number of repetitions to some number (usually 10 repetitions). For example, a Warrior would stand at the position of attention, drop to the push-up position, execute one push-up, return to the position of attention, then return to the push-up position and execute two push-ups, then return to the position of attention. This would continue until the Warrior executed 10 repetitions. Upon reaching 10 repetitions, you may wish the Warrior to continue the exercise back down the pyramid.

Ability Groups Runs

An ability group run is an excellent tool that allows Warriors to improve their individual fitness level. Running in formation is good and does develop morale and esprit de corps, but it can be harmful to the morale and individual fitness level if it provides the basis for the unit running program.

Warriors should be broken down into at least three to four groups based on their APFT run times. Warriors wishing to improve upon their run time should be encouraged to run with the next faster group. Competent Warriors need to be placed in charge of these groups. These Warriors need to be able to maintain accountability and enforce safety requirements.

Rifle PT

One of my personal favorites! See FM 21-20 for the explanation of each exercise. This session can be topped off with a run. In addition, you may use the Partner Resistance Exercises in FM 21-20 with a Rifle. Another way to look at the exercise is to view the weapon as the bar when lifting weights. The 'weight' is provided by the partner. Almost any exercise can then be utilized while doing Rifle PT. The following exercises are a few examples:

1. The military press
2. Pull down
3. Tricep extension
4. Curls
5. Bent over row (with partner holding on to weapon)
6. Partner sit-ups with weapons (Warriors weapon & Partners weapon) across chest
7. Butterfly (partner applies resistance)
8. Formations not currently covered in FM 21-20.

Extended Rectangular Formation

This is the traditional formation for most physical training. The element (squad, platoon, company, etc) is centered on the instructor. The element is in a line formation approximately 5 paces away from the instructor. The element assumes the extended rectangular formation from an in-line formation. If Platoons are in column formation, the instructor adjusts the base platoon so that the company is centered when extended. The extension can also be executed from a company mass formation, without an interval between platoons.

Commands to execute the formation

1. Extend to the left MARCH: (movement: Warriors in the right flank file stand fast with their arms extended to the sides at shoulder level. All other Warriors turn to the left and double-time to the left

2. After taking a sufficient number of steps. All Warriors face the front; each has both arms extended to the sides at shoulder level.

3. The distance between fingertips is about 12 inches and dress is to the right

4. Arms downward, MOVE: (movement: The Warriors lower their arms smartly to their sides).

5. Left, FACE: (movement: Warriors execute a left-face.)

6. Extend to the left, MARCH: (movement: Warriors in the right flank file stand fast with their arms extended to the sides. All other Warriors turn to the left and double-time to the left. Spacing is the same as above and dress is to the right).

7. Arms downward. MOVE: (movement: Warriors lower their arms smartly to their sides).

8. Right, FACE: (movement: Warriors execute the right-face movement).

9. From front to rear, COUNT OFF: (movement: The leading Warrior in each column turns head to the right rear. Calls off, "one", and faces the front. Successive Warriors in each column call off in turn "two," "three," "four," and so on. The last Warrior in each column will not turn the head and eyes to the right while sounding off

10. Even numbers to the left, UNCOVER: (movement: All even-numbered Warriors jump to the left squarely centering themselves between the other elements, bringing their feet together. The unit is now ready for stretching and warm-up exercises

11. Assemble to the right, MARCH: (movement: All Warriors double-time to their original positions in column or line formation).

Circular Formation

The circle formation is recommended for guerilla drills, grass drills, and various circuits. This formation's advantage over the extended rectangular formation is that supervising all Warriors is easier; the moving formation permits effective control. More informal than the rectangular formations, the circle formation is excellent for small groups. When more than 30 Warriors must exercise, separate circles should be used. Concentric circles may be used to accommodate more Warriors. If concentric circles are formed, a squad is designated for each. Each additional circle requires more Warriors than the one inside it. For example, one squad of a platoon may form the inner circle, and the other three squads form the outer circle. When concentric circles are employed, the circles rotate in opposite directions.

Commands to Execute a Circle formation

1. Follow Me: (movement: This command is used when a platoon is to form a circle. The left flank squad of the column moves forward at double time. The platoon gradually forms a circle in a counterclockwise direction. Each succeeding file falls in behind the previous squad. Then the rough outline of the circle is formed)

2. Pick Up A 5-Yard Interval: (movement: This command ensures that the interval between Warriors is uniform. The group may be halted and faced toward the center for instruction. If instruction is not necessary, the exercise may be executed without stopping the platoon.

Summary

Your physical fitness program can be exceptional, meet the standard, or fall below standard. It's up to you! Talk with key leaders and Warriors, and get ideas. Leaders provide direction and motivation. Warriors take care of the rest. Encourage junior Warriors to take charge. Make sure they are properly trained and set them up for success.

Your imagination is the key to a successful PT program. FM 21-20 also offers other suggestions such as: grass drills, guerrilla exercises, log drills, aquatic exercises, and orienteering.

Remember, as leaders we influence the motivation of others. It may also be a good idea to develop squad, section, and platoon PT. This must also be monitored to ensure that quality training takes place.

Resources

Publications for Review

1. DOD Directive 1308.1
2. AR 350-1   Army Training and Leader Development
3. AR 600-9   Overweight Program
4. AR 40-25   Nutritional Standards
5. AR 40-501   Standards of Medical Fitness
6. AR 600-63   Army Health Promotion
7. FM 21-20   Army Physical Training
8. FM 3-22.20   Army Physical Readiness Training (Currently in Development)

Local Information for Review

1. Assess current unit APFT scores
2. Discuss PT program with key leaders and Warriors
3. Assess APFT failure rate
4. Assess special population PT training program
5. Assess unit overweight program
6. Assess the profiles in your unit
7. What are the physical requirements of your unit?
8. Does the PT program adequately address the physical requirements of the unit mission?
9. Does the unit have a Master Fitness Trainer?
10. Is the Master Fitness Trainer used in developing the overall program?

On the Web

1. www.hooah4health.com
2. http://www.runnersworld.com

Chapter Six
After Action Review (AAR)

Introduction

After Action Reviews (AARs) are an extremely useful tool if planned and conducted properly. Conversely AARs that are improperly prepared and executed can be detrimental to the event and the overall morale of the element. The main point to remember when conducting an AAR is not to place blame, or turn the session into a lecture. Remember everyone's opinion is valuable.

Involve everyone in the AAR. As leaders we have not cornered the market on good ideas and advice. Sometimes we need to be good followers or better yet, good listeners. Young Warriors often times have useful insight and a different perspective on a given event or procedure. Use their thoughts and suggestions for the benefit of the team.

Some wise advice I once received from two very good leaders:

1. To be a Great Leader you must first be a Great Listener!
2. God gave you one mouth and two ears for a reason; listen twice as much as you speak.

Planning and Preparation

An AAR allows all participants involved in the event to discover for themselves what happened during the event. It is also a useful method for soliciting new ideas on how training could be improved. The basic questions or areas that should be covered in an AAR are:

1. What was supposed to happen?
2. What happened?
3. Why did it happen that way?
4. How could it be done differently?

Each AAR should be planned into the training event. The Commander must make the AAR a priority. The Commander should develop an AAR plan that should include the following information at a minimum:

1. Who will observe the training and conduct the AAR?
2. Observer/Controllers: During the planning phase, leaders must ensure that they have selected quality observers/controllers. These individuals should not participate in the training and they must be:
    a. Able to perform the tasks to be trained.
    b. Experienced in the duties they are to evaluate.
    c. Knowledgeable in current doctrine.
    d. Know what elements of the task or tasks to evaluate
    e. Fully understand training standards and conditions
3. Who will attend the AAR?
    a. The Commander must ensure that all personnel involved in the training event attend the AAR. This includes Key personnel from the Opposing Forces (OPFOR).

How to Conduct the AAR

Elements of the execution should include:

1. When and where will the AAR be conducted?
2. Plan stop points into the training event that allows a smooth transition into the AAR process.
3. AARs should be conducted as soon as possible after the training event.
4. Approximately one hour should be blocked off for platoon size events.
5. Approximately one and a half to two hours should be blocked off for a company size event.
6. Select a site free from distractions.
7. Warriors should be comfortable and feel free to speak their minds.
8. If possible select clean, well-lit areas and make sure juice, hot soup, or coffee is available.
9. Ensure proper training aids are available during the AAR
   a. Examples of training aids may include: models, terrain boards, maps, video clips, recordings)
   b. Training aids add to the effectiveness of the AAR
   c. Aids should be large enough and positioned so that everyone can see them.
   d. The following questions may help to determine the type of training aid you wish to use:
      i. What points do I need to make during the AAR?
      ii. Will the aid illustrate one or more of the points?
      iii. Can the actual terrain or equipment be used?
      iv. Does the aid have any restrictions or requirements, like additional generators?
      v. Will the participants be able to see and hear it?
      vi. Is the aid really required for the discussion?

Proposed AAR Format

Once all these items have been considered, leaders should rehearse the AAR process and develop a discussion outline. In addition, AAR leaders should put their observations into a chronological order for presentation. A possible format for presenting an AAR may look like this:

1. Introduction
2. Presentation of the Commander's and OPFOR's plan
3. Summary of recent events
4. Discussion of key issues
5. Analysis of key BOS (Battlefield Operation Systems)
6. What happened during the battle?
7. Discussion of training to sustain or improve
8. Conclusion

Conducting the AAR

1. Ask thought-provoking questions.
2. Ask leaders what factors influenced their decisions.
3. Have members describe what happened in their own words.
4. Explore other courses of action.

Note: Discussions concerning leader mistakes should be frank, but should not embarrass the leader. It is important not to destroy the trust of the leader; ensure that other Warriors understand in combat they could become the leader very quickly. Explore why the mistake was made and how to avoid it in the future. Also explore why the leader made the decision (what factors influenced that decision).

Please see the AAR checklist in Chapter Four of this book.

Other Resources

Publications for Review:

1. FM 7-0   Training the Force
2. FM 7-1   Battle Focused Training
3. TC 25-20   A Leader's Guide to After-Action Reviews
4. TC 25-30   A Leader's Guide to Company Training Meetings

Local Information for Review:

Previous AARs concerning your unit

Web sites:

http://call.army.mil

Chapter Seven
LANE TRAINING

Introduction

Lane training is an outstanding tool if properly utilized. The training possibilities are only limited by your imagination and resources. Lanes can be used to facilitate training in all types of scenarios, from war-fighting to peace-keeping. This chapter is designed to provide some basic tips and guidance concerning the planning and execution of lane training.

Lane training should be designed to fit the needs of your unit. Again, this section will provide basic information and a few suggestions based upon past experience.

An excellent example of using lane training was employed by one of my former battalion commanders. Each quarter he would publish his quarterly training guidance. The guidance contained certain critical tasks for that quarter. These tasks were incorporated into a battalion-level lane training exercise at the end of the quarter. Each squad or platoon size element was required to practice these tasks and become proficient in them throughout that quarter. At the end of the quarter the battalion commander would personally select one element from each company to challenge the lane.

It was an exceptional tool that motivated the Warriors and was the source of battalion bragging rights for the quarter. By employing this method the Commander chose tasks that fit together, allowed subordinate leaders to train their Warriors to standard, and then assessed their performance by using the lane.

Lane training provides a sense of realism and motivates the Warrior during the course of the training. Lane training is resource-intensive and therefore should only be undertaken if the command is committed to supporting the training effort and eliminating or minimizing training distracters.

Lane training also utilizes the process of "crawl, walk, and run." In my previous example our Commander supported this process with his training guidance. Once the training guidance was published the units would begin conducting the crawl phase of training. The units would continue to train through the walk phase and eventually achieve the run phase. When an element was selected to challenge the lane it was afforded the opportunity to rehearse at the walk phase and then enter the lane in the run phase. Now let's get down the nuts and bolts of the lane.

Planning the Lane

Our S-3 was responsible for planning, establishing, and resourcing the lane. Subordinate units were tasked to provide observer controllers and required equipment. The lane was set up in the following fashion:

1. Assembly Area: The element was tasked to occupy an assigned area. While at this location the element was briefed by the senior observer/controller (O/C). The element was provided an operations order. In addition, the element was briefed on all administrative and safety requirements. These may include Rules of Engagement (ROE), boundaries, phase lines, objective, task, conditions, and standards.
2. Rehearsal: During this phase the element can rehearse the tasks that will be conducted in the lane. These actions are normally performed at the crawl or walk stage. Rehearsal may be conducted in the following ways: Map, Sand Table or Terrain Model, Rock Drill, Tactical exercise without troops, or utilizing available communications.

3. Lane Execution: During this phase the element is required to enter the lane and perform the tasks identified in the operations order at the run phase.
4. After Action Review (AAR): This is a structured group review and evaluation of the element's performance during the execution of the lane. Sufficient time must be devoted to the AAR process. The idea is to train to standard and not time.
5. Retraining: If retraining is required the element is processed through the lane again.

The following is a list of resources that may assist in developing or deriving tasks to support unit METL tasks.

1. MTPs
2. TCs
3. Common tasks manuals
4. Contingency plans
5. TMs
6. Lane books
7. Drills
8. SOPs
9. Subject mater experts
10. FMs
11. AARs
12. Unit leaders

The following tables will review some of the items that should be considered in the planning and preparation phase of lane training.

Pre-Execution Checks for Lane Training Preparation

Items to Consider	Remarks
Have previous lessons learned been incorporated?	
Have leaders been identified?	
Have training distracters been eliminated?	
Have simulations, simulators and other training aids and devices been included?	
Have T&EO and training outlines been acquired or prepared?	
Have lane books been prepared?	
Have TSPs been prepared?	
Have SOPs been updated?	
Have leaders been trained and their proficiency verified?	
Have OCs been identified, equipped, and trained?	
Has the OPFOR been identified, equipped, trained and verified?	
Have Warriors been trained and verified on individual, collective and battle tasks/drills prior to execution?	
Have pre-lane rehearsals been conducted?	
Have slice units been incorporated into the planning and execution of the training?	
Have sufficient AARs been scheduled?	
Is adequate time available for each AAR?	
Has a risk assessment been completed?	
Have safety considerations been incorporated?	
Have leaders been briefed on environmental protection rules and considerations?	
Have training ranges/facilities been requested and approved?	
Has a recon been conducted?	
Are range and maneuver books on hand?	
Are leaders certified to conduct range operations?	
Have convoy clearances been submitted and approved?	
Has transportation been arranged?	
Are organization and special tools on hand?	
Have TADSS been identified, requested, and acquired?	
Can trainers operate all equipment to include TADDS/Targetry?	
Has all equipment (including communication) been tested?	
Has Class I (rations) been requested and arranged?	
Has Class III (POL) been requested and allocated?	
Has Class IV (construction/barrier material) been requested and picked up?	
Has Class V (ammunition) been requested and picked up and turn-in coordinated?	
Has Class IX (repair parts) been requested/pick-up times coordinated?	
Are latrine facilities adequate? Have portable toilets been pre-positioned?	
Are sufficient expendable supplies on hand? (Have they been requested and arranged?)	
Has a back brief to the chain of command been coordinated?	

Pre-Execution Checks for Lane Training Preparation (Cont.)

Items to Consider	Remarks
Have security issues been resolved?	
Weapons, vehicles, and equipment issued and camouflaged?	
MILES mounted, operational, and zeroed?	
All TADDS on hand and operational?	
Personnel camouflaged?	
OPORD briefed? (Leaders and Warriors know the mission, commander's intent and what is expected of them.)	
Have individual and small element task rehearsals been conducted?	
Safety checks and briefings completed?	
Safety equipment on hand?	
Medical support present and prepared?	
Environmental concerns and controls identified?	
Leader equipment inspected: compass, strip map, binos?	
Warrior equipment inspected: weapons, LBE, ID tags, driver's license, etc.?	
Communications check conducted?	
Are Class I, III, IV, V, and IX available and coordinated?	
Reference material available?	
Transportation coordinated?	
All equipment PMCS'd?	
Vehicle load plans checked (cargo secure)?	
Convoy route and plan briefed?	
Quartering party briefed and dispatched?	
Slice elements incorporated?	
OPFOR Warriors deployed and prepared?	

Rules of Engagement (ROE)

Rules of engagement are important to ensure the safety of those involved and ensure that the main objective of the training will be accomplished. The following is a sample ROE.

1. All personnel will wear MILES from the point of entry into the assembly area until exiting the AAR area.
2. Safety of Warriors always takes precedence over ROE.
3. Any Warrior who becomes a MILES casualty while reacting to a real casualty or equipment damage will not be assessed as a casualty.
4. Blanks will never be fired at personnel within 20 feet.
5. No searches: This exercise will not evaluate the process of searching enemy prisoners of war. Therefore there is no need for physical contact between Warriors and OPFOR.
6. No physical contact
7. No restraint or retraining devices are authorized
8. No confiscation of equipment, food, water, or ammunition
9. At the end of the exercise all weapons will be cleared and remain with the assigned Warrior.
10. Simulators will be under the control of OCs at all times.
11. Careless handling of equipment will be assessed by the OC as damaged. (If the item is ordnance, personnel casualties may be assessed as well.)
12. MILES casualties that occur due to friendly fire while not in contact are still casualties.
13. Warriors will not be assessed as casualties by the OC for taking tactically inappropriate actions.
14. MILES sensors may not be covered in any way.
15. All Warriors must have a casualty card.
16. All Warriors who have been killed must immediately deactivate their MILES and remove their headgear and open their casualty cards.
17. Wounded Warriors may not communicate with other Warriors in any way.

Violations of ROE

1. Warriors who accidentally break ROE or cross a lane boundary will be assessed by the OC as a casualty.
2. Warriors who intentionally cheat will be assessed as casualties and returned administratively to the unit chain of command.
3. MILES will be tested frequently by the OC.
4. Warriors who have tampered with MILES equipment will be ejected from the exercise.
5. Warriors with inoperative MILES cannot continue in the game (if you cannot be killed, you cannot kill).

Phases of Lane Training

The lane training process can be simplified by breaking it down into the three phases:

Plan

1. Conduct long-range planning
2. Conduct short-range planning
3. Conduct near-term planning

Execute

1. Perform assembly procedures
2. Perform rehearsal procedures
3. Perform lane execution procedures
4. Perform AAR procedures
5. Perform retraining procedures as required

Assess

1. Perform AAR planning procedures
2. Perform AAR preparation procedures
3. Conduct AAR
4. Perform follow-up procedures

Summary

As stated previously, each lane will be setup based upon the needs of a given unit. Training will only be as successful as you make it. Planning and resourcing are essential. Again, I found that utilizing the commander's quarterly training guidance was an excellent example for implementing lane training.

When coordinating for OC support we utilized two OCs per element in the lane. For example, an OC remained with the element from the AA to the AAR area. We will call this individual the Main OC. This Main OC never left the element and constantly recorded key points along the way.

In addition, an OC was stationed at each event or task point along the lane. As the element exited a given task or station, the OC for that task passed off a check sheet or mini-AAR to the Main OC. This method gave the main OC a second set of eyes during each task. The Main OC then used his notes and the notes of the other OCs during the exit AAR at the end of the lane. The check sheets must be designed to facilitate clear and concise information to the Main OC.

Key Points

1. Identify tasks to be trained in the quarterly training guidance.
2. Lock in the date for the Lane Training exercise.
3. Coordinate duties and responsibilities for the setup and execution of the lane.
4. Identify, request, and verify training aids.
5. Train OCs and other lane support personnel.
6. Have subordinate units train on lane tasks throughout the quarter (crawl, walk, run).

7. Conduct rehearsal of the lane with OCs and lane personnel.
8. Have an OC with each element entering the lane and one located at each task throughout the lane.
9. Execute the lane.
10. Conduct AAR.
11. Retrain if required.

Resources

Publications for Review

1. FM 25-4   How to Conduct Training Exercises
2. FM 7-0   Training the Force
3. FM 7-1   Battle Focused Training
4. TC 25-10   A Leader's Guide to Lane Training
5. TC 25-20   A Leader's Guide to After Action Reviews
6. TC 25-30   A Leader's Guide to Company Training Meetings

Local Information for Review

1. AARs from previous training events
2. Commander's current unit assessment

On the Web

1. http://call.army.mil
2. Search "AAR" or "Lane Training"

Chapter Eight
WEAPONS TRAINING

Introduction

Weapons qualification draws to the core of our business as Warriors. Each Warrior must be capable of engaging targets with their respective weapon systems.

Weapons qualification is a serious topic and needs command emphasis to be effective. It is not enough to qualify a Warrior twice a year on his/her assigned weapon. Warriors need more training --- preferably live fire --- to stay sharp on marksmanship skills. At times resources may be a problem (ranges not available, not enough ammunition to support additional training); however, I encourage you to utilize all available resources to improve your marksmanship program.

Incorporate marksmanship into training events. For example: if an element is already conducting operations in the field, try to schedule a night scope or night fire range at the same time. Have the unit road march to the range, conduct live fire operations, and then continue on with their mission.

You may even consider working with other units to see if they have ammunition they are not going to utilize. If they do coordinate with them to use their ammunition or piggy back off of their ranges if possible. Working with other units is an excellent way to improve your weapons qualification program and reduce resource burdens.

The possibilities are endless. It takes some imagination, resource management, and command emphasis, but the result will be worth your efforts.

Preparing for Qualification

Most units have established a rifle marksmanship training program, but these are only as good as the individuals in charge of the training. I encourage you to select a trainer that is an expert on the weapon system they will teach. Also ensure this trainer has the skill set to be a good instructor. Remember as leaders we don't necessarily possess all the answers or skills. Be willing to utilize Warriors with the skills and expertise. At times these experts may be junior Warriors.

The following suggestions are actions I have previously used to conduct marksmanship training. The individual you select should become your unit's master small arms trainers for a particular weapon system or systems and be responsible for conducting, preparing, and designing the training.

Three weeks prior to the range I would schedule the appropriate training for each weapon system. These may include:

1. A quick refresher class on the basics of the weapon: how to aim, reduce a stoppage, misfire procedures and engage targets with the weapon.
2. Basic rifle marksmanship including the following areas:
   a. Mechanical Zero
   b. Grouping
   c. Zeroing
   d. Dime washer exercise
   e. Riddle aiming device

    f.   Shadow box

    g.   Review night fire techniques

    h.   Conduct dry fire in NBC gear using the shadow box method

    i.   Supported and non-supported positions

    j.   Breathing techniques

    k.   Estimating ranges

    l.   Methods of observation

    m.   Basic and advanced firing positions

    n.   Malfunctions and corrections

Approximately six-nine weeks prior to the range I would reserve any and all types of computer simulated weapon trainers related to the weapons that will be fired, familiarized, or qualified. Each Warrior, regardless of rank, should be required to qualify using simulators. Remember it is important to expose as many soldiers as possible to weapons systems. Simulators are an excellent tool to expose assistant gunners or alternate personnel to their duties without expending live rounds. The more Warriors that are familiar with a weapon system the stronger your team!

The week of the range I coordinated to have the simulator available at the range (if the system was transportable). Warriors who had difficulty qualifying in the past were sent to the simulator prior to firing. In addition it was used at the range as concurrent or sustainment training.

We also provided intense one on one training for Warriors that had difficulty with previous qualifications or displayed problems during simulation practice.

Tips for Improving your Marksmanship

1. Consider marking the front sight post of the M16 with a small dot of white to provide contrast between the target and front sight.
2. Utilize the entire allotment of ammunition to qualify the Warrior
3. Utilize the entire 18 rounds for qualification (M16)
4. Utilize the 40 rounds of practice ammunition prior to record fire (M16)
5. If a Warrior qualifies expert during the 40 rounds of practice fire let this qualification count and save his 40 alotted for actual qualification for soldiers that may need additional rounds to improve their accuracy.
6. Conduct night fire and NBC fire more than just at range qualification. If ammunition is short conduct these operations in a dry fire sequence.
7. Conduct a night fire range utilizing night scopes for weapons. Review the process of zeroing and engaging targets with night sights mounted on the weapon.
8. Conduct known distance ranges.
9. Conduct moving target exercises. Some techniques that have been utilized in past training (AARs) include:
   a. Constructing simple frames out of 2-by-4s and hang balloons or plastic bottles from them. The wind will move these devices, giving the Warriors an opportunity to engage moving targets.
   b. Placing plastic bottles in the water if on board a ship. The motion of the water provides a moving target. Chem lights can be placed inside the bottle for night fire practices.
   c. Crew drill: insert a 4-by-4 post into the ground. Have the element train its weapons on the 4-by-4 and attempt to cut it in half. Make it a competition among squads.
   d. Consider conducting a quick-fire training exercise. This involves live fire of squad-size elements.
   e. Utilize MOUT sites or room clearing procedures

The possibilities are endless and only limited by your imagination, resource, and range policies.

These techniques helped make our marksmanship program successful. We required each Warrior to complete the gates. The repetitive nature of the training built confidence and enforced the fundamentals of firing. Weapons qualification is a perishable skill; many Warriors need the training prior to range qualification. Using these techniques will dramatically improve your marksmanship program.

NOTE: Check with your local range control prior to conducting any of the above exercises. Ensure that your chain of command supports the actions. Do not implement the training without proper approval. Ensure that a risk assessment is completed and approved by the appropriate approving authority.

Make the training realistic. Add a sense of competition by offering an incentive to the best marksman or squad, with awards like Best Shooter in the Company/Battalion for both the individual, crew, or squad. This doesn't sound like much, but it does motivate Warriors.

Lessons Learned

Always conduct AARs after your range events. Incorporate lessons learned into future training. I suggest keeping them on file in the unit training room. Here are a few examples of lessons learned:

1. Regardless of how busy your unit is, make time to properly PMCS the weapon.
2. Warriors need to set their weapon to mechanical zero prior to arrival at the range (it saves valuable time in the zeroing process).
3. We used computer simulator as much as possible in our unit areas. These included: MACs, Weaponeer or The Skills Engagement Trainers.
4. As a Warrior is zeroed pull him off the range and replace him with a new Warrior. This keeps the pace of the zero range going and prevents a backlog.
5. When Warriors zeroed but failed to qualify: Bring the Warrior back to the zero range and have them fire six rounds instead of three. This allows the leader to clearly identify the Warrior's center of mass. Warriors were able to qualify after this adjustment.
6. If Warriors are unable to zero in 18 rounds: It was observed that after making corrections to the weapon the Warrior adjusted his point of aim. Remind Warriors to consistently aim center of mass.

The Best Lesson Learned of All: As a BN CSM I observed an M249 gunner not returning fire. They stated they had no ammo. I Yelled "you have magazine don't you?" They replied "Yes". I jumped into the foxhole and loaded the weapon and began to fire. After the incident. I asked the Warrior if this was their assigned weapon. They stated yes but they had never fired it, torn it down, loaded it...etc.

Implement a weapons certification program that requires all leaders to know how to load, unload, reduce a stoppage, clear, disassemble, assemble, and perform a function check on all weapons assigned to the unit.

Never assume that leaders know how to do a task simply because they are wearing a the rank of a leader. Many leaders have not had the exposure to multiple weapon systems. Teach them so they can train their soldiers.

Resources

Publications for Review

1. AR 350-1   Army Training and Leader Development
2. DA PAM 350-38 Standards in Weapons Training

3. FM 3-22.9   RIFLE MARKSMANSHIP M16-/M4-SERIES WEAPONS
4. FM 3-22.27   MK 19, 40-MM GRENADE MACHINE GUN
5. FM 3-22.31   40-MM GRENADE LAUNCHER, M203
6. FM 3-22.34   TOW WEAPON SYSTEM
7. FM 3-22.37   JAVELIN -- CLOSE COMBAT MISSLIE SYSTEM
8. FM 3-22.40   TACTICAL EMPLOYMENT OF NONLETHAL WEAPONS
9. FM 3-22.65   BROWNING MACHINE GUN CALIBER .50 HB, M2
10. FM 3-22.68   CREW-SERVED MACHINE GUNS 5.56-MM AND 7.62-MM
11. FM 3-23.24   M47 DRAGON MEDIUM ANTITANK WEAPON SYSTEM
12. FM 3-23.25   SHOULDER-LAUNCHED MUNITIONS
13. FM 3-23.30   GRENADES AND PYROTECHNIC SIGNALS
14. FM 3-23.35   COMBAT TRAINING WITH PISTOLS, M9 AND M11
15. FM 3-23.25   LIGHT ANTI-ARMOR WEAPONS
16. FM 23-10   SNIPER TRAINING
17. FM 23-23   M18A1 CLAYMORE MINE
18. TC 23-11   STAR LIGHT SCOPE SMALL HAND HELD OR INDIVIDUAL WEAPONS MOUNTED
19. TC 23-13   CREW SERVED WEAPON NIGHT VISION SIGHT
20. Related TMs

Local Information for Review

1. Previous weapon qualification scores
2. Unit's marksmanship training program prior to range operations
3. Identify Warriors with previous qualification problems

On the Web

1. http://call.army.mil
2. Search "AARs", "marksmanship", or "weapons"

Chapter Nine
FAMILY READINESS GROUP

Introduction

Family Readiness Groups (FRG) are an integral part of the unit, but they are sometimes overlooked. This chapter will focus on the basics of a FRG, but please keep in mind there is no exact model for forming and organizing a FRG. A FRG should be tailored to the individual needs of the unit. A program that works in one unit may not necessarily work in another unit. This program needs command emphasis! The support of a FRG should be strongly encouraged but is not mandatory

The Basics

The purpose of the FRG is to allow people within a unit to help each other. FRGs provide a communication network to pass information to families and identify needs to the command. The unit chaplain should be utilized as a key advisor and resource for the FRG. In addition, the unit should appoint a military member to act as the liaison with the FRG.

The FRG should be given access to a meeting place within the unit (day rooms, lawns, dining facilities, chapels, theaters, or other facilities). In addition, the FRG should have access to other types of support such as unit phones, reproduction capabilities, mailing privileges, and equipment.

There are several agencies that can provide support to the unit FRG. These agencies include: the unit chaplain, ACS, AER, and Installation Volunteer Coordinator (IVC). Some installations establish Family Assistance Centers (FAC) during deployments and mobilizations. These facilities furnish information, assistance, guidance, and referrals for family members.

Prior to a deployment or extended field exercise it is a good idea to conduct pre-deployment briefings for the family members. As such you should incorporate FRG tasks into your unit METL matrix.

Goals and Activities for FRGs

1. Provide an opportunity for family members to mutually support one another.
2. Develop and operate systems to provide information and education programs and orient new families, promote involvement, and prevent isolation.
3. Interact with military family members, the unit commander, and rear detachment commander.
4. Help involve families in unit activities.
5. Refer family needs that cannot be met by the FRG.
6. Provide information to families who remain in the local area while Warriors serve unaccompanied tours.
7. Assist units in developing and evaluating mobilization and deployment handbooks.

Activities FRGs Should Avoid

1. Becoming surrogate parents.
2. Becoming social workers.
3. Lending money, cars, or expensive items.
4. Dividing into groups (enlisted vs. officer spouses, ethnic groups, or religious groups).

5. Becoming a babysitting or errand service.

6. Duplicating on post or community activities (providing food or money, etc.).

Tips For Starting and Maintaining a Successful FRG

1. A genuine concern, interest, and willingness to establish and sustain a FRG

2. Family member leadership and participation in organizing and operating the FRG

3. Early contact of new spouses by unit leaders and FRG volunteers

4. Establish a command and family member committee to develop the organization of the total family support system

5. Maintain record of volunteer performance and contributions.

6. Will assist in providing recognition (awards, letters)

7. Delineate respective roles of each position

8. DA PAM 608-47 (now obsolete but can usually be found by doing an internet search. It has some good information in it. Just remember this is no longer policy. It contains some ideas, or good to know information) to include:

   a. Sample FRG support worksheet

   b. Sample FRG responsibilities

   c. Guidelines for Telephone Contact

   d. Volunteer job description

9. Appoint FRG volunteer leaders at the company and battalion levels

10. Make the FRG part of the unit written deployment family assistance plan

11. Studies have shown that the overriding factor in the success of an FRG is that the volunteer is truly a volunteer. Remember the FRG leader does not have to be the Commander's or 1SG's spouse. It should be the best person for the job.

12. Volunteers can be elected by the group or selected because they emerge from the group as a leader

Rosters Made Available to the FRG

The following rosters should be provided to or be generated by the FRG. These include:

1. Unit roster: updated names, addresses, and telephone numbers of Warriors assigned to the unit

2. FRG membership roster updated names, addresses, and telephone number of Warriors and families in the unit. Participation must be on a voluntary basis.

3. FRG volunteer roster. Roster: names, addresses, and telephone numbers of each unit volunteer. In addition, it would be a good idea to identify volunteers for specific types of duties based upon their individual skills. For example, someone who does not have good people skills may be better at working on the unit newsletter, while some who has good people skills may be the person to contact individuals by phone

These rosters must be used IAW with Privacy Act considerations.

Possible Uses for the FRG

1. Warrior and family sponsorship

2. Unit welcoming or newcomers orientation

3. Holiday and unit parties or outings

4. Deployment briefings

5. Relocation briefings
6. Workshops (military benefits, prenatal care, preparing for deployments, service for coping with stress, reunions, and homecomings)
7. Use of Government Equipment, Services, and Funds
8. The following items may be available to your FRG. Review DA PAM 608-47 for in-depth details and check with local policies.
   a. Official mail services are authorized under certain conditions for FRGs.
   b. FRG newsletters can be printed with appropriate funds provided the information is considered official and approved by the commander.
   c. FRG volunteers may use government facilities to include dedicated office space, desk(s), equipment, supplies, and telephones needed to accomplish assigned duties.
   d. Use of military vehicles may be authorized IAW AR 58-1.
   e. It may be possible for Commanders to authorize either appropriated or non-appropriated funds to pay for travel and training of volunteers, to improve their effectiveness in assigned roles or to enable them to accept increasingly responsible challenges. See your local ACS advisor.
   f. Reimbursement of incidental expenses may be authorized. See AR 608-1 and AR 215-1 for possible details.

FRG-Generated Funds

See your ACS or MWR advisor for Rules in generating funds for your FRG. They can point you to the proper regulation

FRG funds are considered informal and do not have to apply for Private Organization status as long as their funds do not exceed $1000. They may exceed the $1,000 limit under certain conditions. Please review the regulation for specifics.

Only one person is responsible for maintaining, accounting for, and documenting spending of the funds. This does not mean that only one signature is required to spend money. However, the individual responsible for supervision of the fund will provide an annual financial report to the commander.

Use of the funds is limited to the expenses that support the purpose and mission of the FRG.

It is recommended that FRG funds not be invested in interest or dividend bearing accounts. Otherwise the FRG may be liable for local, state, or federal taxes.

FRGs can raise money for their activities through authorized fund-raising activities. These activities must be approved by the appropriate local authority.

Methods to Elicit Volunteer Involvement

1. Send command letter to all family members in each company inviting them to participate on a committee or attend a briefing.
2. Send a command invitation to key family member of leaders within the unit asking them to attend a committee meeting or briefing.
3. Conduct a command briefing for Warriors and spouses of each unit, outlining the family support system and the importance placed on FRG involvement. The briefing may include the following information:
   a. Mission of the unit
   b. The basic concepts and goals of the FRG

c. Why family member involvement is so important

d. Personal or written testimonials about successful FRG initiatives

e. Let attendees ask questions and make comments.

f. Limit demands placed on one individual (avoid burn-out).

g. Employ people in areas where they can excel.

h. Develop a pro-family atmosphere.

Training that Will Assist FRG Volunteers

1. Effective communication
2. Coping with stress
3. Active listening
4. Conflict resolution
5. Problem-solving
6. Effective meetings
7. Crisis intervention
8. Management and leadership skills
9. Use of community resources
10. Time management
11. Principles of information and referral
12. Volunteer management and motivation
13. Use of a telephone tree
14. Preparing a newsletter
15. Military correspondence
16. Team-building

Possible Fund-raisers

1. Bake sales
2. Making and selling unit cookbooks
3. Car washes
4. Selling of unit T-shirts, hats, pins
5. Potluck dinners (with a different ethnic theme each time)

Note: Try to have fund raisers that bring money in from other people. Do not rely on the soldiers in your unit to by items to support their own events.

Possible FRG Sponsored Functions/Events

1. Potluck dinners
2. Sporting events (softball, bowling, skating)
3. Unit recreational days
4. Sending birthday cookies to deployed Warriors
5. Formal dinners
6. Exchanging video tapes (sending them to deployed Warriors)
7. Stuffing stockings for deployed Warriors

8. Conducting homecoming for returning Warriors (some local merchants may donate food to support these functions)
9. Unit newsletter

Items to Consider

1. Write a letter of introduction to the members of the unit
2. How often should we conduct meetings?
3. Who will be in charge of the meeting?
4. Who will be responsible for maintaining rosters?
5. Who will be responsible for maintaining and accounting for funding?
6. Who will be in charge of the FRG?
7. How should the group be structured?

Important Documents Checklist

DOCUMENTS	LOCATION
Marriage certificate	
Birth certificate	
Baptismal certificate	
Adoption papers	
Citizenship papers	
Passports	
Armed Forces ID cards (Expiration date?)	
Wills	
Family medical records	
Family dental records	
Shot records	
Social Security cards/numbers	
Court Orders (divorce/child custody)	
Copy of emergency data card	
Copy of SGLI election form	
Addresses/phone numbers of immediate family	
Powers of attorney	
Copies of TDY/PCS orders	
Insurance policies (life, auto, home, property)	
Leave and Earnings Statement	
Bank account numbers (checking/savings)	
Checkbook	
List of investments/bonds	
Deed mortgage papers	
Copies of installment contracts	
Credit card/club cards	
Federal and state tax records	
Driver's license	
Car registration, title, inspection certificates	
POV shipping documents	
Warranties on car or appliances	
Inventory of household goods	
Pet health/vaccination records	
Ration book	
Gas coupons	
Extra key (car, house, safe deposit box)	
Diplomas/school transcripts	
Spouse's employment resume	
Family photo album	
List of important numbers (FRG, rear det)	
Dependent child care plan	

Family Readiness Group Questionnaire

Note: A Privacy Act statement must be furnished to the individual before this form is completed.

Name:_____

Military Member's Name:_____

Home Address:_____

Phone:_____

Children
Name/Age:_____
_____
_____
_____

Do you have transportation?   Y   N

Do you speak a language other than English?   Y   N

    If so which language(s) do you speak:_____

Do you have any other family members in the area?   Y   N

Telephone numbers of family members in the area_____

Name and telephone number of a local friend or neighbor:_____

Other than your spouse, who would we notify in case of an emergency: (name, phone, address, relationship)_____

Are you willing to assist other family members in your unit?   Y   N

    What would you like to do?

        Telephoning   Y   N

        Babysitting   Y   N

        Occasional transportation   Y   N

        Planning company activities   Y   N

        Assisting with the company newsletter   Y   N

        Other_____   Y   N

What would you like to see the FRG accomplish?_____

_____
_____
_____
_____

Do you have any skills/talents that you would be willing to share with the FRG?

_____
_____
_____
_____

Resources

Publications for Review

1. AR 608-1   Army Community Service Center
2. The Military Spouse   Available at your local clothing sales store

Local Information for Review

1. Unit SOPs
2. Rear detachment Policies
3. Phone Rosters
4. Volunteer Lists
5. AARs on Family Support Group Past Activities
6. ACS
7. AER

On the Web

1. Search for Family Support Groups or FRG
2. CALL: http://call.army.mil
3. ACS: http://www.myarmylifetoo.com
4. AER: http://www.aerhq.org/
5. MWR: http://www.armymwr.com/
6. BOSS: http://www.armymwr.com/portal/recreation/single
7. Red Cross: http://www.redcross.org/
8. Military One Source: http://www.militaryonesource.com

Chapter Ten
CONSOLIDATED TRAINING SUBJECTS

This chapter contains numerous subjects related to training, it was not feasible to list all the training publications or websites that may be available. I tried to mention significant publications by subject area. Do not limit yourself to the publications listed in this book. Quality training means thinking of real-world situations and putting them to use in the training environment. Use the suggestions in this chapter to stimulate your thought process and develop training that is realistic and challenging to your Warriors. Look at real world events, the evening news, world news, etc.

There are several approaches you may choose to use. For instance, training can be planned using the crawl, walk, and run method. This means that the Warriors are aware the training is to take place, it is explained to them, demonstrated to them and finally they are asked to perform the training. Another approach would be to simply place the Warriors in a training situation and evaluate their performance.

Each method has its benefits and shortfalls, but basically if the Warriors have not been trained in the tasks, or require refresher training, use the crawl, walk, and run methods.

If the Warriors have received training or should be proficient in the task, simply place them in a training scenario and evaluate them. The more you challenge your Warriors the more they will excel.

I have listed subject areas that I believe are important and require training. Below each subject area will be topics or scenarios that I believe are important for Warriors to know or understand. Do not let this be a stand-alone list, use your thoughts and experience to modify or add to these items.

Be innovative! Challenge your Warriors. Do your best to minimize risks and complete the training as safely as possible. Any training that is high-risk should be approved at the appropriate level.

Utilize all available resources for your training. Tap the experts! For example, have a military intelligence interrogation team teach a class on resisting interrogation efforts, or have legal give a class on chapter separations, etc.

As I mentioned earlier, it is very important to implement training in a realistic manner. At times our training opportunities may be restricted due to limited resources such as time, mission, money, or lack of training areas. It is very important to take advantage of every training opportunity.

For example, you may determine that your element needs training in CBRN operations, but you lack the available time for training. Previously we have discussed incorporating training into your schedule by altering the task, conditions, and standards of your current day's mission. Here is an example of how to incorporate CBRN training into a daily work schedule.

1. During motor stables, have your Warriors perform PMCS in MOPP4
2. Conduct services in MOPP4
3. Recover/repair a vehicle in MOPP4.

These conditions may add additional time to the required task, but it helps to prepare the Warrior for working under these conditions. It also offers an opportunity to discover other methods of conducting procedures while in MOPP gear, and provides an overall training benefit to the Warrior and unit. Ensure that appropriate safety precautions are taken and inform your chain of command of any changes in the training schedule.

CBRN Training

References: AR 350-1, FM 21-20, FMs related to CBRN

CBRN training plays an important role in military operations and is extremely important to the survivability of our forces. At times CBRN may not receive appropriate emphasis; consider incorporating CBRN tasks into your daily mission requirements.

Methods of Incorporating

1. Conduct CBRN physical fitness training
    a. CBRN Football
    b. CBRN Soccer
    c. CBRN Frisbee Football
    d. CBRN Road March
    e. CBRN Rifle PT
    f. CBRN 2 Ball Soccer
    g. CBRN Frisbee Football
2. Conduct daily operations in an CBRN environment
    a. All sections or platoons work in a level of MOPP 0-4.
    b. Increase MOPP posture throughout the day.
    c. Send information over unit communications net. See if the information to upgrade MOPP posture is being passed by leaders and is accurate/timely.
    d. Have Warriors conduct conversations over the phone and radio in MOPP 4.
3. Conduct maintenance operations in an CBRN environment.
    a. PMCS
    b. Conduct PMCS on all CBRN equipment on a weekly/monthly basis; make it part of motor stables
    c. Prepare your vehicles to cross a contaminated area during motor stables.
    d. Services
    e. Recovery/repair operations
    f. Ordering parts

Tasks to Consider

1. Conduct Deliberate Decontamination
2. Ask a chemical company to establish a decontamination point for your unit complete with shower points. Utilize this at a mid-point in a field training exercise or at the end of the exercise.
3. Conduct Hasty Decontamination.
4. Coordinate with Chemical Company for a Decontamination exercise.
5. Send CBRN Reports.
6. Cross a Contaminated Area.
7. Conduct CBRN Survey and Monitoring.
8. Assess Unit CBRN Team.
9. During a unit alert gather your unit CBRN teams and require them to conduct a survey of an area, to include all duties they would normally be required to conduct in an actual CBRN environment. By evaluating a slice you do not tie up all the assets within your element. This process can be applied to other sections such as maintenance recovery or the reaction force.

10. Conduct Unmasking Procedures.
11. Conduct MOPP Gear Exchange.
12. Administer First Aid to Nerve Agent Casualty.
13. Administer First Aid to Blister Agent Casualty.
14. Use Latrine in MOPP 4.
15. Prepare CBRN Alarm for Use.
16. Operate Cam.
17. Conduct CBRN advance Party Operations.
18. Conduct an CBRN Lane Competition.

Incentives

Consider providing recognition in the form of

1. Certificates of achievement
2. Special unit awards
3. Coins
4. Letters of appreciation/achievement
5. A pat on the back for:
6. Best CBRN team

Physical Fitness Training

References: AR 350-1, FM 21-20

Since PT is already a part of a Warrior's life most of the events listed below can easily be incorporated into a PT program.

Tasks to Consider

1. Log Drills
2. Guerrilla Drills
3. Grass drills
4. Partner Resistance Exercises
5. Runs:
   a. Long Slow Runs
   b. Laps (run one lap fast then jog a lap, or run a certain distance and then jog twice the distance); builds endurance and speed.
   c. Last Person Up Runs
   d. Ability Group Runs
   e. Short Fast Runs
   f. Flak Vest Run
   g. Rifle PT Run
   h. Run with exercise stations along the route
   i. Run in conjunction with an orienteering exercise

      j.   Scavenger runs: a competition in which individuals or teams are provided a hint and must figure out where to go next in order to claim an artifact. Individuals/Teams with the fastest times and the correct artifacts are considered the winners.

6. Road March
   a. Distance
   b. CBRN March
7. Circuit Training
   a. Sandbag Circuit
   b. Upper Body Circuit
   c. Lower Body Circuit
   d. Mixed Circuit
8. Water Training
   a. Drown Proofing
   b. Swimming
   c. Water Aerobics
9. Aerobics
10. Sports
    a. Two Ball Soccer
    b. Frisbee Football
    c. Football
    d. Exercise Pyramids (sit-up, push up improvement)
    e. Playing Card Exercises
11. Alternate Event Familiarization: (to show Warriors what it is like to take this event)
    a. 6.2 Mile Bike
    b. 800 yard Swim
    c. 2.5 Mile Walk
12. CBRN Sports
    a. Football
    b. Soccer
    c. 2 Ball Soccer
    d. Frisbee Football

Incentives

Consider providing recognition in the form of

1. Certificates of achievement
2. Special unit awards
3. Coins
4. Letters of appreciation/achievement,
5. Pat on the back for:
6. Iron person (highest score over 300)
7. 270 and above club
8. Element with the highest APFT average (semi-annually)
9. Best PT instructor

10. Consider creating a hall of fame on the unit bulletin board for scores of 270 or above

Driver's Training

References: AR 385-10, 385-40, 385-55, FM 21-305, TC 21-305 through 21-306, Applicable Operator's manual. Check local policies and procedures.

Driver's training is essential to a unit's ability to accomplish the mission. Attempt to have your Warriors licensed on every piece of equipment in the unit. The best method I have found is to establish a detailed training program that consists of a written test, hands-on testing, and other training events. If time is a factor, consider implementing the training in conjunction with unit motor stables or other activities that require vehicle operations.

Methods of Incorporation

1. During motor stables:
    a. Have the unlicensed Warrior perform PMCS on the vehicle.
    b. Have the Warrior take a written test on the vehicle during motor stables.
2. If the Warrior has a learner's permit have the Warrior operate the vehicle during motor stables with a licensed operator. I found this not only helped train the Warriors but it also significantly reduced my deadline rate by exercising the vehicles on a weekly basis.
3. If possible consider conducting your motor stables at night. Have vehicle operator's drive with night vision devices; utilize black drive and blackout markers. This also provides an excellent training opportunity for new drivers.
4. Construct a Driver's Training Program that includes:
    a. Mandatory Classroom training
    b. Familiarization of New Equipment Training
    c. Written Test
    d. Hands-on Test
    e. Maintenance Test
    f. Proper PMCS
    g. Dispatching Procedures
    h. Fall and Winter Safe Driving
    i. Spring and Summer Safe Driving
    j. Senior Occupant Duties and Responsibilities
    k. Driving Habits and Techniques
    l. Proper Load Distribution
    m. Securing Cargo
    n. Host Nation Laws
    o. Properly Fill out Report of Motor Vehicle Accident
    p. Driver's Award Program
    q. Vehicle Movement Signals
    r. Properly Fill out 5988-E
    s. Identification of Indicators, and Controls on each type of Vehicle
    t. Operation During Daylight Hours

u. Operation During Hours of Reduced Visibility

v. Operate Vehicle in Rough Terrain

Tasks to Consider

1. Operate vehicle under normal conditions.
2. Operate vehicle under adverse conditions (snow, sand, mud, cold, heat).
3. Self recovery of vehicle.
4. Assisted recovery of vehicle.
5. Drive using blackout drive/markers.
6. Drive utilizing night vision devices.
7. Actions during an air attack.
8. Actions at a halt.
9. Actions during a mine strike.
10. Actions during an ambush (blocked/unblocked).
11. Actions during a riot or demonstration.

Incentives

Consider providing recognition in the form of

1. Certificates of achievement
2. Special unit awards
3. Coins
4. Letter of appreciation/achievement
5. Or a pat on the back for:
6. Vehicle Rodeo (award for best vehicle handler by class of vehicle)
7. Driver's badge.
8. Most accident-free miles (month, quarter, year).
9. Vehicle with the least amount of down time (month, quarter, year).
10. Section with best readiness rating.
11. Elements in which all members are licensed on all unit equipment.

Family Readiness Group Training

References: AR 608-1, 608-10, 608-18, 608-99; DA PAM 608-38 (no longer exist but can be found on the internet and used as a tool to gain insight and information. Remember while they are no longer official they may provide useful information).and Local SOPs/policies

While some FRGs may depend upon a few core individuals, it is a good idea to involve as many people as possible and get the training out to as many people as possible. The Family Support Group is an outstanding activity that benefits everyone. It can be a great morale builder. Incorporate the FRG as much as possible into your unit activities.

Methods of Incorporation

Consider having the FRG set up a "welcome back from the field" or "deployment" brunch. This has been an outstanding success in previous units. As we rolled into the motor pool or unit area, the FRG had a nice spread of food prepared. The Warriors spent some time with family members while cleaning up the equipment. This encouraged an understanding of the Warrior's job and involved family members.

Family days at work: Encourage family members to come and join their spouses/parents at work. One unit I was in had a family one-day FTX. The family members got to go to the field with us, experiencing the alert, deployment, attacks, and the clean-up. It was a day for all to remember

Consider the following events

1. Bake sales
2. Making and selling a unit cookbook
3. Car washes
4. Developing unit T-shirts

Tasks to Consider

1. Classes (most classes may be coordinated with on post activities)
2. Opening and maintaining a FRG account
3. Effective communications
4. Active listening
5. Problem solving
6. Use of community resources
7. Military correspondence
8. Recognition Program
9. Funding
10. Ideas for events

Weapons Training

References: AR 350-1, DA PAM 350-38, FMs related to specific weapon systems, TC 23-11, 23-13, and all technical manuals associated with each individual weapon system.

Methods of Incorporation

Warriors can only become better at shooting by shooting. The more opportunity you give them to shoot the more efficient they will become.

Try to design your training events with ranges in mind. For example, if you are going on an FTX, develop a scenario that will utilize ranges while you are in the field. This also allows you consolidate ranges with FTX's thereby conserving resources.

Consider incorporating a live fire moving vehicle range. Your unit is road marching when the convoy comes under fire. Select the ambush site close to the moving vehicle firing range. Conduct the safety briefing and have each vehicle enter the moving vehicle firing range.

The realism is incredible. It provides Warriors the opportunity to fire from a moving vehicle and engage targets.

Training should be conducted in the crawl and walk phase before attempting the live fire exercise. (Strongly enforce safety and conduct a risk assessment). Other methods may include conducting night fire ranges, CBRN ranges, and night vision ranges in conjunction with FTXs.

In garrison, weapons training could consist of setting up a weapons lane. In the lane the Warrior may be required to perform any task on the particular weapon system: assembly, disassembly, maintenance, grazing fire, load, unload, reduce stoppage, or fire on targets utilizing the weaponeer or MAC's simulators.

In previous units we would have utilized computerized simulators and consistently scheduled sections with times to bring their Warriors in to fire. We were able to support three Warriors at a time. Some were able to be brought directly to the unit location. This also provided the opportunity to have the Warriors fire on three-round burst and CBRN fire. Our weapon qualification scores significantly improved.

We applied the same concepts to other weapon systems. We established our own practice grenade range, utilized in conjunction with Sergeant's Time Training. We extensively trained gun crews on the M60, M249, M240 and M203. We invited experts from infantry units or Special Forces units and utilized their expertise. Gunners were taught how to use grazing fire, defilade position, how to effectively utilize the Traverse and Elevation (T&E) mechanism, and use of overhead fire.

Our gun crews received crew drill training and we dedicated portions of Sergeant's Time Training to crew or team drills. While we may have only had one crew officially-trained (fully qualified during live fire), we had at least one additional crew trained in all other aspects of the weapon system. The results were outstanding.

Tasks to Consider

1. Perform Maintenance on a Given Weapon
2. Zero Weapon
3. Establish Mechanical Zero
4. Engage Targets on a Known Distance Range
5. Engage Moving Targets (Known Distance Range)
6. Engage Hostile Aircraft with Small Arms (FM 44-8)
7. Conduct marksmanship training on:
    a. M16A2
    b. M60
    c. M249
    d. M240
    e. 9mm
    f. M203
8. Employ/Recover
    a. Claymore
    b. Mines
9. Engage targets with AT4, LAW, Dragon, Javelin
10. How to use windage and elevation to engage targets beyond 300 meters or in high winds
11. Conduct weapons lane training
12. Utilize weapons in MOPP 4
13. Perform crew served weapon drills
14. Conduct Known distance ranges
15. Conduct a moving target range

16. Conduct a range utilizing night vision devices

Incentives

Consider providing recognition in the form of

1. Certificates of achievement
2. Special unit awards
3. Coins, letters of appreciation/achievement
4. A pat on the back for: Best marksman in the unit give the award a name, honoring a heroic sharpshooter from the past Bill Hickok (Civil War), Alvin York (WWI), Audie Murphy (WWII).
5. Best crew served weapons team
6. Consider creating a hall of fame on the unit bulletin board for experts
7. Most competent weapons expert

First Aid

References: FM 4-25.11, CTT manual

Methods of Incorporating

Place emphasis on first aid events. These skills may be required in day to day life from an automobile accident to a gunshot wound. I found that by implementing a program that required one to two first aid tasks to be either taught or evaluated during Sergeant's Time, our Warriors became more proficient in first aid skills.

These tasks were listed on the training schedule and Warriors were evaluated by squad/section leaders. Since the tasks were on the training schedule Warriors knew the task would be tested and were instructed to prepare for the task. As we placed command emphasis on training, most Warriors performed well and received first time Go's. We tested to standard. Warriors became motivated and involved in the training.

At times we utilized immediate action drills, in which Warriors had no previous knowledge that a task was to be evaluated. Perhaps at formation we would hand out injury cards (one or two per squad) and at a designated time casualties would be inflicted. The other members of the squad had to provide first aid, move the Warrior to cover, fill out casualty feeder reports, witness statements, and move the injured Warrior by field expedient methods.

During one such evaluation I was acting as a casualty with a sucking chest wound. Our combat lifesaver was told to treat the incident as if it were real-world. The Warrior was performing in an outstanding manner, when he said "Now I would start an IV." When the Commander said, "Don't tell me, do it," the Warrior became concerned. It took three attempts for the Warrior to start the IV. That event was a great teaching tool. We utilized it in future training events and the ability of our combat lifesavers to start an IV significantly improved.

Tasks to Consider

1. Evaluate a Casualty
2. Combat Lifesaver Administers IV
3. Treat Sucking Chest Wound
4. Splint a Fracture

5. Treat an Abdominal Wound
6. Give First Aid for Burns
7. Give First Aid for Heat Injuries
8. First Aid Lane Training
9. Move a Casualty by Field Expedient Methods
10. Treat Casualty for Nerve Agent
11. Conduct CPR
12. Conduct CPR in MOPP4
13. Mask and Clear an Unconscious Warrior
    a. How do you get an unconscious Warrior to breathe out and clear the mask? One method (depending upon injuries) may be to place your hands over the appropriate vents and sit on the Warrior's stomach, forcing the air out.
14. Move Casualty to Cover
15. Request MEDEVAC
16. Consider coordinating with a MEDEVAC unit and have each element conduct a request.
17. Use make-up kits to construct more realistic injuries (may be available from the battalion aid station, TMC, or training devices on post).

Financial Training

References: TC 21-7 "Personal Financial Readiness and Deployment Handbook"; coordinate with ACS and unit financial advisor

Methods of Incorporation

Financial training provides several benefits for our Warriors. It can help a Warrior understand the problems associated with poor financial management, encourage financial stability at an early point in a Warrior's career, show that the command has a sincere desire to assist the Warrior, and inform the Warrior of possible consequences for improper management of funds.. We also found it beneficial to encourage spouses to attend this training. We conducted the training in conjunction with the Family Support Group, Better Opportunities for Single Soldiers, and during lunch hours.

Our classes were conducted by Army Community Service. They were informational only and no outside agencies were invited to sell a product. This was simply a tool to educate Warriors and their spouses on financial management. The classes were conducted in a specific order approximately three to four times a year.

As a result, the problems the command experienced concerning financial problems were drastically reduced. This allowed leaders to concentrate their efforts on accomplishing the mission and training the Warriors.

Tasks to Consider

1. Check Writing
2. Balancing a Checkbook
3. Basic Investing
4. Advance Investing
5. Budgeting
6. Indebtedness
7. Support of Family Members

8. Credit Cards
9. Explanation of the Leave and Earning Statement
10. Pay entitlement (family separation, hazardous duty, jump pay, etc.)
11. Bonds
12. Certificates of Deposit
13. Consequences for
    a. Non-support of family members
    b. Indebtedness

Professional Development

References: AR 350-1, All tactical FMs, Mission Training Plans, Army Regulations/programs

Methods of Incorporation

I have found that, at times, we have forgotten the basics. My professional development programs focused on the basics and then became more advanced.

I began with administrative topics. My rationale for reviewing administrative actions was that these situations appeared to be monopolizing the time of my key leaders. By giving them the tools to solve these problems, or prevent them in the first place, I reasoned that I would have more time for tactical training. Some of the administrative topics included counseling, NCOER preparation, record preparation for promotion, chapter actions, revocation of privileges, finance, etc. Once we had covered the basic administrative topics we moved on to tactical topics.

I also found it important to relate the importance of the training. In other words, make the training meaningful to the leader. Don't just tell them why it is important --- show them. This helps prevent the attitude that this would be another BORING CLASS, taken just to check the block.

Some of the methods I used to stress the importance of classes were: a short skit at the beginning of the class, a movie clip, a short exercise, or real-world examples. People tend to learn and understand more if they understand the purpose of the training and how it will help them.

I taught the first few classes to set the example and then I established a list of tasks I thought were important, and implemented a roster of leaders who would instruct future sessions. The instructors had to brief me on the class and have all the information prepared at this briefing. These briefings were conducted one to two weeks out from the scheduled training.

Professional development training is also an excellent time to bring in the experts from legal, ACS, AER, PSB, and other areas that may contain information useful to your leaders. Shape the program to benefit your unit and its ability to accomplish the mission, but don't overlook administrative tasks that bury your leaders.

This also provides an excellent opportunity to speak with your leaders about topics that concern them directly. Use this time to hammer out issues that may be affecting leaders and do your best to resolve the issues. Also encourage officers to attend the training. Officers and NCOs should work together; do not divide your ability to solve problems by separation Officers and NCOs during training. Never call something "NCO business." The bottom line is: it's LEADER BUSINESS. Officers and NCOs should work together as a team.

Tasks to Consider

1. Conduct Route Recon
2. Coordinate with Adjacent Elements
3. Conduct staff rides
4. Tour local battlefields. Consider dividing the tour into key events, and assigning them to NCOs in your unit to provide a short briefing on the key events. For example, topics for the battle of Gettysburg may include: how the battle started, biographies of key figures, events at the Round Top, absence of the Confederate cavalry, or Pickett's charge. Explain the purpose of the training, involve the leaders, and by having them present the briefing you prepare them for future responsibilities and schooling.
5. Conduct Advance Party Operation
6. Lead Convoy Operations
7. Supervise Recovery Operations
8. Emplace Crew-served Weapons
9. Supervise Crossing of Contaminated Area
10. Use and Construct a Map Overlay
11. Develop a Unit Sector Sketch
12. Supervise Unmasking Procedures
13. Duty Rosters (AR 220-45)
14. Indebtedness (AR 600-15)
15. Military Justice, Article 15 Proceedings (AR 27-10)
16. Family Support, Child Custody and Paternity (608-99)
17. Chapter Actions (AR 600-20)
18. Revocation of privileges
19. Flags and Bars (AR 600-8-2)
20. Promotions (decentralized and centralized) (AR 600-8-19)
21. Reviewing Records for a Promotion Board
22. Leaves and Passes (AR 600-8-10)
23. Enlisted promotions (AR 600-8-19)
24. Military Awards (AR 600-8-22)
25. NCOERS (AR 623-3)
26. Weight Control Program (AR 600-9)
27. Equal Opportunity Training (AR 600-20)
28. Army Command Policy (AR 600-20)
29. Drug and Alcohol Program (AR 600-85)

Maintenance Training

References: Appropriate TMs for equipment, Army Maintenance Regulations, DA PAMs

Methods of Incorporation

Maintenance keeps our fighting force operational. Every piece of equipment requires maintenance. Therefore it is important to establish standards and practices that ensure high levels of maintenance within your element.

Our maintenance programs focused on driver's training, maintenance of all associate equipment (radios, CBRN, weapons, etc.) and inspections. I have found the best way to achieve success in maintenance is to tell the Warrior (class), show the Warrior (hands-on), and evaluate the Warrior (hands-on/written evaluation). This sounds like a lot of work and it is, in the beginning but as the program develops it will greatly increase your readiness rate.

I began by speaking with my motor officer and motor sergeant, CBRN NCO, communications NCO, and arms room personnel. They explained the problems they were having and offered possible solutions. Some of the common problems cited were lack of proper PMCS; lack of leader emphasis; leaders who lacked knowledge of equipment; lack of accountability for equipment; and other unit missions taking priority.

To correct these issues we instituted some changes. Monthly maintenance classes were given to leaders. All Warriors had to take a PMCS class (hands-on and written on each vehicle). Also, vehicles were assigned primary and alternate operators, maintenance operations were spot-checked by key leaders, and all items requiring services or maintenance were listed on the training schedule. In addition, the Commander and I would check three items each week during motor stables. These items were picked at random so the Warriors never knew what we would check; every vehicle was checked with the operator and NCO standing by the vehicle.

During weekly training (Sergeant's Time) I would spot-check weapons, communications, and CBRN equipment. Another useful tool is to routinely check your arms room and CBRN room. One problem I noted was that equipment not assigned was not being checked. I have two suggestions for this problem. First, assign all unassigned equipment to squads for maintenance or second, make the arms room or CBRN room responsible for cleaning unassigned equipment.

Another useful tool is to have the motor pool, CBRN room, arms room, and communications NCO brief you weekly on maintenance status. For example, my arms room would make a list of weapons that had not been cleaned properly.

It takes a lot of work to maintain equipment, but with the proper command emphasis and proper procedures and processes in place and the installation of pride in unit equipment, your readiness rate will improve. A previous unit of mine won three USAREUR Army Awards for Maintenance Excellence and placed second at the Department of the Army level. Like I said, leaders get the ball rolling and the Warriors become motivated to excel. Challenge them and they will excel.

Tasks to Consider

1. Written test on equipment
2. Hands-on Application for each piece of equipment
3. Operator handling courses (operating vehicles under different conditions)
4. Snow
5. Mud
6. Rain
7. Blackout drive
8. Night Vision device
9. Recovery operations
10. Power generation operations
11. How to properly change each category of tire
12. Conducting services on equipment
13. Supervise Maintenance Operations
14. Spot check all maintenance operations

15. Hold individuals accountable

Incentives

1. Consider providing recognition in the form of
2. Certificates of achievement
3. Special unit awards
4. Coins
5. Letters of appreciation/achievement
6. A pat on the back for:
7. Element with the least amount of down time (best readiness rating for the quarter or year)
8. Most accident-free miles
9. Most tonnage handled
10. Best maintainer of equipment (annual award)

Missions Other Than War

References: Applicable FMs, Lessons Learned, and Local Policies

Methods of Incorporation

Consistently we have been called upon to execute missions other than war. This is not a new concept for the U.S. Army. During our expansion westward, the Army was called upon to protect our own citizens as our country moved into new territories. However, the challenges we face today are different and require intense training to ensure mission accomplishment. One of the best methods I have found to maintain readiness in this area is lane training.

I incorporated missions other than war into my lane training and weekly training activities. Warriors would have to negotiate for information, establish checkpoints and perform other tasks that were easily incorporated into Sergeant's Time Training.

Tasks to Consider

1. Regional orientation of culture and people of the area
2. Negotiating skills
3. Utilize role players or host nation Warriors to assist you
4. Mine, booby trap training
5. Contact a local EOD or engineer unit and ask for assistance in teaching classes or practical application
6. Unexploded ordnance training
7. Checkpoint operations
8. Utilize experience from Warriors who have conducted these operations in the past
9. Information collection
10. Utilize the S-2 or military intelligence units for assistance
11. Consider role-playing exercises that will drive your points home
12. Patrolling
13. Consider asking for assistance from infantry, ranger, or SF units
14. Media relations

15. Contact your PAO for assistance
16. During your training, utilize Warriors posing as reporters asking hard, pointed questions; use video cameras
17. Establish a place of lodging
18. Establish a buffer zone
19. Supervise truce or cease fire
20. Assist in maintaining law and order
21. Contact military police units for possible assistance
22. Monitor boundaries
23. Rules of engagement
24. React to drive-by shooting
25. React to riot
26. React to demonstration
27. React to media
28. Fight a meeting engagement
29. Conduct movement to contact
30. Conduct a search (personnel and property)
31. Disarm belligerents
32. Open secure routes
33. Law of war
34. Treatment of civilians engaged in hostile acts
35. Customs and basic language of the area
36. Field sanitation
37. Reaction to hostage situations
38. U.N. format procedures
39. React to minefield
40. Apprehension of civilian criminal

UCMJ Training

References: AR 27-10, Manual for Courts-Martial; local regulations, supplements and policies

Methods of Incorporation

Increasingly our leaders are faced with situations that require a more in-depth understanding of the legal system. Training leaders in these areas helps to develop them professionally and implement procedures that will prevent future problems. I utilized the JAG, PSB, and other experts as often as possible in both professional development classes and unit classes. It is important that Warriors understand the possible consequences for their actions and what actions they can legally take.

Tasks to Consider

1. Corrective Training
2. Chapter Actions
3. Counseling requirements
4. Documentation
5. Article 15s

6. Maximum Punishments
7. Procedures
8. Types of Court Martial
9. Revocation of privileges
10. Conducting health and welfare inspections
11. Search requirements
12. Detaining Warriors
13. When to use the rights warning card
14. Actions when you suspect illegal activity in government buildings
15. Warrior in possession or using drugs
16. Warrior selling drugs
17. Displaying extremist material

School Training

Reference: Applicable school handouts, read ahead packets, FMs or ARs that would cover material to be taught in the course

Methods of Incorporation:

This training is designed to address subjects that have high failure rates in a given course. For example, in WLC the primary failure, historically, is land navigation. In order to prepare a Warrior for this course we would implement a pretest (written and hands-on) to determine the solder's current readiness level. After assessing the pretest we would provide classroom instruction, hands-on evaluation and retaining as required. This helps set the Warrior up for success.

The schools that appear to be conducive to this type of pre-training are WLC, BNCOC, ANCOC, Battle staff, and the Master fitness course. Some skills, like land navigation, may be incorporated into normal training and therefore only a refresher may be required. This training should be tailored to the individual.

Tasks to Consider

1. Consider the subjects that have high failure rates
2. Land Navigation Test
3. Review of Common Subject
4. Inventory and inspect equipment
5. Weapons qualification training
6. D & C training
7. Construct a written test
8. Construct a hands-on test

Lane Training

References: Appropriate titles for tasks to be taught or evaluated

Methods of Incorporation

I have found that lane training is one of the best tools, because it allows flexibility and can be tailored to any scenario. The downside is that it is usually resource-intensive. Consider conducting a lane on a monthly basis and use it as a method to evaluate training levels. The lane should be the last stage of training. Prior to the lane the Warriors should have already received the appropriate training.

Tasks to Consider

1. CBRN
   a. React to Chemical Attack
   b. Cross contaminated area
   c. Treat Nerve Agent Casualty
   d. Use M256 kit
   e. Conduct Decontamination
   f. Conduct MOPP Gear Exchange
   g. Evacuate a Chemical Casualty
   h. Send a Salute Report

2. Maintenance
   a. Trouble shoot vehicle break down
   b. Repair vehicle during hours of darkness
   c. Conduct Recovery operations
   d. Vehicle stuck in mud, water, or sand
   e. Conduct self recovery
   f. Conduct Convoy to new unit area

3. Consolidated lane:
   a. React to Media
   b. React to demonstration (riot)
   c. React to Minefield
   d. React to Sniper
   e. Evaluate and Treat Casualty
   f. Peacekeeping Operations:
   g. Establish a Checkpoint
   h. Operate a Checkpoint
   i. Apply Rules of engagement
   j. React to Media
   k. React to riot/demonstration
   l. React to indirect fire
   m. Send Salute Report

Tactical Training

References: Appropriate FMs

Methods of Incorporation

While dedicated training in the field or urban environment is the preferred method, some of the tasks below can be conducted in local unit areas or in motor pools. A little imagination can go a long way in establishing effective training.

Tasks to Consider

1. Conduct an Ambush
2. React to an Ambush (near and far)
3. Conduct Convoy
4. Utilize the task during motor stables and assembly a small group of vehicles to conduct a road march (this exercises the vehicles and provides training).
5. Actions at a Halt (mounted, dismounted as well as short halt and long halt)
6. Issue a Warning Order
7. Utilize in day-to-day operations
8. Issue an Operations Order
9. Utilize in day-to-day operations. All my unit level activities utilized the operations order format.
10. Issue a Frago
11. Report Enemy Information (Salute)
12. Warriors can observe traffic on a road or parade field and send report
13. Incorporated into Sergeant's Time training
14. Recognize Friendly and Threat Vehicles and Aircraft
15. Actions When Crossing a Danger Area
16. Prepare Convoy for movement
17. Utilize during motor stables
18. React to Mine strike (mounted/dismounted)
    a. Construct a small minefield in your local unit area.
    b. Consider burying soda cans or other objects at random depths and patterns for use by mine detecting teams
    c. Mark minefields with rocks and other unconventional methods. See if your Warriors react properly.
19. Request Fire Support
    a. Use simulator
    b. Utilize a forward observer to the teach the class
    c. Untrained observer
    d. Howe to call in Tactical Air support
    e. Coordinate with Adjacent Units/Elements
    f. Conduct Graves Registration
    g. Conduct Road march
    h. Process Enemy Prisoner of War
    i. Gather battlefield intelligence
    j. Conduct Patrol

    k.   React to indirect fire

    l.   React to direct fire

20. React to Air Attack

    a.   Conduct Aircraft Recognition Exercises

    b.   Conduct Training on Engaging Aircraft

    c.   Set up a remote control aircraft shoot down range

    d.   Coordinate Live Fire Remote Control Shoot Down Exercise

    e.   Employ Passive and Active Air Defense Measures

21. Conduct River Crossing

    a.   Coordinate with the Engineers (mounted or dismounted)

    b.   Conduct risk assessments (swimmers/non swimmers)

    c.   OIF/OEF numerous lost theirs or were injured due to vehicles being to close to edge of embankments that could not support the weight of vehicles

    d.   Exercise rollover procedures, and water exit drills, along with buddy assist recovery procedures

22. Drown Proofing

    a.   Utilize the local pool

23. Move unit by Ground

24. Move unit by Air

    a.   Construct a mock-up of the air frame

    b.   Use engineer tape and chalk to diagram the layout of the aircraft on the ground

    c.   Coordinate with air liaison for use of an actual aircraft

25. Move unit by Rail

    a.   Construct a mock-up of a rail car

    b.   Use engineer tape or chalk to layout the rail care on the ground

    c.   Coordinate with unit movement NCO/officer for a rail car

26. Move unit by Sea

Land Navigation

References: FM 3-25.26 and Orienteering Handbook

Methods of Incorporation

Land navigation is a perishable skill and should be incorporated into your training as often as possible. Be sure to include field-expedient methods of navigation, mounted and dismounted navigation, and urban terrain navigation. Encourage leaders to utilize opportunity training.

Tasks to Consider

Never allow our dependency on technology to be the factor that causes a Warriors' death that makes the difference between success or failure on the battle field. Remember the BASICS!

Do not depend on technology too much. It is a good thing but Warriors need to remember the basics. Batteries go dead and equipment breaks remember the basics.

1.   Use the compass

2. Shadow tip method
3. Watch method
4. North Star method
5. Intersection/Resection
6. Map Orientation
7. Determine location by using GPS
8. Operate GPS
9. Maintain GPS
10. Convert Azimuth
11. Conduct Land Navigation Exercise using Field Expedient Methods
12. Use Military Map to Navigate Mounted/Dismounted
13. Conduct an orienteering exercise

Survival Training

References: Appropriate FMs and related civilian material

Tasks to Consider

1. Edible plants
2. Methods to find water
3. Methods to determine direction
4. Methods to avoid capture
5. How to resist interrogation efforts
6. Contact your local MI unit to see if they can teach the class
7. Methods used by interrogators
8. Use MI to teach and demonstrate
9. Methods to resist torture

Safety Training

References: Appropriate ARs and local polices and supplements, Army safety Website (excellent tool)

Methods of Incorporation

Safety is a critical factor in preserving life and limb. Ensure that you conduct training prior to the start of summer and winter. Awareness and education are keys to preventing accidents and injuries. In the past I have observed unit safety days in which the unit was shut down for either a ½ a day or full day. Classes were conducted in a round robin format on all types of safety subjects.

Tasks to Consider

1. Summer Safety
2. Drown proofing
3. Authorized swimming areas
4. Driving methods
5. Electrical safety

6. Lightning strikes
7. Cooking stoves
8. Winter Safety
9. Stove/heater operation
10. Winter driving
11. Power generation
12. Cooking stoves
13. Conducting Risk Assessment
14. Identify risk
15. Identify risk reduction methods
16. Implement reduction methods

Adventure Training

Methods of Incorporation

Adventure training is great for developing skills and motivating Warriors. Again it is another method to challenge the Warrior.

Tasks to Consider

1. Hand-to-Hand Combat
2. Combatives training have become a hot issue
3. Use them as part of your training Ensure you use proper risk assessments. Warriors need to know what it is like to take and give a punch and kick
4. Female and male Warriors need to be able to square off with one another (in a supervised safe environment that is established in such a manner that teaches them the skills they need to survive in combat or hostile situations.
5. Warriors are trained in NCOES in varying degrees of combative use them but Safety is a MUST Ensure your plan is approved by Senior Leaders!
6. Consider other actions or activities that will teach contact and instill self confidence and the ability to take a blow and get up and give it back again it must be supervised, planned, approved by senior leaders, and have an approved risk assessment.
   a. Unit Karate or similar program (someone in the unit may be able to teach or someone from the local community may be willing to volunteer their time
   b. A Game known as PT Battle Ball:
      i. Set up: 4 sand bags placed in the corners to mark off the field one sand bag place in the middle of the field
      ii. One soft ball
      iii. 2 platoons
      iv. one platoon is given the softball. The goal is for the platoon to get the softball place under the sand bag in the center of the field without the other platoon stopping them.

      v.   Rules: rules of engagement are laid out by the command the goal is to limit injuries, but provide Warriors the ability be aggressive without hurting one another. Teaching them to protect each other, work as a team, learn how to fall, how to take a blow, and how to give a blow. However no blows will be allowed that will hurt a Warrior or effect the unit's combat readiness. AGAIN APPROVAL OF SENIOR LEADERS REQUIRED, SAFETY APPROVAL REQUIRED.

7. Orienteering
8. Rappelling
9. Force March with Tactical skills along the way
10. Military stakes competition
11. Rock climbing
12. White water rafting
13. Water survival

NOTE: Many items mentioned in this training section regarding weapons, SOPs, Family Readiness Groups, Classes, can be found in some of other products like:

1. Tools of the Trade Volume 1
2. Tools of the Trade Volume 2
3. The Military Spouse

Chapter 11
TRAINING CIRCULARS

Training Circulars

TC 1-05	RELIGIOUS SUPPORT HANDBOOK FOR THE UNIT MINISTRY TEAM
TC 1-210	AIRCREW TRAINING PROGRAM: COMMANDER'S GUIDE TO INDIVIDUAL, CREW, AND COLLECTIVE TRAINING
TC 1-210-1	UNITED STATES ARMY SPECIAL OPERATIONS AVIATION AIRCREW TRAINING PROGRAM COMMANDER'S GUIDE TO INDIVIDUAL AND CREW STANDARDIZATION
TC 1-211	AIRCREW TRAINING MANUAL - UTILITY HELICOPTER UH-1H/V SERIES
TC 1-218	AIRCREW TRAINING MANUAL - UTILITY AIRPLANE C-12
TC 1-219	AIRCREW TRAINING MANUAL GUARDRAIL COMMON SENSOR AIRPLANE RC-12
TC 1-228	AIRCREW TRAINING MANUAL OH-58A/C KIOWA SS TC 1-215
TC 1-237	AIRCREW TRAINING MANUAL UTILITY HELICOPTER H-60 SERIES
TC 1-238	AIRCREW TRAINING MANUAL ATTACK HELICOPTER AH-64A SS TC 1-214
TC 1-240	AIRCREW TRAINING MANUAL CARGO HELICOPTER CH-47D/F
TC 1-248	AIRCREW TRAINING MANUAL OH-58D KIOWA WARRIOR
TC 1-251	AIRCREW TRAINING MANUAL - ATTACK HELICOPTER AH-64D
	CHANGE 1, 28 MAY 2007
TC 1-400	BRIGADE AVIATION ELEMENT HANDBOOK
TC 1-600	UNMANNED AIRCRAFT SYSTEMS COMMANDER'S GUIDE AND AIRCREW TRAINING MANUAL
TC 1-611	SMALL UNMANNED AIRCRAFT SYSTEM AIRCREW TRAINING MANUAL
TC 2-22.303	THE 2X HANDBOOK
TC 2-22.601	ARMY COUNTER-RADIO CONTROLLED IMPROVISED EXPLOSIVE DEVICE ELECTRONIC WARFARE HANDBOOK
TC 2-91.701	INTELLIGENCE ANALYTICAL SUPPORT TO COUNTER IMPROVISED EXPLOSIVE DEVICE OPERATIONS
TC 3-10	COMMANDER'S TACTICAL NBC HANDBOOK
TC 3-11-55	JOINT SERVICES LIGHTWEIGHT INTEGRATED SUIT TECHNOLOGY (JSLIST)
TC 3-15	NUCLEAR ACCIDENT AND INCIDENT RESPONSE AND ASSISTANCE (NAIRA)
TC 3-17	COMBAT IDENTIFICATION (CID) TRAINING INTEGRATION

TC 3-34.489	THE SOLDIER AND THE ENVIRONMENT SS TC 5-400; CHANGE 1, 26 OCT 2001
TC 5-210	MILITARY FLOAT BRIDGING EQUIPMENT
TC 5-230	ARMY GEOSPATIAL GUIDE FOR COMMANDERS AND PLANNERS
TC 5-340	AIR BASE DAMAGE REPAIR (PAVEMENT REPAIR)
TC 7-9	INFANTRY LIVE-FIRE TRAINING
TC 7-21	STRYKER DRIVER TRAINING
TC 7-98-1	STABILITY AND SUPPORT OPERATIONS TRAINING SUPPORT PACKAGE
TC 8-226	DENTAL LABORATORY SPECIALIST
TC 8-502	NUTRITION CARE OPERATIONS
TC 8-800	SEMI-ANNUAL COMBAT MEDIC SKILLS VALIDATION TEST (SACMS-VT)
TC 9-21-01	SOLDIERS IMPROVISED EXPLOSIVE DEVICE (IED) AWARENESS GUIDE IRAQ & AFGHANISTAN THEATERS OF OPERATION
TC 9-60	COMMUNICATIONS-ELECTRONICS FUNDAMENTALS: BASIC PRINCIPLES OF ALTERNATING CURRENT AND DIRECT CURRENT SS FM 11-60 & FM 11-61
TC 9-62	COMMUNICATIONS-ELECTRONICS FUNDAMENTALS: SOLID STATE DEVICES AND SOLID STATE POWER SUPPLIES AND AMPLIFIERS SS FM 11-62 & FM 11-66
TC 9-64	COMMUNICATIONS-ELECTRONICS FUNDAMENTALS: WAVE PROPOGATION, TRANSMISSION LINES, AND ANTENNAS SS FM 11-64
TC 9-72	COMMUNICATIONS-ELECTRONICS FUNDAMENTALS: DIGITAL COMPUTERS SS FM 11-72
TC 9-237	OPERATOR'S CIRCULAR WELDING THEORY AND APPLICATION: REPORTING ERRORS AND RECOMMENDING IMPROVEMENTS
TC 9-524	FUNDAMENTALS OF MACHINE TOOLS
TC 10-10	COMBINED ARMS TRAINING STRATEGY (CATS) FOR QUARTERMASTER UNITS
TC 12-43	PERCUSSION TECHNIQUES CHANGE 1, 4 NOVEMBER 2003
TC 12-44	ARMY BAND SECTION LEADER HANDBOOK SS TC 12-02 SERIES
TC 12-45	THE MARCHING BAND
TC 19-138	CIVILIAN LAW ENFORCEMENT AND SECURITY OFFICER TRAINING
TC 19-210	ACCESS CONTROL HANDBOOK
TC 20-32-3	FOREIGN MINE HANDBOOK (BLAKAN STATES)
TC 20-32-4	FOREIGN MINE HANDBOOK (ASIA)
TC 20-32-5	COMMANDER'S REFERENCE GUIDE LAND MINE AND EXPLOSIVE HAZARDS (IRAQ)

TC 21-3	SOLDIER'S HANDBOOK FOR INDIVIDUAL OPERATIONS AND SURVIVAL IN COLD-WEATHER AREAS
TC 21-7	PERSONAL FINANCIAL READINESS AND DEPLOYABILITY HANDBOOK
TC 21-21	WATER SURVIVAL TRAINING
TC 21-24	RAPPELLING
TC 21-305	TRAINING PROGRAM FOR WHEELED VEHICLE ACCIDENT AVOIDANCE
TC 21-305-1	TRAINING PROGRAM FOR THE HEAVY EXPANDED MOBILITY TACTICAL TRUCK (HEMTT)
TC 21-305-2	TRAINING PROGRAM FOR NIGHT VISION GOGGLE DRIVING OPERATIONS
TC 21-305-3	TRAINING PROGRAM FOR THE M939 SERIES 5-TON TACTICAL CARGO TRUCK
TC 21-305-4	TRAINING PROGRAM FOR THE HIGH MOBILITY MULTIPURPOSE WHEELED VENICLE (HMMWV)
TC 21-305-5	TRAINING PROGRAM FOR EQUIPMENT TRANSPORTERS (C-HET, MET, AND LET)
TC 21-305-6	TRAINING PROGRAM FOR THE TRACTOR AND SEMITRAILER (M915, M931, AND M932)
TC 21-305-7	TRAINING PROGRAM FOR LIGHT VEHICLES
TC 21-305-8	TRAINING PROGRAM FOR MEDIUM VEHICLES
TC 21-305-9	TRAINING PROGRAM FOR THE HEAVY EQUIPMENT TRANSPORTER SYSTEM
TC 21-305-10	TRAINING PROGRAM FOR THE PALLETIZED LOAD SYSTEM
TC 21-305-11	TRAINING PROGRAM FOR THE FAMILY OF MEDIUM TACTICAL VEHICLES OPERATOR
TC 21-305-100	THE MILITARY COMMERCIAL DRIVER'S LICENSE DRIVER'S MANUAL
TC 21-306	TRACKED COMBAT VEHICLE DRIVER TRAINING
TC 23-2	66-MM ROCKET LAUNCHER M202A1
TC 23-11	STARLIGHT SCOPE, SMALL HAND-HELD OR INDIVIDUAL WEAPONS MOUNTED, MODEL NO. 6060
TC 23-13	CREW-SERVED WEAPON NIGHT VISION SIGHT
TC 24-20	TACTICAL WIRE AND CABLE TECHNIQUES
TC 24-21	TACTICAL MULTICHANNEL RADIO COMMUNICATIONS TECHNIQUES
TC 24-34	COMSEC LOGISTICS AND OPERATIONAL SUPPORT IN THE FIELD
TC 25-1	TRAINING LAND
TC 25-8	TRAINING RANGES
TC 25-10	A LEADER'S GUIDE TO LANE TRAINING
TC 25-20	A LEADER'S GUIDE TO AFTER-ACTION REVIEWS
TC 25-30	A LEADER'S GUIDE TO COMPANY TRAINING MEETINGS

TC 26-6	COMMANDER'S EQUAL OPPORTUNITY HANDBOOK
TC 31-20-2	SPECIAL FORCES HANDBOOK FOR THE FINGERPRINT IDENTIFICATION SYSTEM
TC 31-73	SPECIAL FORCES ADVISOR GUIDE
TC38-3	GUIDE FOR BASIC MILITARY PRESERVATION AND PACKING
TC 43-4	COMMANDER'S AND SHOP OFFICER'S GUIDE FOR SUPPORT MAINTENANCE MANAGEMENT
TC 44-117-21	AVENGER TEAM CREW TRAINING SS ARETP 44-117-21-DRILL
TC 44-635-11	PATRIOT ELECTRIC POWER PLANT III AND ANTENNA MAST GROUP CREW TRAINING SS ARTEP 44-635-11-DRILL
TC 44-635-12	PATRIOT INFORMATION COORDINATION CENTRAL WITH ELECTRIC POWER UNIT, COMMUNICATIONS RELAY GROUP, AND TACTICAL COMMAND SYSTEM CREW TRAINING SS ARTEP 44-635-12-DRILL
TC 44-635-13	PATRIOT ENGAGEMENT CONTROL STATION, RADAR SET, AND BATTERY COMMAND POST CREW TRAINING ARTEP 44-635-13-DRILL
TC 44-635-14	PATRIOT PAC-2/PAC-3 LAUNCHING STATION AND MISSILE RELOAD CREW TRAINING SS ARTEP 44-635-14-DRILL
TC 44-635-15	PATRIOT PAC-2/PAC-3 LAUNCHING STATION FORKLIFT MISSILE RELOAD CREW TRAINING SS ARTEP 44-635-15-DRILL
TC 44-646-15	SENTINEL AND COMMAND AND CONTROL SUBSYSTEMS CREW TRAINING SS ARTEP 44-176-15-DRILL
TC 44-677-17	COUNTER-ROCKETS, ARTILLERY, AND MORTAR (C-RAM) COMMAND AND CONTROL (C2) INTERCEPT CREW TRAINING
TC 55-HEAT	TRAINING PROGRAM FOR THE HIGH MOBILITY MULTIPURPOSE WHEELD VEHICLE (HMMWV) EGRESS ASSISTANCE TRAINER (HEAT)
TC 55-60-17	TRAINING PROGRAM FOR THE 50,000-POUND ROUGH-TERRAIN CONTAINER HANDLER
TC 55-60-18	TRAINING PROGRAM FOR THE KALMAR 53,000-POUND ROUGH TERRAIN CONTAINER HANDLER (RTCH)
TC 55-88-1	RAIL HANDBOOK FOR AIR BRAKE AND TRAIN HANDLING RULES
TC 55-509-1	MARINE ELECTRICITY
TC 63-1	WARFIGHTER HANDBOOK FOR COMBAT SERVICE SUPPORT LIVE FIRE EXERCISES
TC 90-1	TRAINING FOR URBAN OPERATIONS
TC 90-11-1	MILITARY SKIING

Chapter Thirteen
FIELD MANUAL 7-0

Introduction

This chapter contains FM 7-0 for your reference. This Field Manual is entitled 'Training for Full Spectrum Operations.' This is the December 2008 revision. As FM 7-1 was last revised in September of 2003, FM 7-0 is the most current training FM. Generally speaking, 7-0 contains the principles and the concepts of training while 7-1 provides more in-depth examination and specific instruction.

*FM 7-0

Field Manual
No. 7-0

Headquarters
Department of the Army
Washington, DC, 12 December 2008

Training for Full Spectrum Operations

Contents

Distribution Restriction: Approved for public release; distribution is unlimited.

*This publication supersedes FM 7-0, 22 October 2002.

Figures

Tables

Preface

FM 7-0, *Training for Full Spectrum Operations*, establishes the Army's keystone doctrine for training. Since FM 7-0 was last published, enough has changed in the nature of operational environments worldwide to merit a full review of its content and form. FM 7-0 is the guide for Army training and training management. It addresses the fundamental principles and tenets of training.

FM 7-0 addresses the fundamentals of training modular, expeditionary Army forces to conduct full spectrum operations—simultaneous offensive, defensive, and stability or civil support operations—in an era of persistent conflict. Conducting effective training for full spectrum operations must be a top priority of senior leaders during both force generation and operational deployments.

FM 7-0 incorporates new tenets for training modular organizations to conduct full spectrum operations. However, the manual has further developed the concepts in the 2002 version as well. The Army must not lose the many sound training practices used before 11 September 2001. In addition, the manual emphasizes that commanders should leverage the combat experience of seasoned individuals and their leaders in developing training plans.

FM 7-0 cannot answer every training challenge of today's complex operational environments. It should, however, generate reflection and introspection on how Soldiers and units train for full spectrum operations as an expeditionary Army.

FM 7-0 is organized as follows:

- Chapter 1 discusses the environment in which training and operations occur. It stresses the need for the Army to prepare for full spectrum operations. The chapter concludes by discussing the aim point concept used to focus training on the most likely operational environments.
- Chapter 2 focuses on the Army's seven principles of training and the supporting tenets that apply at all organizational levels and across all components.
- Chapter 3 describes the Army Training System, defines training and education, describes the three training domains, and provides a brief discussion of leader development.
- Chapter 4 describes Army training management. It begins by describing the effects of Army force generation and modular organizations on training management. Then it addresses how to develop the mission-essential task list. The bulk of the chapter discusses how to use the Army's training management model to plan, prepare, execute, and assess training.

FM 7-0 applies to all leaders at all organizational levels. All leaders are trainers. Leaders include officers, warrant officers, noncommissioned officers, and Army civilians in leadership positions.

FM 7-0 applies to the Active Army, Army National Guard/Army National Guard of the United States, and U.S. Army Reserve unless otherwise stated.

FM 7-0 uses joint terms where applicable. Most terms with joint or Army terms are defined in both the glossary and the text. *Glossary references*: Terms for which FM 7-0 is the proponent publication (the authority) have an asterisk in the glossary. *Text references*: Definitions for which FM 7-0 is the proponent publication are in boldfaced text. These terms and their definitions will be in the next revision of FM 1-02. For other definitions in the text, the term is italicized and the number of the proponent publication follows the definition.

FM 7-0 uses *individuals* as a collective expression for Soldiers and Army civilians.

Headquarters, U.S. Army Training and Doctrine Command, is the proponent for this publication. The preparing agencies are the Combined Arms Doctrine Directorate and the Collective Training Directorate, both subordinate to the U.S. Army Combined Arms Center. Send written comments and recommendations on DA Form 2028 (Recommended Changes to Publications and Blank Forms) to Commander, U.S. Army

Preface

Combined Arms Center and Fort Leavenworth, ATTN: ATZL-CTD (FM 7-0), Bldg 275, 513 Grant Ave, Fort Leavenworth, KS 66027-6900; by e-mail to leav-fm7-0_revision@conus.army.mil; or submit on an electronic DA Form 2028.

131

Chapter 1

Training for Full Spectrum Operations—Changing the Army's Mindset

The primary mission of the Army is to fight and win the Nation's wars. Conducting offensive and defensive operations has long been the Army's core capability. However, the recent experience of operations in the Balkans, Iraq, and Afghanistan, coupled with today's operational environments, clearly indicates that the future will be an era of persistent conflict—one that will engage Army forces around the world to accomplish the Nation's objectives. This all points to the fact that the Army must adopt a new mindset that recognizes the requirement to successfully conduct operations across the spectrum of conflict, anytime, anywhere. FM 3-0 codified this forward-looking paradigm shift in the Army's operational concept:

Army forces combine offensive, defensive, and stability or civil support operations simultaneously as part of an interdependent joint force to seize, retain, and exploit the initiative, accepting prudent risk to create opportunities to achieve decisive results. They employ synchronized action—lethal and nonlethal—proportional to the mission and informed by a thorough understanding of all variables of the operational environment. Mission command that conveys intent and an appreciation of all aspects of the situation guides the adaptive use of Army forces.

THE STRATEGIC LANDSCAPE

1-1.   The future will be one of persistent conflict. Today's operational environments are being shaped by multiple factors. These include science and technology, information technology, transportation technology, the acceleration of the global economic community, and the rise of a networked society. The international nature of commercial and academic efforts will also have dramatic effects. The complexity of today's operational environments guarantees that future operations will occur across the spectrum of conflict.

FUTURE OPERATIONAL ENVIRONMENTS

1-2.   An *operational environment* is a composite of the conditions, circumstances, and influences which affect the employment of military forces and bear on the decisions of the commander (JP 3-0). Operational environments of the future will remain arenas in which bloodshed is the immediate result of hostilities between antagonists. Operational goals will be attained or lost not only by the use of lethal force but also by how quickly a state of stability can be established and maintained. Operational environments will remain dirty, frightening, and physically and emotionally draining. Death and destruction resulting from environmental conditions, as well as conflict itself, will create humanitarian crises. Due to the high lethality and long range of advanced weapons systems and the tendency of adversaries to operate among the population, the danger to combatants and noncombatants will be much greater than in past conflicts. State and nonstate actors, can be expected to use the full range of options, including every diplomatic, informational, military, and economic measure at their disposal. This applies to all adversaries, regardless of their technological or military capability. In addition, operational environments will extend to areas historically immune from battle, including the homeland—the United States and its territories—and the territory of multinational partners, especially urban areas. Operational environments will probably include areas not defined by geography, such as cyberspace. Computer network attacks already cross borders and may soon be able to hit anywhere, anytime. With the exception of cyberspace, all operations will be conducted "among the people." Outcomes will be measured in terms of effects on populations.

1-3. Operational environments will remain extremely fluid. Coalitions, alliances, partnerships, and actors will change continually. Interagency and joint operations will be required to deal with this wide and intricate range of players. International news organizations, using new information and communications technologies, will no longer depend on states to gain access to the area of operations. These organizations will greatly influence how operations are viewed. They will have satellites or their own unmanned aerial reconnaissance platforms from which to monitor the scene. Secrecy will be difficult to maintain, making operations security more vital than ever. Finally, complex cultural, demographic, and physical factors will be present, adding to the fog of war. Such factors include humanitarian crises and ethnic and religious differences. In addition, complex and urban terrain will often become major centers of gravity and havens for potential threats. Tomorrow's operational environments will be interconnected, dynamic, and extremely volatile.

TYPES OF THREATS

1-4. States, nations, transnational actors, and nonstate entities will continue to challenge and redefine the global distribution of power, concept of sovereignty, and nature of warfare. Threats are nation-states, organizations, people, groups, conditions, or natural phenomena able to damage or destroy life, vital resources, or institutions. Preparing for and managing these threats requires employing all instruments of national power—diplomatic, informational, military, and economic. Threats may be described through a range of four major categories or challenges: traditional, irregular, catastrophic, and disruptive. While helpful in describing threats the Army is likely to face, these categories do not define the nature of an adversary. In fact, adversaries may use any and all of these challenges in combination to achieve the desired effect against the United States.

1-5. Traditional threats emerge from states employing recognized military capabilities and forces in understood forms of military competition and conflict. In the past, the United States optimized its forces for this challenge. The United States currently possesses the world's preeminent conventional and nuclear forces, but this status is not guaranteed. Many nations maintain powerful conventional forces, and not all are friendly to the United States. Some of these potentially hostile powers possess weapons of mass destruction. Although these powers may not actively seek armed confrontation and may actively avoid U.S. military strength, their activities can provoke regional conflicts that threaten U.S. interests. Deterrence therefore remains the first aim of the joint force. Should deterrence fail, the United States strives to maintain capabilities to overmatch any combination of enemy conventional and unconventional forces.

1-6. Irregular threats are those posed by an opponent employing unconventional, asymmetric methods and means to counter traditional U.S. advantages. A weaker enemy often uses irregular warfare to exhaust the U.S. collective will through protracted conflict. Irregular warfare includes such means as terrorism, insurgency, and guerrilla warfare. Economic, political, informational, and cultural initiatives usually accompany, and may even be the chief means of, irregular attacks on U.S. influence.

1-7. Catastrophic threats involve the acquisition, possession, and use of nuclear, biological, chemical, and radiological weapons, also called weapons of mass destruction. Possession of these weapons gives an enemy the potential to inflict sudden and catastrophic effects. The proliferation of related technology has made this threat more likely than in the past.

1-8. Disruptive threats involve an enemy using new technologies that reduce U.S. advantages in key operational domains. Disruptive threats involve developing and using breakthrough technologies to negate current U.S. advantages in key operational domains.

NATURE OF FUTURE CONFLICT

1-9. By combining traditional, disruptive, catastrophic, and irregular capabilities, adversaries will seek to create advantageous conditions by quickly changing the nature of the conflict and moving to employ capabilities for which the United States is least prepared. The enemy will seek to interdict U.S. forces attempting to enter any crisis area. If U.S. forces successfully gain entry, the enemy will seek engagement in complex terrain and urban environments as a way of offsetting U.S. advantages. Methods used by adversaries include dispersing their forces into small mobile combat teams—combined only when required to strike a common objective—and becoming invisible by blending in with the local population.

1-10. Threats can be expected to use the environment and rapidly adapt. Extremist organizations will seek to take on statelike qualities. They will use the media, technology, and their position within a state's political, military, and social infrastructures to their advantage. Their operations will become more sophisticated, combining conventional, unconventional, irregular, and criminal tactics. Threats will focus on creating conditions of instability, seek to alienate legitimate forces from the population, and employ global networks to expand local operations. Threats will employ advanced information engagement and will not be bound by limits on the use of violence.

1-11. Future conflicts are likely to be fought "among the people" instead of "around the people." This fundamentally alters the manner in which Soldiers can apply force to achieve success. Enemies will increasingly seek populations within which to hide as protection against the proven attack and detection means of U.S. forces, in preparation for attacks against communities, as refuge from U.S. strikes against their bases, and to draw resources. War remains a battle of wills—a contest for dominance over people. The essential struggle of future conflicts will occur in areas where people are concentrated. It will require U.S. security dominance across the population.

EFFECTS OF TODAY'S OPERATIONAL ENVIRONMENTS

1-12. Because the Army, the threats, and the Army's operational concept have changed, thinking about Army missions and capabilities must also change. The Army cannot train for the last war. Major combat operations include more than large-scale offensive and defensive operations; they also include stability operations. All overseas Army operations combine simultaneous offensive, defensive, and stability operations. Operations within the United States and its territories simultaneously combine civil support, defense, and offense. Army forces must be not only capable of defeating the enemy's armed forces but also able to work in concert with the other instruments of national power—diplomatic, informational, and economic (the "whole of government")—to achieve national objectives. Army forces must be campaign capable as well. Once deployed, they may be required to operate for extended periods across the spectrum of conflict, from stable peace through general war, until strategic objectives are achieved. This campaign capability is the ability to sustain operations for as long as necessary to conclude operations successfully.

BASING STRATEGY AND ORGANIZATIONS

1-13. The Army's basing strategy and formations have changed. Formerly, Army forces were forward-based and sustained with individual replacements; today Army forces are based primarily in the United States, with complete units deploying to and from operations. The Army has transformed itself into a modular, brigade-based, deployable force capable of expeditionary full spectrum operations. The Army National Guard and U.S. Army Reserve are converting from a strategic reserve to an operational force.

FULL SPECTRUM OPERATIONS

1-14. The Army's new operational concept has changed Army operations significantly. All operations are now full spectrum operations. At present, the operational training domain is developing leaders with significant competencies in counterinsurgency operations. However, the Army's strategic depth requires leaders, Soldiers, and units with competencies in major combat and limited intervention operations as well. The other training domains must adjust to build and sustain these competencies. (Paragraphs 3-26 through 3-50 discuss the training domains.)

1-15. Full spectrum operations require mentally agile leaders able to operate in any operational theme across the spectrum of conflict. Effective command and control focuses on commanders rather than staffs. Commanders, not staffs, drive effective decisionmaking. Commanders must be able to mass fires at decisive points and times and effects over time. Decentralized rather than centralized operations are the norm today and will likely remain so. All leaders, from the highest to the lowest levels, must understand both the art and the science of operations and battle command.

1-16. Leaders synchronize not only combined arms forces but also lethal and nonlethal effects. Training can no longer focus only on anticipated enemies. In any conflict, the population in the area of operations will be a key factor—especially in conditions of insurgency and unstable peace. Operations in this part of the spectrum of conflict occur among the people throughout a campaign; they are not just part of post-conflict operations. The military alone cannot solve all the problems faced in this environment. Unified action—involving joint and multinational forces, and interagency, nongovernmental, and intergovernmental organizations—now reaches to the tactical level. Leaders at each level must be prepared to operate in this environment. In addition, Soldiers will continue to depend on the support of Army civilians and contractors throughout a campaign.

1-17. Civil support operations will continue to involve Regular Army and Reserve Component Soldiers and civilians operating with nongovernmental, local, state, and federal agencies. Since the homeland is vulnerable to attacks and natural disasters, all components must be prepared to conduct civil support operations on short notice. Regular Army forces are normally involved in civil support when natural or man-made disasters and incidents within the United States and its territories exceed the capabilities of Reserve Component organizations and domestic civilian agencies.

THREATS

1-18. In the past, the Army primarily trained to fight against other armies with conventional capabilities within clearly defined military and political boundaries. However, yesterday's Cold War enemies who planned to fight in predictable formations have been replaced by unpredictable, fleeting enemies who hide among the population. Today's enemies are adaptive, smart, and innovative. Their actions cannot be predicted with assurance. They will look for ways to attack friendly vulnerabilities. Rather than directly confront the Army's overwhelming superiority, enemies will attack with asymmetric means. In a single campaign, Army forces may fight multiple enemies with different agendas, rather than a single enemy unified by purpose or command.

1-19. Army forces will not only have to deal with conventional armed forces but also interact with vastly different cultures and languages of civilian populations. In addition, they will have to deal with both crumbling infrastructures and irregular forces. Nonlethal capabilities and information engagement will often be the primary weapons. Interactions between deployed Army units and the media have increased exponentially. Today's information environment means that everything Soldiers do will be subject to viewing and listening by friends and enemies. The ability to get the Army's message out and compete in the information environment is often as important as physical actions on the battlefield. Commanders use information engagement to fight this battle. Information engagement influences perceptions and behavior by communicating information, building trust and confidence, and promoting support for Army operations. (See FM 3-0, chapter 7.)

SOLDIERS

1-20. Today's dangerous and complex operational environments require Soldiers who are men and women of character and intellect. Their character and competence represent the foundation of a values-based, trained, and ready Army. Soldiers train to perform tasks while operating alone or in groups. Soldiers and leaders develop the ability to exercise mature judgment and initiative under stress. The Army requires agile and adaptive leaders able to handle the challenges of full spectrum operations in an era of persistent conflict. Army leaders must be—

- Proficient in their core competencies.
- Flexible enough to operate across the spectrum of conflict.
- Able to operate with joint and multinational, military and civilian organizations, and to leverage the capabilities of others to achieve their objectives.
- Culturally astute and able to use this awareness and understanding to conduct innovative operations.
- Courageous enough to see and exploit opportunities in challenging and complex operational environments.
- Grounded in the Army Values and Warrior Ethos.

1-21. Commanders at all levels ensure their Soldiers operate in accordance with the law of war. The *law of war* [also called the law of armed conflict] is that part of international law that regulates the conduct of armed hostilities (JP 1-02). It is the customary and treaty law applicable to the conduct of warfare on land and to relationships between belligerents and neutral states. The law of war includes treaties and international agreements to which the United States is a party as well as applicable customary international law. The purposes of the law of war are to—

- Protect both combatants and noncombatants from unnecessary suffering.
- Safeguard certain fundamental human rights of persons who become prisoners of war, the wounded and sick, and civilians.
- Make the transition to peace easier.

LEARNING AND ADAPTING

1-22. Contemporary operations challenge Army forces in many ways. The Army has always depended on its ability to learn and adapt. German Field Marshal Erwin Rommel observed that American Soldiers were initially inexperienced but learned and adapted quickly and well. Today's Army is more experienced than the one in North Africa during World War II; however, today's complex operational environments require organizations and Soldiers able to adapt equally quickly and well. Adaptable organizations learn constantly from experience (their own and others') and apply new knowledge to each situation. Agility and innovation are at a premium, as are creative and adaptive leaders. As knowledge increases, the Army continuously adapts its doctrine, organization, training, materiel, leadership and education, personnel, and facilities.

1-23. The Army as a whole must be versatile enough to operate successfully across the spectrum of conflict—from stable peace through unstable peace and insurgency to general war. Change and adaptation that once required years to implement must now be recognized, communicated, and enacted far more quickly. Technology played an increasingly important role in increasing lethality on twentieth century battlefields. Now it is assuming more importance and will require greater and more rapid innovation in tomorrow's conflicts. No longer can the Army take months to respond to hostile, asymmetric approaches. Solutions must be disseminated across the force in weeks—and then adapted quickly and innovatively as the enemy adapts to counter the newfound advantages.

1-24. Despite the many changes in today's operational environments, one thing remains constant: the Army and the other Services must retain the ability to fight and win. To do otherwise would create vulnerabilities for enemies to exploit. Retaining this ability requires tough, realistic training.

THE ROLE OF TRAINING

1-25. Effective training is the cornerstone of operational success. Through training, leaders, Soldiers, and units achieve the tactical and technical competence that builds confidence and agility. These characteristics allow Army forces to conduct successful operations across the spectrum of conflict. Army forces train using training doctrine that sustains their expeditionary and campaign capabilities. Focused training prepares leaders, Soldiers, and units to deploy, fight, and win. Achieving this competence requires specific, dedicated training on offensive, defensive, stability, and civil support tasks. The Army trains Soldiers and units daily in individual and collective tasks under challenging, realistic conditions. Training continues in deployed units to sustain skills and adapt to changes in the operational environment.

1-26. The United States' responsibilities are global; therefore, Army forces prepare to operate in any environment. Training management links training with missions. Commanders focus their training time and other resources on tasks linked to their doctrinal or directed mission. (See paragraph 4-29.) Because Army forces face diverse threats and mission requirements, senior commanders adjust their training priorities based on the likely operational environment. As units prepare for deployment, commanders adapt training priorities to address tasks required by actual or anticipated operations.

1-27. Army training includes a system of techniques and standards that allows Soldiers and units to determine, acquire, and practice necessary skills. Candid assessments, after action reviews, and applying lessons learned and best practices produce quality Soldiers and versatile units, ready for all aspects of an opera-

136

tional environment. The Army Training System prepares leaders, Soldiers, and units to employ Army capabilities adaptively and effectively in today's varied and challenging conditions.

1-28. Through training, the Army prepares Soldiers to win in land combat. Training builds teamwork and cohesion within units. It recognizes that Soldiers ultimately fight for one another and their units. Training instills discipline. It conditions Soldiers to operate within the law of war and rules of engagement. Training prepares unit leaders for the harsh reality of land combat. It emphasizes the fluid and disorderly conditions inherent in land operations.

1-29. Within these training situations, commanders emphasize mission command. (See FM 6-0.) To employ mission command successfully during operations, commanders and subordinate leaders must understand, foster, and frequently practice its principles during training.

1-30. Managing training for full spectrum operations presents challenges for leaders at all echelons. Training develops discipline, endurance, unit cohesion, and tolerance for uncertainty. It prepares Soldiers and units to address the ambiguities and complexities inherent in operations. During the Cold War, Army forces prepared to fight and win against a near-peer competitor. The Army's training focus was on offensive and defensive operations in major combat operations. As recently as 2001, the Army believed that forces trained to conduct the offense and defense in major combat operations could conduct stability and civil support operations just as effectively. However, the complexity of today's operational environments and commanders' legal and moral obligations to the population of an area of operations has shown that approach to be incorrect. Recent operational experience has demonstrated that forces trained exclusively for offensive and defensive tasks are not as proficient at stability tasks as those trained specifically for stability. For maximum effectiveness, stability and civil support tasks require dedicated training, similar to training for offensive and defensive tasks. Similarly, forces involved in protracted stability or civil support operations require intensive training to regain proficiency in offensive and defensive tasks before engaging in large-scale combat operations. Therefore, a balanced approach to the types of tasks to be trained is essential to readiness for full spectrum operations.

1-31. Leaders, Soldiers, and units must be prepared to achieve military objectives throughout all phases of a campaign. Army forces must be trained to conduct full spectrum operations under the conditions of any operational environment, anywhere along the spectrum of conflict. The Army must train, organize, and develop capabilities for stability operations with the same intensity and focus that it does for combat operations. Figure 1-1 displays the relationship of full spectrum operations to the spectrum of conflict and operational themes. The challenges of today's operational environments require a change in the Army mindset. The oval on the diagram—called the aim point—indicates that the focus of Army training and leader development must shift leftward from the right side of the spectrum of conflict—from training under conditions of general war to conditions midway between general war and insurgency. Doing this enables Army forces to sustain the proficiency in irregular warfare and limited intervention developed over the last seven years of conflict while sustaining their capability for major combat operations.

1-32. The aim point concept is a major cultural change for Army leaders, Soldiers, and units. To be successful in future operations, the Army cannot look at operations today as temporary interruptions in preparing for major combat operations against a near-peer enemy. Nor can it afford to view operations dominated by the offense and defense and those dominated by stability as either/or propositions. Both usually occur simultaneously. Army forces must be well-trained and able to deploy rapidly to conduct and win engagements and wars while remaining ready to conduct sustained stability operations. Similarly, in operations dominated by stability they must remain prepared to conduct offensive and defensive operations. The predominate operation—offense, defense, or stability—is determined by the situation, objectives, or conditions to be achieved, desired end state, and level of violence. Commanders consider the simultaneous execution of these three elements of full spectrum operations in their mission analysis.

1-33. The art of command takes on even greater significance in today's operational environments. Land operations occur among the people. While technology can enhance Army forces' effectiveness, land operations are basically a human endeavor involving human interactions. As a result, they are conducted in a complex realm dominated by fog, friction, and uncertainty. Command in this environment is an art, not a science. It requires leaders who can think creatively, understand their environment to a degree not required before, and can provide original solutions to ever changing problems posed by adaptable foes applying asymmetric capabilities.

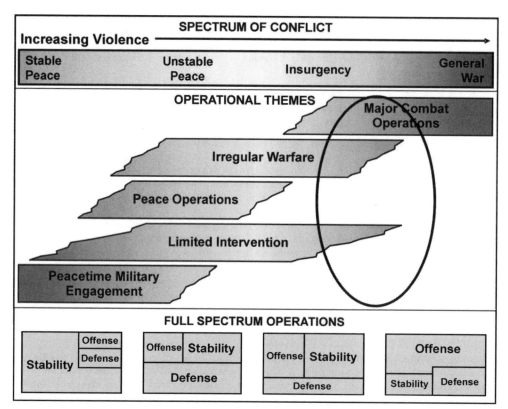

Figure 1-1. Aim point for Army training and leader development

1-34. A commander's fundamental challenge is conducting training that develops proficiency in all elements of full spectrum operations. The fact that units have not had as much time as they would have liked to train on offensive and defensive operations magnifies this challenge.

MEETING THE CHALLENGES OF FULL SPECTRUM OPERATIONS

1-35. In an era of persistent conflict, uncertainty exists as to where Army forces will operate and what the mission will be. Therefore, commanders face two training challenges: preparing their units for the most likely missions, and developing the skills needed to adapt quickly and easily to operations anywhere on the spectrum of conflict.

1-36. To focus training and leader development in the operational training domain, Headquarters, Department of the Army, establishes core mission-essential task lists (core METLs, or CMETLs) for each brigade and higher echelon unit. (See chapter 4, section II.) CMETLs rarely change. They provide a mix of mission-essential tasks that cover offensive, defensive, stability, and civil support operations. Units train on collective and individual tasks derived from and appropriately supporting those broad CMETL tasks.

1-37. Units do not have the time or other resources required to train under the conditions of all operational environments along the spectrum of conflict. Therefore, Headquarters, Department of the Army, analyzes possible operational environments and determines the likely force package requirements for each operational theme at the points along the spectrum of conflict where Army forces are most likely to operate. Based on this analysis and Headquarters, Department of the Army, guidance, Army command, Army Service component command, and direct reporting unit commanders focus their subordinate units' training on specific operational themes.

1-38. Commanders should leverage the experience of their combat-seasoned Soldiers. These veterans can help train other Soldiers and reduce the training time required for certain tasks. However, commanders should not assume that Soldiers and leaders who have served in combat are proficient in all tasks associated with a new position.

IMPLICATIONS OF THE AIM POINT ON TRAINING AND LEADER DEVELOPMENT

1-39. The aim point and standardized CMETL represent a change in mindset. They underlie a revision in how commanders prepare long- and short-range training plans. Previously, these plans focused solely on mission-essential tasks and how to train them. Now, developing these plans is a two-step process. The first step is a commander-to-commander dialog that discusses the following:

- Training conditions and corresponding resources required.
- The proportion of effort to be allocated among offensive, defensive, stability, and civil support tasks.
- The risks to readiness.
- The core capabilities required of a unit as it adjusts its training focus to prepare for a directed mission.

The second step is a training briefing during which the senior commander enters into a "contract" with subordinate commanders. The contract addresses the tasks to be trained, training conditions, risks associated with the training focus and conditions, and the resources required. (See chapter 4, section III.)

1-40. Army units must have the capability to train on stability tasks, such as "Providing essential services" and "Support to economic and infrastructure development," while sustaining proficiency in offensive and defensive operations. This training should include collecting accurate bottom-up intelligence and receiving and acting on top-down intelligence at the tactical level.

1-41. As much as possible, unit training conditions realistically replicate the projected operational environment. For example, besides an opposing force, conditions should incorporate the cultures, languages, and key leaders in the projected area of operations. Training tasks should also address dealing with the news media, unified action partners, and special operations forces. In addition, training should incorporate the contributions of both lethal and nonlethal actions.

1-42. Operations require well-trained leaders, Soldiers, and units who are not only proficient in core warfighting competencies but also mentally agile and able to adapt those competencies across the spectrum of conflict. Effective leaders and Soldiers are agile enough to readily seize fleeting opportunities. Their competencies can expand from those required for warfighting to those supporting stability operations, for example, language skills, cross-cultural communication, enabling economic development and governance, and conflict resolution through negotiation and mediation. These leaders and Soldiers use their knowledge of culture and language to enable operations and leverage the instruments of national power to achieve objectives.

1-43. Complex operational environments have required the generating force's role to change from that of the pre-2001 institutional Army. Meeting the significant challenges of today's operational environments requires an integrated, coordinated team effort from both the operational Army and the generating force. The *operational Army* consists of those Army organizations whose primary purpose is to participate in full spectrum operations as part of the joint force (FM 1-01). In contrast, the *generating force* consists of those Army organizations whose primary mission is to generate and sustain the operational Army's capabilities for employment by joint force commanders (FM 1-01). The generating force recruits, helps train, and equips Soldiers and units. It provides doctrine, mobile training teams, training support, and reachback resources to help prepare leaders, Soldiers, and units for missions. The generating force supports training and education in institutions, at home stations, and in deployed units. The generating force remains ready to adjust course content to maintain a balance of capabilities for operations across each of the operational themes. (FM 1-01 addresses generating force support to operations.)

1-44. Training the modular force is different from training division- and corps-based organizations. Commanders of some modular organizations need a greater breadth of skill than their predecessors required. Training during an era of persistent conflict is different from training for no-notice contingencies. While the need for trained divisions and corps has not changed, Army Service component commands have a new requirement for trained deployable command posts. These conditions require Army leaders to think differently about how they train their organizations. For example, they should assess whether the benefit of training overhead (such as external support and the level of evaluators desired) is worth the cost. They should look for ways to leverage a combat-seasoned force to reduce the ramp-up time to readiness. And they must look for opportunities to train smartly as the level of funding varies over time.

1-45. Operational environments, threats, and the Army's operational concept have changed since 2001. Army forces are now expected to conduct full spectrum operations across the spectrum of conflict. Therefore, the mindset of all members of the Army—leaders and Soldiers, military and civilian, Regular Army and Reserve Component—needs to change. All need to adapt to new concepts and think about how the Army can train more wisely, efficiently, and effectively. In a changing training environment, the constant of demanding training that focuses on the basics and achieves tough standards under challenging conditions remains immutable.

Chapter 2

Principles of Training

This chapter discusses the Army's seven principles of training. The principles of training provide a broad but basic foundation to guide how commanders and other leaders plan, prepare, execute, and assess effective training. Each principle contains an associated set of tenets that support and expand it.

TRAINING CONCEPT

2-1.   The Army provides combatant commanders with agile individuals, units, and their leaders. These expeditionary forces are trained and ready to conduct (plan, prepare, execute, and assess) full spectrum operations in support of unified action anywhere along the spectrum of conflict. The Army accomplishes this by conducting tough, realistic, standards-based, performance-oriented training. Live, virtual, constructive, and gaming training enablers enhance this training. Units train while deployed, at home station, and at maneuver combat training centers (CTCs). Commanders lead and assess training to ensure the training is high-quality and that individuals meet established standards. To meet the challenge of preparing for full spectrum operations, the Army takes advantage of the training capabilities found in the three training domains: institutional, operational, and self-development. (See paragraphs 3-26 through 3-50.) Commanders apply seven principles to plan, prepare, execute, and assess effective training. (See table 2-1.)

Table 2-1. The Army's seven principles of training

> - Commanders and other leaders are responsible for training.
> - Noncommissioned officers train individuals, crews, and small teams.
> - Train as you will fight.
> - Train to standard.
> - Train to sustain.
> - Conduct multiechelon and concurrent training.
> - Train to develop agile leaders and organizations.

COMMANDERS AND OTHER LEADERS ARE RESPONSIBLE FOR TRAINING

2-2.   Commanders are ultimately responsible for the training, performance, and readiness of their Soldiers, Army civilians, and organizations. However, leaders across all echelons and throughout the operational Army and generating force are responsible for training their respective organizations. For example, a commander is responsible for training a unit, an operations officer for training the operations staff section, and a platoon leader and platoon sergeant for training a platoon. These leaders ensure their organizations are trained and mission-ready. Leaders fulfill this responsibility by actively engaging in all aspects of training and adhering to eight tenets:

- Commanders are the unit's primary training managers and primary trainers.
- Commanders train their direct subordinate units and guide and evaluate training two echelons down.
- A leader's primary objective is to train subordinates and organizations for mission success.

141

- Leaders motivate their subordinates toward excellence and encourage initiative and innovation.
- Leaders place high priority on training and leader development.
- Leaders ensure training is executed to standard.
- Leaders continually assess individual and organizational proficiency.
- Leaders enforce safety and manage risks.

COMMANDERS ARE THE UNIT'S PRIMARY TRAINING MANAGERS AND PRIMARY TRAINERS

2-3.   The commander is the unit's primary training manager and primary trainer. Commanders develop their organization's mission-essential task list (METL), approve subordinate organizations' METLs, publish training and leader development guidance, and make resource decisions that allow subordinate leaders to train effectively. Senior noncommissioned officers (NCOs) at every level of command are vital to helping commanders meet their training responsibilities. Senior NCOs are often the most experienced trainers in the unit; they are therefore essential to a successful training program.

2-4.   Company commanders personally manage their company's training. Commanders at battalion level and higher manage training through their operations officer, who develops the unit's training plans. (See paragraphs 4-137 through 4-160.) However, to ensure effective unit training, those commanders remain involved in the training process. Effective training leads to well-trained units and ensures the welfare of Soldiers and civilians.

2-5.   Commanders set the training direction by providing subordinates clear guidance without stifling initiative and innovation. Commanders ensure the unit is focused on the right tasks, conditions, and standards. To perform their responsibilities as the unit's primary training manager and primary trainer, commanders—

- Use mission command in training as well as operations. (See FM 6-0.)
- Supervise the planning, preparation, execution, and assessment of training that results in proficient leaders, individuals, and organizations.
- Ensure training supports the unit's needs.
- Focus training on the unit's METL.
- Provide and protect the required resources.
- Incorporate safety and composite risk management (CRM) into all aspects of training.
- Ensure training is conducted to standard.
- Assess subordinate leader and unit proficiency and provide feedback.
- Develop and communicate a clear vision for training.
- Ensure the training environment replicates the anticipated operational environment.

COMMANDERS TRAIN THEIR DIRECT SUBORDINATE UNITS AND GUIDE AND EVALUATE TRAINING TWO ECHELONS DOWN

2-6.   Commanders are responsible for training their direct subordinate units. They guide and evaluate two echelons down. For example, brigade commanders train battalions and evaluate companies; battalion commanders train companies and evaluate platoons. Commanders develop leaders at one and two levels below their own through personal interaction and by providing them clear guidance.

A LEADER'S PRIMARY OBJECTIVE IS TO TRAIN SUBORDINATES AND ORGANIZATIONS FOR MISSION SUCCESS

2-7.   Training subordinates, teams, and units for mission success involves training the unit to established standards under a variety of rapidly changing and stressful conditions. Leaders set intermediate objectives to prepare their units to reach this primary objective. They employ the Army's training management model to ensure mission accomplishment. (See chapter 4, section III.) Leaders focus training on the tasks most important to mission accomplishment. They avoid trying to do too much, since there is not enough time to do everything.

LEADERS MOTIVATE THEIR SUBORDINATES TOWARD EXCELLENCE AND ENCOURAGE INITIATIVE AND INNOVATION

2-8.   Leaders create training conditions that prompt subordinates to be self-starters and creatively overcome challenges. Effective commanders practice mission command during training to create these opportunities. *Mission command* is the conduct of military operations through decentralized execution based on mission orders. Successful mission command demands that subordinate leaders at all echelons exercise disciplined initiative, acting aggressively and independently to accomplish the mission within the commander's intent (FM 3-0).

2-9.   Textbook answers seldom solve a problem exactly. Commanders intentionally create complex, ambiguous, and uncertain situations that challenge subordinates and organizations. Subordinate leaders then grow accustomed to making decisions with incomplete information. They learn to work outside their comfort zone. Under mission command, leaders require subordinates to assess the situation, determine tasks that lead to a solution, and execute the tasks to standard. Finally, leaders should reward subordinates by recognizing those who adapt to unfamiliar situations, seize the initiative, and develop creative solutions.

LEADERS PLACE HIGH PRIORITY ON TRAINING AND LEADER DEVELOPMENT

2-10. A leader's primary focus is preparing subordinates and organizations to conduct full spectrum operations in a variety of operational environments. Preparation includes training for ongoing operations as well as likely contingencies. It means making the training tougher than the expected operation. Leaders at all levels make the most of every available training opportunity or event to build organizations and develop individuals. Good training develops good leaders, and good leaders provide good training.

2-11. Training and leader development remain a priority throughout a deployment. Keeping this priority improves task performance, hones skills needed for the current operation, and minimizes the degradation of key skills for future operations.

2-12. Responsibility for training and leader development includes developing staffs. Well-trained staffs are as important to operational success as well-trained squads, platoons, and companies.

LEADERS ENSURE TRAINING IS EXECUTED TO STANDARD

2-13. The Army is a standards-based organization. Its leaders enforce established standards or establish and enforce standards where none exist. To ensure training meets standards, leaders stay involved during all training phases—planning, preparation, execution, and assessment.

2-14. Leaders inspect training for quality and effectiveness. They ensure individuals and organizations meet training objectives and that training is supported by sufficient resources and qualified trainers. Leaders establish discipline in training by creating and maintaining a climate that drives individuals and organizations to meet the standards. A disciplined unit trains to standard, even when leaders are not present. Leaders who enforce standards in training prepare their units to meet those standards in operations. They set the example for future generations of leaders.

LEADERS CONTINUALLY ASSESS INDIVIDUAL AND ORGANIZATIONAL PROFICIENCY

2-15. Leaders continually assess their own proficiency, that of subordinates, and that of their organizations. Leaders ensure training is relevant to individual and organizational needs so their subordinates are prepared to meet mission requirements. Leaders assist the commander by continually assessing not only individual performance and organizational proficiency but also training efficiency and effectiveness. Equally important, leaders provide feedback on performance to individuals and the organization through coaching, individual performance counseling (see FM 6-22, appendix B), and after action reviews (AARs). Leaders develop learning organizations by ensuring these processes are fully integrated into the unit's culture and climate.

LEADERS ENFORCE SAFETY AND MANAGE RISKS

2-16. Involved leaders minimize damage, injury, and loss of equipment and personnel. They do this by providing effective supervision, enforcing standards, and applying CRM. In some of the most dangerous operational environments and during the most complex missions, Army forces have experienced fewer losses than expected. This success is due to good leadership, comprehensive planning, effective supervision, and enforcing standards. Leaders influence first-line leader risk management decisions and guide first-line leaders to influence individual risk decisions at the lowest echelons. Leaders—

- Mitigate identified training risks by developing and implementing control measures that target specific risks. Leaders use CRM to match solutions to risks they identify. (FM 5-19 contains CRM doctrine. Paragraphs 2-37 through 2-39 of this manual discuss applying CRM to training.)
- Make risk decisions at the appropriate level. As a matter of policy, commanders establish and publish approval authority for risk decisions. Doing this requires leaders to identify risks and mitigating measures. It also ensures that the right leaders make decisions involving safety.

NONCOMMISSIONED OFFICERS TRAIN INDIVIDUALS, CREWS, AND SMALL TEAMS

2-17. NCOs are the primary trainers of enlisted Soldiers, crews, and small teams. Officers and NCOs have a special training relationship; their training responsibilities complement each other. This relationship spans all echelons and types of organizations. NCOs are usually an organization's most experienced trainers. Their input is crucial to a commander's overall training strategy (see paragraph 4-93) and a vital ingredient of the "top-down/bottom-up" approach to training. This approach is characterized by direction from commanders ("top-down") and subsequent input from subordinate officers and NCOs ("bottom-up"). (See paragraphs 4-72 through 4-73.) This two-way communication helps ensure the organization trains on the most important tasks. Five tenets support NCOs as they train individuals, crews, and small teams:

- Training is a primary duty of NCOs; NCOs turn guidance into action.
- NCOs identify Soldier, crew, and small-team tasks, and help identify unit collective tasks that support the unit's mission-essential tasks.
- NCOs provide and enforce standards-based, performance-oriented, mission-focused training.
- NCOs focus on sustaining strengths and improving weaknesses.
- NCOs develop junior NCOs and help officers develop junior officers.

TRAINING IS A PRIMARY DUTY OF NCOS; NCOS TURN GUIDANCE INTO ACTION

2-18. NCOs train, lead, and care for Soldiers and their equipment. They instill in Soldiers the Warrior Ethos and Army Values. NCOs take the broad guidance given by their leaders and identify the necessary tasks, standards, and resources. Then they execute the training in accordance with their leader's intent.

NCOS IDENTIFY SOLDIER, CREW, AND SMALL-TEAM TASKS, AND HELP IDENTIFY UNIT COLLECTIVE TASKS THAT SUPPORT THE UNIT'S MISSION-ESSENTIAL TASKS

2-19. To identify Soldier, crew, and small-team tasks, NCOs begin with individual Soldier tasks. Then they identify the individual, crew, and small-team tasks that link to or support the unit's mission-essential tasks. NCOs also help officers identify the collective tasks that support the unit's mission-essential tasks.

NCOS PROVIDE AND ENFORCE STANDARDS-BASED, PERFORMANCE-ORIENTED, MISSION-FOCUSED TRAINING

2-20. Disciplined, mission-focused training ensures Soldier proficiency in the individual tasks that support an organization's mission-essential tasks. NCOs ensure key individual tasks are integrated into short-range and near-term training plans. NCOs plan, prepare, execute, and assess training. They help commanders and other leaders assess training by conducting internal AARs and participating in external AARs. NCOs provide candid feedback to commanders and other leaders on all aspects of training—especially individual, crew, and small team training. They base feedback on their observations and evaluations before, during, and after training. NCOs identify problems with training and implement solutions on their own initiative.

NCOs FOCUS ON SUSTAINING STRENGTHS AND IMPROVING WEAKNESSES

2-21. NCOs quickly assimilate new Soldiers into the organization, continuously coach and mentor them, and hone their newly acquired skills. NCOs cross-train their Soldiers in critical skills and duties. Cross-training prepares Soldiers to accept positions of increased responsibility and take another Soldier's place if necessary. NCOs are dedicated to helping each Soldier grow and develop, both professionally and personally. This dedication is vital to developing future leaders. It is essential to ensuring the organization can successfully accomplish its mission, even when its leaders are absent. While developing Soldiers' skills and knowledge, NCOs foster initiative and agility in subordinates.

NCOs DEVELOP JUNIOR NCOs AND HELP OFFICERS DEVELOP JUNIOR OFFICERS

2-22. NCOs train and coach Soldiers. Senior NCOs train junior NCOs for the next higher position well before they assume it. Senior NCOs help form high-performing officer-NCO teams and help clarify to junior officers the different roles of officers and NCOs in training. NCOs also help officers develop junior officer competence and professionalism and explain NCO expectations of officers.

TRAIN AS YOU WILL FIGHT

2-23. For twenty-first century full spectrum operations, "fight" includes lethal and nonlethal skills. "Train as you fight" means training under the conditions of the expected operational environment. To train as they expect to fight, leaders adhere to the following eight tenets:

- Train for full spectrum operations and quick transitions between missions.
- Train for proficiency in combined arms operations and unified action.
- Train the fundamentals first.
- Make training performance-oriented, realistic, and mission-focused.
- Train for challenging, complex, ambiguous, and uncomfortable situations.
- Integrate safety and CRM throughout training.
- Determine and use the right mix of live, virtual, constructive, and gaming training enablers to provide conditions for training events that replicate the anticipated operational environment.
- Train while deployed.

TRAIN FOR FULL SPECTRUM OPERATIONS AND QUICK TRANSITIONS BETWEEN MISSIONS

2-24. Army organizations are required to conduct simultaneous offensive, defensive, and stability or civil support operations as well as support diplomatic, informational, and economic efforts. Effective training challenges leaders and organizations with rapidly changing conditions, requiring them to adapt to accomplish evolving missions. Commanders create training conditions that force subordinate leaders to quickly assess situations and develop innovative solutions. Doing this requires being able to train functionally diverse subordinate organizations. Leaders and subordinates put as much emphasis on rapid decisionmaking and execution as on deliberate planning and preparation. They exercise their mental agility to transition quickly between offensive, defensive, and stability or civil support operations.

TRAIN FOR PROFICIENCY IN COMBINED ARMS OPERATIONS AND UNIFIED ACTION

2-25. Combined arms proficiency is met through effectively integrating the warfighting functions. It is fundamental to all Army operations. Individuals, units, and their leaders are trained to fight and win the Nation's wars; however, they also contribute to implementing the peace alongside and in support of the diplomatic, informational, and economic instruments of national power. (See FM 3-0.)

2-26. Unified action and joint interdependence require leaders aware of the institutional cultures of organizations making up or working with a joint force. This awareness includes understanding how joint and multinational, military and civilian partners operate and make decisions. Individuals, units, and their leaders develop that understanding only by continuous education and by regular training with these partners. Deployed units prepare to participate in unified action with minimal additional training or lengthy adjustment periods.

2-27. Commanders and leaders should replicate unified action as much as possible during training. Live, virtual, constructive, and gaming training enablers can help replicate the conditions of an actual operational environment, including the contributions of unified action partners. Where possible, commanders establish predeployment training relationships that mirror the operational task organization. These habitual relationships help build a team prepared for unified action.

TRAIN THE FUNDAMENTALS FIRST

2-28. Fundamentals, such as warrior tasks and battle drills, are a critical part of the crawl-walk-run concept. (See paragraphs 4-180 through 4-184.) Warrior tasks are individual Soldier skills critical to Soldier survival. Battle drills are group skills designed to teach a unit to react and survive in common combat situations. Both focus individual training on performing basic tasks to a high degree of proficiency. Leaders assess whether or not their subordinates need to begin at the crawl stage. Training fundamentals first can ease training on more complex individual and collective tasks, such as those related to culture and foreign languages. It helps Soldiers become more agile and innovative. Soldiers well-trained in basic tasks—such as physical fitness, lifesaving skills, marksmanship, and small-unit drills—are essential to units confidently and successfully completing collective tasks.

MAKE TRAINING PERFORMANCE-ORIENTED, REALISTIC, AND MISSION-FOCUSED

2-29. Performance-oriented training involves physically performing tasks. It is an active, hands-on approach as opposed to a passive, listening one. Performance-oriented training focuses on results rather than process. It lets individuals and units train all tasks to standard. That training should be stressful physically and mentally to prepare individuals for conditions encountered during operations. Commanders and subordinate leaders plan realistic training. They integrate training support resources that replicate operational environment conditions as much as possible.

2-30. Training usually starts with a unit's core METL. (See paragraph 4-41.) METLs include core capability and general mission-essential tasks. Core capability mission-essential tasks are those the organization is designed to perform. General mission-essential tasks are those that all units, regardless of type, must be able to accomplish. (See paragraph 4-46.)

2-31. The Army has learned that developing proficiency in performing offensive and defensive tasks does not automatically develop proficiency in performing stability or civil support tasks. Similarly, an army that focuses only on stability or civil support tasks may have significant difficulties quickly transitioning to offensive and defensive operations.

2-32. Effective training incorporates conditions that allow execution of both core capability and general mission-essential tasks using lethal and nonlethal actions to adapt to different situations. While no organization can be completely proficient on all types of operations at all times, all can become proficient in the tasks it will most likely perform in the near term. As operational environments become more complex and resources (such as time, money, land, and airspace) become scarcer, the value of live, virtual, constructive, and gaming training enablers increases. These enablers enhance training effectiveness by replicating the conditions of an actual operational environment. Leaders are responsible for integrating and effectively using training aids, devices, simulators, and simulations (TADSS) to enhance realism.

TRAIN FOR CHALLENGING, COMPLEX, AMBIGUOUS, AND UNCOMFORTABLE SITUATIONS

2-33. Leaders train their subordinates and organizations to deal with challenging, complex, ambiguous, and uncomfortable situations. Such conditions require agile individuals and their leaders to show initiative and creativity and to be comfortable with fog and friction. Under mission command, leaders require subordinates to exercise initiative by trying different solutions to challenging problems.

2-34. Effective training builds competent and confident units and leaders. It includes situations where varied and tough conditions test their discipline and resolve. Training under those conditions develop individuals with the ability to remain calm in chaotic uncertain conditions.

2-35. Challenging training requires individuals to conduct continuous operations and different elements of full spectrum operations simultaneously. All Soldiers must develop the ability to assess quickly the level of force required. Training under realistic conditions requires Soldiers to use force commensurate with the situation. It also trains them to anticipate the second- and third-order effects of their actions.

2-36. Training should also challenge commanders. Some training should place them in situations requiring quick decisionmaking based on rapid analysis without staff support. Such training prepares individuals, organizations, and their leaders for the complexities inherent in today's operational environments. Proficiency in full spectrum operations requires leader-trainers who understand the requirements of those environments and effectively train their units for them.

INTEGRATE SAFETY AND COMPOSITE RISK MANAGEMENT THROUGHOUT TRAINING

2-37. Risk management and safety are not risk aversion. Risk is inherent in Army training, since success in operations depends on tough, realistic, and challenging training. Managing risk applies to individual and collective training under any operational or training environment, regardless of the echelon, component, mission, or type of force. *Composite risk management* is the decisionmaking process for identifying and assessing hazards, developing and implementing risk mitigation actions to control risk across the full spectrum of Army missions, functions, operations, and activities (FM 5-19). CRM underpins the protection element of combat power. Leaders manage risks without degrading training realism. They identify hazards, mitigate risks, evaluate environmental considerations, and make decisions at the appropriate level. CRM provides knowledge leaders need to take prudent risks.

2-38. Leaders use the risk management process to determine the right balance between the potential gains and losses associated with risk in operations and training. (See FM 5-19.) For example, an infantryman who adjusts the prescribed combat load to maximize combat power and mobility while balancing weight requirements is making a risk decision.

2-39. CRM expands the scope of the compliance-based Army Safety Program to identify, analyze, and manage risks that doctrine may or may not address. Individuals and organizations continuously apply CRM to training and establish control measures to mitigate risks. In training, CRM helps leaders identify the hazards inherent in tough, realistic, and challenging training environments. Leaders can then decide whether achieving the training objectives merits accepting the risk associated with those hazards. In operations, commanders use CRM to identify hazards and mitigate the risks those hazards pose to the force. This contributes to preserving the force so commanders can apply maximum combat power to the current operation and sustain combat power for future operations. Since individuals operate as they have trained, practice in integrating CRM into the operations process while training is essential.

DETERMINE AND USE THE RIGHT MIX OF LIVE, VIRTUAL, CONSTRUCTIVE, AND GAMING TRAINING ENABLERS

2-40. A combination of live, virtual, constructive, and gaming training enablers can help replicate an actual operational environment. Based on resources available—such as time, fuel, funds, and training areas—commanders determine the right mix of live, virtual, constructive, and gaming training enablers to effectively and efficiently train for a mission or rehearse an operation.

TRAIN WHILE DEPLOYED

2-41. Training does not stop when a unit is deployed. Commanders should periodically review their directed METL to sustain or retrain certain tasks as needed. (See paragraphs 4-55 through 4-68.) As time and resources allow, they should also train METL tasks to maintain proficiency during long deployments. Commanders consider the effects of the operational variables (political, military, economic, social, infrastructure, information, physical environment, and time [PMESII-PT]) on the area of operations before undertaking such training. (See FM 3-0, paragraphs 1-21 through 1-44.)

TRAIN TO STANDARD

2-42. Army training is performed to standard. Leaders prescribe tasks with their associated standards that ensure their organization is capable of accomplishing its doctrinal or directed mission. A standard is the minimum proficiency required to accomplish a task under a set of conditions. (See paragraph 4-91.) The goal in training is achieving mastery, not just proficiency. Leaders continually challenge individuals and organizations by varying training conditions to make achieving the standard more challenging. The following tenets focus on standards-based training:

- Leaders know and enforce standards.
- Leaders define success where standards have not been established.
- Leaders train to standard, not to time.

LEADERS KNOW AND ENFORCE STANDARDS

2-43. Enforcing standards provides individuals and organizations with a sound basis for training. Effective training is executed to Army standards, joint standards, or both. Standards include measures of performance that leaders use to evaluate the ability of individuals and organizations to accomplish tasks. Standards usually are established in such publications as doctrine, combined arms training strategies, and unit standing operating procedures.

LEADERS DEFINE SUCCESS WHERE STANDARDS HAVE NOT BEEN ESTABLISHED

2-44. Individuals and organizations may be required to perform tasks based on emerging tactics, techniques, and procedures or new conditions. These tasks may not have established standards. Leaders adapt by redefining an existing task or establishing a standard to meet the situation.

2-45. Leaders create achievable standards based on any or all of the following: commander's guidance; observations, insights, and lessons from similar operations; their professional judgment; and common sense. The next higher commander approves these standards. Doctrine describes common tactics, techniques, and procedures that permit commanders, other leaders, and units to adjust rapidly to changing situations. Where possible, commanders base new standards on doctrine, since doctrine provides the basis for a common vocabulary and evaluation criteria.

LEADERS TRAIN TO STANDARD, NOT TO TIME

2-46. Leaders allocate enough time to train tasks to standard. When necessary, they allocate time to retrain tasks under the same or different, preferably more difficult, conditions. Good leaders understand that they cannot train on everything; therefore, they focus on training the most important tasks. Leaders do not accept substandard performance in order to complete all tasks on the training schedule. Training a few tasks to standard is preferable to training more tasks below standard. Achieving the standard may require repeating tasks or restarting a training event. Leaders should allocate time for remedial training. When a unit meets the standard in less time than expected, it can use that time for training related tasks—or leaders can end training early. Training plans should allow for this.

TRAIN TO SUSTAIN

2-47. Units must be capable of operating continuously while deployed. Maintenance is essential for continuous operations and is, therefore, an integral part of training. Maintenance is more than maintaining equipment; it includes maintaining and sustaining performance levels, personnel, equipment, and systems over extended periods. Leaders create training conditions that require units to do this. Leaders incorporate sustainment into individual and collective training by following these nine tenets:

- Make maintenance of equipment, individuals, and the organization part of every training event.
- Equipment maintenance is the cornerstone of sustainment.
- Soldiers and civilians maintain entire systems.

- Leaders train and retrain critical tasks to sustain proficiency.
- Train to sustain core individual and collective skills and knowledge.
- Sustain leader presence.
- Train staffs routinely.
- Leaders develop a sense of stewardship in subordinates.
- Preventable loss is unacceptable.

MAKE MAINTENANCE OF EQUIPMENT, INDIVIDUALS, AND THE ORGANIZATION PART OF EVERY TRAINING EVENT

2-48. Commanders allocate time for individuals and units to maintain themselves and their equipment to standard during training events. This time includes scheduled maintenance periods (such as for preventive maintenance checks and services), assembly area operations, and physical training. Leaders train their subordinates to appreciate the importance of maintaining themselves and their equipment. Organizations perform maintenance during operations to the standards they practice in training. Maintenance training in this context includes not only taking care of equipment but also sustaining critical individual and collective skills. Maintenance training helps sustain mental and physical fitness, essential skills, and equipment readiness rates. Effective training prepares individuals and organizations to operate for long periods by including the maintenance tasks required to sustain operations.

EQUIPMENT MAINTENANCE IS THE CORNERSTONE OF SUSTAINMENT

2-49. Functional, reliable, and maintained equipment is essential to mission success. All Soldiers are responsible for maintaining their equipment during training and operations. Leaders are responsible for ensuring they do so. Leaders ensure subordinates execute scheduled maintenance with the same intensity as other training events. These periods should have clear, focused, and measurable objectives. As with other types of training, leaders supervise, enforce standards, complete AARs, and hold subordinates accountable. They lead by example to underscore that maintenance training is important to readiness. Effective maintenance training ensures organizational equipment is available when needed. It also reduces the effect of frequent deployments and high personnel tempo.

SOLDIERS AND CIVILIANS MAINTAIN ENTIRE SYSTEMS

2-50. Leaders train subordinates to maintain entire systems. For example, maintaining a fighting vehicle involves maintaining its components—weapons; radios; basic issue items; and chemical, biological, radiological, and nuclear equipment—as well as the vehicle itself. Units are systems that require sustainment in the form of rest, resupply, rotation of shifts, and special training as required.

LEADERS TRAIN AND RETRAIN CRITICAL TASKS TO SUSTAIN PROFICIENCY

2-51. Sustaining proficiency applies to maintaining skill proficiency, since physical health, memory, and skills deteriorate without regular use and periodic challenges. Limited training time requires leaders to pick the most important tasks to sustain or improve, for example, those tasks that are essential to mission accomplishment and perishable without frequent practice. Retraining tasks that individuals can perform to standard while not training tasks that individuals cannot perform wastes valuable training time. Commanders select the most important tasks when they prepare their METL. (See chapter 4, section II.) They consider AARs, trends, new equipment, and collaboration among leaders at all levels when they do this. Commanders use the mix of live, virtual, constructive, and gaming training enablers that best sustains individual and collective skills.

TRAIN TO SUSTAIN CORE INDIVIDUAL AND COLLECTIVE SKILLS AND KNOWLEDGE

2-52. Leaders balance the time spent training on METL tasks with time spent on such skills as physical and mental fitness, marksmanship, and navigation.

149

SUSTAIN LEADER PRESENCE

2-53. A leader's physical presence determines how others perceive that leader. It is more than the leader just showing up; it involves the image that the leader projects. Presence is conveyed through actions, words, and the manner in which leaders carry themselves and make decisions. Setting the example for health, physical fitness, resilience, and calmness under pressure is the foundation of leader presence. (See FM 6-22, chapter 5.)

TRAIN STAFFS ROUTINELY

2-54. The staff is an extension of the commander. It is a vital part of the commander's command and control system. (See FM 6-0.) Operations require staffs to operate continuously without losing proficiency. Staffs should train regularly and often, rather than in short bursts just before a major evaluation. An effective staff maintenance program progresses to a high level of proficiency. It includes—

- Operating over extended periods and distances.
- Enforcing rest plans.
- Maintaining tactical command and control information systems and other equipment.
- Establishing security measures.
- Cross-training.

LEADERS DEVELOP A SENSE OF STEWARDSHIP IN SUBORDINATES

2-55. Resources include the following: individual and organizational equipment, installation property, training areas, ranges, facilities, time, the environment, and organizational funds. Protection of these assets is both a leader's and an individual's responsibility. Subordinates follow the example leaders set. Preserving readiness requires enforcing accountability for property and other resources across all echelons.

2-56. Well-disciplined individuals willingly take ownership of and properly care for their equipment. This sense of stewardship avoids costly and unnecessary expenditures on replacements. In addition, mission accomplishment requires individuals to be physically and mentally ready and have their equipment properly functioning and maintained. This readiness ensures their safety and security, as well as that of everyone else in the organization. Good stewardship is learned during tough training in which individuals learn to respect and trust themselves and their leaders. Good training also develops appreciation for the importance of well-maintained equipment and other resources.

PREVENTABLE LOSS IS UNACCEPTABLE

2-57. Soldiers, Army civilians and their leaders are professionally obligated to protect the Nation's resources—human, financial, materiel, environmental, and informational. Preventable loss can be mitigated by integrating CRM throughout Army training.

CONDUCT MULTIECHELON AND CONCURRENT TRAINING

2-58. *Multiechelon training is a training technique that allows for the simultaneous training of more than one echelon on different or complementary tasks*. It is the most efficient way to train, especially with limited resources. It requires synchronized planning and coordination by commanders and other leaders at each affected echelon.

2-59. Multiechelon training optimizes the use of time and resources. This is important in an environment characterized by frequent deployments and limited resources. Multiechelon training can occur when an entire unit trains on a single task or when different echelons of a unit simultaneously train on different tasks. Multiechelon training allows individuals and leaders to see the effects of one echelon's execution on another echelon. This type of training offers commanders an opportunity to reduce training resource requirements. For example, when a lower echelon requires less attention than a higher one, observer controller/trainers can be consolidated at the higher echelon and be required to observe both echelons. While multiechelon training involves as many echelons as a commander desires, the focus can seldom exceed two echelons.

2-60. Concurrent training occurs when a leader conducts training within another type of training. It complements the execution of primary training objectives by allowing leaders to make the most efficient use of available time. For example, an artillery battery commander supporting an infantry battalion during a non-firing maneuver exercise might conduct howitzer section training while the fire direction center maintains communications with fire support officers moving with the infantry. Similarly, while Soldiers are waiting their turn on the firing line at a range, their leaders can train them on other tasks. Leaders look for ways to use all available training time. Concurrent training can occur during multiechelon training.

2-61. While large-scale training events provide the best opportunity to conduct multiechelon training, smaller scale events can provide conditions conducive to training multiple echelons simultaneously. Leaders should exercise initiative and create their own training events within a larger training exercise, based on the needs of their unit and through coordination with the larger or supported unit.

TRAIN TO DEVELOP AGILE LEADERS AND ORGANIZATIONS

2-62. The Army trains and educates its members to develop agile leaders and organizations able to operate successfully in any operational environment. The Army develops leaders who can direct fires in a firefight one minute and calmly help a family evacuate a destroyed home the next. The Army trains leaders who accept prudent risks to create opportunities to seize, retain, and exploit the initiative. This agility requires educated, highly trained, and well-disciplined individuals. They must also be physically tough, mentally agile, and well-grounded in their core competencies and the Warrior Ethos. The Army needs people experienced and knowledgeable enough to successfully accomplish any mission along the spectrum of conflict and in any operational theme. Such individuals—expeditionary individuals and their leaders—can adapt to any situation and operate successfully in any operational environment. These seven tenets underlie developing competent and agile leaders and organizations:

- Train leaders in the art and science of battle command.
- Train leaders who can execute mission command.
- Develop an expeditionary mindset in Soldiers and Army civilians.
- Educate leaders to think.
- Train leaders and organizations to adapt to changing mission roles and responsibilities.
- Create a "freedom to learn" environment.
- Give subordinates feedback.

TRAIN LEADERS IN THE ART AND SCIENCE OF BATTLE COMMAND

2-63. *Battle command* is the art and science of understanding, visualizing, describing, directing, leading, and assessing forces to impose the commander's will on a hostile, thinking, and adaptive enemy. Battle command applies leadership to translate decisions into actions—by synchronizing forces and warfighting functions in time, space, and purpose—to accomplish missions (FM 3-0). During the Cold War, the Army thought it knew what was necessary to succeed against a predictable enemy. Now the Army faces different challenges. These challenges result from multiple circumstances. Some have military causes; others result from actions by the population in the area of operations. These conditions require an unprecedented understanding of a wide variety of factors. Commanders think about these factors in terms of the operational variables (PMESII-PT) and mission variables (mission, enemy, terrain and weather, troops and support available, time available, civil considerations [METT-TC]). That understanding is essential to successful battle command.

2-64. Battle command is guided by professional judgment gained from several sources: experience, knowledge, education, intelligence, and intuition. Leaders improve their battle command skills through realistic, complex, and changing training scenarios. Training gives commanders greater understanding that enables them to make qualitatively better decisions than their opponents. Simultaneously, they focus their intuitive abilities on visualizing the current and future conditions of their operational environment.

151

2-65. Successful battle command involves timely, effective decisions based on combining judgment with information. It requires knowing when and what to decide. It also requires commanders to assess the quality of information and knowledge. Commanders identify important information requirements and focus subordinates and the staff on them. Commanders anticipate the activities that follow decisions, knowing that once executed, the effects of those decisions are often irreversible. In exercising battle command, commanders combine analytical and intuitive approaches for decisionmaking. These skills are developed and honed through rigorous training and mentoring by senior commanders at every echelon.

TRAIN LEADERS WHO CAN EXECUTE MISSION COMMAND

2-66. Commanders who train using mission command develop leaders who practice mission command and subordinates who are comfortable with and expect to operate using mission orders. (*Mission orders* is a technique for developing orders that emphasizes to subordinates the results to be attained, not how they are to achieve them. It provides maximum freedom of action in determining how to best accomplish assigned missions [FM 3-0].) If mission command is not practiced in training, leaders will not use it in operations.

2-67. Mission command requires an environment of trust and mutual understanding. Training under mission command increases trust and allows the unit to achieve unity of effort by focusing on the commander's intent. Subordinates develop initiative and the ability to develop creative solutions to problems—in short, they become more agile. Effective mission command requires leaders who can develop clear intent statements—brief statements that provide a clear purpose and end state. As with battle command, commanders and other leaders at every level employ mission command in training and operations.

DEVELOP AN EXPEDITIONARY MINDSET IN SOLDIERS AND ARMY CIVILIANS

2-68. Organizations are only as agile as their people are, especially their leaders. Expeditionary individuals and their leaders are knowledgeable and experienced enough to conduct full spectrum operations in any operational theme anywhere along the spectrum of conflict—and they know it. Persistent conflict is producing a force of seasoned Soldiers with multiple operational experiences. Home station training and rotations at the maneuver CTCs are incorporating offensive, defensive, and stability operations into major combat operations and irregular warfare scenarios—and in others as needed. However, developing an expeditionary mindset requires complementing operational experiences with self-development through reading and simulations. It also requires institutional training that provides broadening and introspective experiences. Effective institutional training allows Soldiers and Army civilians to reflect on their strengths and weaknesses and take the steps necessary to develop and enhance their skills and knowledge. Reading AARs and lessons learned by individuals and units in operations augments personal knowledge and experiences. Expeditionary leaders are versatile in their knowledge, skills, behaviors, and competencies. These leaders master the skills and competencies associated with other branches in order to train their modular units. Institutional experiences, home station training, CTC exercises, and self-development all contribute to producing expeditionary leaders and units.

EDUCATE LEADERS TO THINK

2-69. Expeditionary leaders are trained to think critically and originally. These leaders know how to conduct operations. Just as important, they know how to develop novel, original solutions to complex tactical situations in actual operational environments. Effective training cultivates a leader's ability to develop workable tactical concepts, quickly choose among alternatives, and modify their actions as the operational environment changes. These skills involve a mix of education and experience, reinforced through training, exercises, and day-to-day operations. Expeditionary leaders understand that no single solution to a problem exists; what worked yesterday may not work today. They can apply their skills and knowledge to solve recurring problems—and new ones as they arise. Leaders also develop their subordinate leaders' skills by creating a training environment that challenges subordinates to think beyond familiar drills and common solutions. Leaders teach subordinates that operations do not always occur under the same conditions, in sequence, or with logical transitions.

TRAIN LEADERS AND ORGANIZATIONS TO ADAPT TO CHANGING MISSION ROLES AND RESPONSIBILITIES

2-70. Training adaptable leaders and organizations requires creativity and imagination. Commanders and other leaders prepare themselves, their subordinates, and their units for unfamiliar situations, to include employing both lethal and nonlethal means. Leaders develop flexible subordinates—subordinates who do not freeze in unfamiliar situations. Leaders train subordinates to perform at both their current and the next level of responsibility. That training prepares individuals to assume the next higher position quickly when needed. Live, virtual, constructive, and gaming training enablers let leaders inexpensively train and retrain tasks under varying conditions.

2-71. To make units agile, commanders and senior NCOs help subordinates develop their intuition. Leaders coach subordinates through various situations comprising varying conditions and degrees of force. That coaching helps subordinates recognize similar situations and intuitively know how to handle them without being limited by a single "approved solution." Leaders help subordinates recognize alternative—even non-standard—solutions to complex challenges rather than relying on past solutions that may not fit the situation. Battle drills are important combat skills; they teach Soldiers how to react instinctively in life-and-death situations, where aggressiveness may be more important than finesse or where immediate action is more important than deliberate decisionmaking. However, well-trained Soldiers can quickly identify situations where battle drills do not fit, think their way through them, and act to resolve the situation.

CREATE A "FREEDOM TO LEARN" ENVIRONMENT

2-72. Leaders foster an organizational climate that allows subordinate leaders to think their way through unanticipated events and react to unfamiliar situations. (See FM 6-22, chapter 8.) Freedom to learn does not mean accepting substandard performance. It means establishing a standard that rewards creativity, innovation, and initiative—and a command climate that allows honest mistakes. Leaders focus on what was completed and how individuals responded to the situation. If results are unsatisfactory, subordinates learn from mistakes through feedback. They analyze why they failed to achieve the desired results, discover how to adapt, and then try again. Leaders also solicit recommendations from subordinates being trained.

2-73. Subordinates who think they are not allowed to fail or try innovative means to accomplish tasks avoid taking risks and attempting imaginative solutions. The best lessons are often learned through failure. However, repeated failures of the same task can indicate an inability to learn or the need to reassess the training technique, training, or both. Today's dynamic operational environments require individuals and their leaders to learn while operating. This important skill requires agile leaders who can learn from their mistakes under pressure and adapt successfully to a new but similar situation. Learning while operating is not the same as having the freedom to learn; it is the product of it. A training environment in which individuals have the freedom to make mistakes produces individuals better able to learn and adapt during operations.

GIVE SUBORDINATES FEEDBACK

2-74. The Army's primary feedback technique is the AAR. (See paragraphs 4-202 through 4-208.) Leaders use AARs to provide feedback based on observations and assessments of performance during training and operations. AARs are essential for developing agile leaders and subordinates. Feedback helps all individuals learn from training. It allows them to reflect on what they did and how they can improve future performance. AARs are not critiques; they are a means of self-discovery led by a facilitator. AARs help leaders and subordinates understand how and why actions unfolded as they did and what should be done next time to avoid the same mistakes or repeat successes. Leaders can use AARs to gauge training effectiveness and whether changes are needed in future training. Well-planned and well-executed AARs form the building blocks of learning organizations. (See FM 6-01.1, appendix B, for using AARs during operations.)

Chapter 3

The Army Training System

This chapter discusses the Army Training System, which prepares Soldiers, Army civilians, organizations, and their leaders to conduct full spectrum operations. This discussion addresses the importance of discipline in training and the complementary nature of the institutional, operational, and self-development training domains. The chapter defines training and education, reinforces the importance of leader development, and describes the lifecycle of training and education.

FOUNDATIONS OF ARMY TRAINING

3-1.   The foundations of Army training are discipline, sound principles and tenets, and a responsive training support system.

DISCIPLINE

3-2.   The essential foundation of any good training program is discipline. Good commanders and leaders instill discipline in training to ensure mission success. Discipline in training can be summed up this way:

- Disciplined individuals do the right thing when no one is looking, even under chaotic or uncertain conditions. Discipline demands habitual and reasoned obedience, even when leaders are absent.
- Disciplined individuals perform to standard, regardless of conditions. They have repeatedly practiced tasks to standard, sustained training standards, and trained under conditions closely replicating expected operational environments.
- Discipline is an individual, leader, and organizational responsibility. It is essential to mission success. Well-trained, disciplined individuals and organizations increase the likelihood of success in any operation.
- Discipline in training relates to the Army Values. Success in all three training domains demands it.

PRINCIPLES

3-3.   The purpose of Army training is to provide combatant commanders with trained and ready Army forces. Training builds individual confidence and competence while providing individuals with essential skills and knowledge. Individuals and organizations need skills and knowledge to operate as part of expeditionary Army forces conducting full spectrum operations in any operational environment. The principles of training established in chapter 2 apply to all Army training, regardless of topic, component, location, or duration. The Army applies these principles to planning, preparing, executing, and assessing individual and organizational training in three distinct but linked training domains: institutional, operational, and self-development. (See figure 3-1, page 3-2.)

TRAINING SUPPORT

3-4.   Developing leaders and preparing Soldiers, Army civilians, staffs, and units for full spectrum operations requires a team effort. The generating force and operational Army share this responsibility. Fulfilling it requires close coordination, integration, and synchronization. While each training domain has specific responsibilities, some intentional overlap ensures all tasks needed for full spectrum operations are trained. The ability to conduct quality training relies on a training infrastructure designed to prepare subordinates and leaders for the challenges of an operational environment. The Army's training support system provides training support products, services, and facilities necessary to replicate a relevant training environment. (See paragraphs 4-120 through 4-122.)

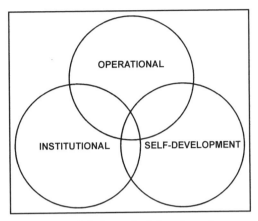

Figure 3-1. Army training domains

TRAINING AND EDUCATION

3-5.   The Army Training System comprises training and education. Training is not solely the domain of the generating force; similarly, education continues in the operational Army. Training and education occur in all three training domains. Training prepares individuals for certainty. Education prepares individuals for uncertainty. Education enables agility, judgment, and creativity. Training enables action.

3-6.   Training develops tactical and technical, individual and collective skills through instruction and repetitive practice. Training uses a crawl-walk-run approach that systematically builds on the successful performance of each task. (See paragraphs 4-180 through 4-184.) The stage at which a Soldier or unit enters training depends on the leader's assessment of the current readiness level; not everyone needs to begin at the crawl stage. Mastery comes with practice under varying conditions and by meeting the standards for the task trained.

3-7.   Army training prepares individuals and organizations by developing the skills, functions, and teamwork necessary to accomplish a task or mission successfully. Training is generally associated with "what to do." Well-trained organizations and individuals react instinctively, even in unknown situations. Training also helps develop leaders and organizations able to adapt to change under unfamiliar circumstances. Soldiers and teams who execute a battle drill to standard in a new situation under the stress of combat exemplify the result of good training. Repetitive training on a task under varying conditions develops intuition on how to approach the task under new or unfamiliar conditions.

3-8.   Education, in contrast, provides intellectual constructs and principles. It allows individuals to apply trained skills beyond a standard situation to gain a desired result. It helps develop individuals and leaders who can think, apply knowledge, and solve problems under uncertain or ambiguous conditions. Education is associated with "how to think." It provides individuals with lifelong abilities that enable higher cognitive thought processes. Education prepares individuals for service by teaching knowledge, skills, and behaviors applicable to multiple duty positions in peace or war. Educated Soldiers and Army civilians have the foundation needed to adapt to new and unfamiliar situations.

3-9.   Traditional training and education may not meet all the needs of an expeditionary Army. The Army is adapting training and education as appropriate to meet the conditions of today's operational environments. Developing new approaches may be necessary to ensure Soldiers and Army civilians are confident in their ability to conduct full spectrum operations anywhere along the spectrum of conflict with minimal additional training.

TRAINING AND EDUCATION LIFECYCLE OF SOLDIERS AND ARMY CIVILIANS

3-10. Soldiers and Army civilians begin training the day they enter the Army. They continue training until the day they retire or separate. Individuals train to build the skills and knowledge essential to a trained, expeditionary Army. Training prepares individuals, units, staffs, and their leaders to conduct full spectrum operations anytime and anywhere along the spectrum of conflict. This lifelong learning occurs in all three training domains—institutional, operational, and self-development—and involves self-assessment.

INSTITUTIONAL

3-11. The Soldier is, first of all, a warrior. Soldier training begins in the generating force. In schools and training centers, Soldiers train on individual tasks that ultimately support their projected unit's core capability mission-essential tasks. Soldiers are also exposed to the skills of other branches while in schools and training centers. Finally, Soldiers train on warrior tasks—critical tasks that all Soldiers must perform in full spectrum operations. Armed with basic skills from the institution, Soldiers are assigned to a unit. There they integrate into a team and begin training in the operational training domain.

3-12. In contrast, most Army civilians enter the Army with the skills and knowledge required for their position. Civilians enhance their knowledge, skills, and abilities through the Civilian Education System, functional training, self-development, and assignments. Army civilians are key contributors to Army readiness.

OPERATIONAL

3-13. Operational assignments build on the foundation of individual skills learned in schools. Unit leaders introduce new skills required by a Soldier's specialty. In addition, Soldiers master collective tasks that support the unit's mission-essential tasks. In units, individuals train to standard on individual and collective tasks—first with their unit and then as an integrated component of a combined arms team, which may participate in unified action. Major training events, combat training center (CTC) exercises, and operational deployments provide additional experiences necessary for building fully trained units. Regardless of where individuals train—in the generating force or the operational Army—effective training is relevant, rigorous, realistic, challenging, and properly resourced. Conditions replicate the projected operational environment as much as possible. This training environment provides the full range of experiences needed to produce capable, bold, and agile individuals and units.

3-14. Army civilians usually gain operational experience in the generating force; however, civilians support both the operational Army and the generating force. They fill positions that make it possible to man, equip, resource, and train operational Army units. Army civilians provide the skills and continuity essential to the functioning of Army organizations and programs.

SELF-DEVELOPMENT

3-15. Self-development is just as important as other individual training. It allows individuals to expand their knowledge and experience to supplement training in the institutional or operational training domains. Self-development can enhance skills needed for a current position or help prepare an individual for future positions. It can mean the difference between failure and success. Individuals are responsible for their own professional growth and for seeking out self-development opportunities. (FM 6-22, paragraphs 8-30 through 8-50, addresses self-development.)

3-16. Civilian knowledge, skills, and abilities are key contributors to Army readiness. They are enhanced through the Civilian Education System and focused, continuous learning. Commanders and first-line leaders monitor and annually assess individual performance and development. In schools, individuals monitor their own progress. Regardless of who tracks the self-development plan, the burden of self-development rests on the individual. It is a function of each person's desire to improve.

3-17. Soldiers and Army civilians complete self-assessments with or without supervision. They thoroughly assess their competencies and seek advice and counsel from others to determine strengths and weaknesses. Guidance on self-development can come from schools, leaders, mentors, and peers.

3-18. As professionals, Soldiers and Army civilians discipline themselves to pursue training and education on and off duty. Self-development can take many forms. Examples include the following: reading Army and joint manuals, professional journals, and military history; taking college courses; completing self-paced online training modules; or pursuing academic degrees. Such training and education is critical to developing the agility and breadth of skills needed during full spectrum operations. Individuals can use Army or commercial training and education products to become more proficient in any area.

LIFELONG TRAINING AND EDUCATION

3-19. Soldiers and Army civilians cycle between the institutional and operational domains for training and education throughout their careers. They supplement training, education, and experience with structured, guided, and individualized self-development programs. Individuals return to schools and centers at certain points to gain new skills and knowledge needed for the next duty assignment and to prepare them for higher levels of responsibility. They return to units, sometimes at the next higher grade, assume new responsibilities, and apply the knowledge and experience gained in school to operations.

3-20. Leaders should encourage subordinates to increase their skills and knowledge through training and education in all three domains. Commanders and other leaders supplement and reinforce what individuals learn in schools. Subordinates and leaders identify gaps in learning and fill those gaps through self-development. Similarly, Army civilians hone their skills in the institutional training domain through functional training courses and the Civilian Education System. They return to their current positions more knowledgeable or move to positions of greater responsibility. This three-pronged, Armywide, team approach to broadening individual training and education helps develop agile leaders.

FOUNDATIONS OF LEADER DEVELOPMENT

3-21. The Army is committed to training, educating, and developing all its leaders—officers, warrant officers, noncommissioned officers, and Army civilians—to lead organizations in the complex and challenging operational environments of the twenty-first century. Training and education develop agile leaders and prepare them for current and future assignments of increasing responsibility. Army leaders require character, presence, and intellectual capacity (see FM 6-22, part two):

- Leaders of character practice the Army Values, empathize with those around them, and exemplify the Warrior Ethos.
- Leaders with presence display military bearing; are physically fit, composed, and confident; and are resilient under stress.
- Leaders with intellectual capacity possess mental agility, make sound decisions, are innovative, employ tact in interpersonal relations, and know their profession.

3-22. The Army training and leader development model helps develop trained and ready units led by competent and confident leaders. (See figure 3-2.) Leader development is a deliberate, continuous, sequential, and progressive process. It develops Soldiers and Army civilians into competent and confident leaders who act decisively, accomplish missions, and care for subordinates and their families. It is grounded in the Army Values. The aptitude for command, staff leadership, and special duties (such as teaching, foreign internal defense team leadership, attaché duties, and joint staff assignments) all contribute to leader development and affect future assignments and promotions.

3-23. Leader development occurs through the lifelong synthesis of knowledge, skills, and experiences gained through the three training domains. Each domain provides distinct experiences and has specific, measurable actions that develop leaders. The domains interact, with feedback and assessments from various sources and procedures contributing to individuals' development. Performance feedback and formal and informal assessments help individuals improve performance in their current position and prepare them to serve successfully at the next level of responsibility.

3-24. Competent and confident leaders are essential to successfully training units, and ultimately to employing those units in operations. Uniformed leaders are inherently Soldiers first; they remain technically and tactically proficient in basic Soldier skills. Civilian leaders master the skills and knowledge required of their position. They hone their leadership abilities to provide organizations with both leadership and management skills. All leaders seek to be agile and able to observe, understand, and react to the operational environment. These leaders exercise mission command and apply relevant knowledge, skills, and experiences acquired through training and education to accomplish missions.

3-25. Commanders and other leaders play key roles in the three training domains by developing subordinate leaders with the following characteristics:

- Are tactically and technically competent, confident, and agile.
- Can successfully employ their units across the spectrum of conflict.
- Possess the knowledge and skills needed to train and employ modular force units and operate as a part of a unified action.
- Are culturally astute.
- Can prepare mission orders that meet their commander's intent.
- Are courageous, seize opportunities, and effectively manage risk.
- *Take care of their people.*

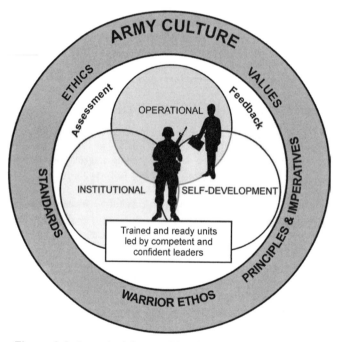

Figure 3-2. Army training and leader development model

TRAINING DOMAINS

3-26. The three training domains complement each other, providing a synergistic system of training and education. The integration of the domains is critical to training Soldiers, Army civilians, and organizations. That integration is especially vital to developing expeditionary Army forces that can successfully conduct full spectrum operations on short notice anywhere along the spectrum of conflict. Conducting full spectrum operations requires competent, confident Soldiers experienced and knowledgeable in a multitude of areas. Skills not developed in one domain are made up in the others. For example, Soldiers who have not deployed on disaster relief operations need to read and understand observations, insights, and lessons from these operations. Leaders assess subordinates' competencies to determine capability gaps. Armed with this knowledge and knowing what individuals will learn on the job, leaders identify subordinates' capability gaps and provide appropriate self-development guidance.

INSTITUTIONAL TRAINING DOMAIN

3-27. The *institutional training domain* **is the Army's institutional training and education system, which primarily includes training base centers and schools that provide initial training and subsequent professional military education for Soldiers, military leaders, and Army civilians**. It is a major component of the generating force. The institutional domain provides initial military training, professional military education, and civilian education. Comprised of military and civilian schools and courses, this domain provides the foundational skills and knowledge required for operational assignments and promotions. Army centers and schools teach specialty skills, warrior tasks, battle drills, and individual skills. These are enhanced and broadened through operational assignments and self-development. It also provides functional training and support to the operational training domain. Leaders and individuals master the basics of their profession in institutional training. This allows units to focus on collective training, while also sustaining and enhancing individual skills and knowledge. The institutional training domain supports Soldiers and Army civilians throughout their careers. It is a key enabler for unit readiness.

3-28. The institutional training domain provides a framework that develops critical thinkers. These leaders can visualize the challenges of full spectrum operations and understand complex systems. They are mentally agile and understand the fundamentals of their profession and branch. Branch schools provide a basic understanding of how their branch and the other branches interact. Institutions of higher learning, such as senior service colleges and civilian graduate schools, take leaders out of their "comfort zone," helping them become mentally agile.

3-29. The Army systematically develops Soldiers and Army civilians over time and prepares units to accomplish their missions. Training and education becomes progressively more advanced throughout an individual's career. Institutional training complements and forms the foundation for the operational training in units.

3-30. The institutional training domain includes four major components:

- Support to the field.
- Initial military training.
- Professional military education and the Civilian Education System.
- Functional training.

Support to the Field

3-31. Training for full spectrum operations requires closely linking the institutional training domain with the operational training domain. The institutional training domain does more than train and educate; it is where Army doctrine is developed and taught. Doctrine establishes the framework for all the Army does. It provides the basis for establishing standards for tasks and missions. The institutional domain is an extensive resource that exists to support the operational domain.

3-32. The institutional training domain, as requested and as available, provides training products to help commanders and other leaders train their units. These products include the following: combined arms training strategies, training support packages, mobile training teams, on-site courses, distance training, and distributed learning courses.

3-33. Mobile training teams are a particularly valuable resource. They can provide subject matter expertise; help commanders train Soldiers, teams and units; and can develop Soldiers by bringing courses to them. Individuals and units reach back to the generating force for subject matter expertise and for self-development training and education. Army Service component commands prioritize unit requirements for support from the generating force. (See FM 1-01.)

Initial Military Training

3-34. Initial military training provides the basic knowledge, skills, and behaviors individuals need to become Soldiers, succeed as members of Army units, contribute to mission accomplishment, and survive and win on the battlefield. Initial military training is given to all new Soldiers. It motivates Soldiers to become dedicated and productive and qualifies them in warrior tasks and knowledge. It instills an appreciation for the Army's place in a democratic society, inspires the Warrior Ethos, and introduces the Army Values.

3-35. Newly commissioned officer training focuses on developing competent, confident small-unit leaders trained in tactics, techniques, procedures, and fieldcraft. Newly appointed warrant officer training focuses on developing competent and confident leaders technically proficient in systems associated with individual functional specialties. Enlisted Soldier training focuses on qualifications in the designated military occupational specialty tasks and standards defined by the branch proponent. When Soldiers arrive in their first unit, leaders continue the socialization and professional development process.

Professional Military Education and the Civilian Education System

3-36. Professional military education and the Civilian Education System help develop Army leaders. Training and education for officers, warrant officers, noncommissioned officers, and Army civilians is continuous and career-long. These programs integrate structured programs of instruction—both resident (at a school or center) and nonresident (distance training, distributed learning, or mobile training teams).

3-37. Formal training and education are broadening experiences. They provide time to learn and to teach others. Student leaders can use this time to reflect and introspectively assess the status of their knowledge, skills, and abilities—and how to improve them. Professional military education and the Civilian Education System are progressive and sequential. They provide a doctrinal foundation and build on previous training, education, and operational experiences. These programs provide hands-on technical, tactical, and leader training focused on preparing leaders for success in future assignments. Professional military education and the Civilian Education System teach individuals how to think, helping them become mentally agile leaders.

Functional Training

3-38. Functional training qualifies Soldiers, Army civilians, and their leaders for assignment to positions requiring specific skills and knowledge. Functional training supplements the basic skills and knowledge gained through initial military training, professional military education and the Civilian Education System. Functional courses accomplish one or more of the following:

- Meet the training requirements for particular organizations (for example, airborne or contracting officer training).
- Meet the training requirements of a particular individual's assignment or functional responsibility (such as language or sniper training).
- Address force modernization training requirements and meet theater- or operation-specific training requirements (such as detainee operations or high-altitude, rotary-wing flight training).

OPERATIONAL TRAINING DOMAIN

3-39. Soldier, civilian, and leader training and development continue in the operational training domain. The *operational training domain* consists of the training activities organizations undertake while at home station, at maneuver combat training centers, during joint exercises, at mobilization centers, and while operationally deployed. The four areas of the operational training domain are—

- Commander and leader responsibilities.
- Unit training.
- Major training events.
- Operational missions.

Commander and Leader Responsibilities

3-40. Commanders are responsible for unit readiness. Subordinate leaders help commanders achieve mission readiness by ensuring all training and leader development contribute to proficiency in the unit's mission-essential tasks and meet the Army standard.

Unit Training

3-41. Unit training reinforces foundations established in the institutional training domain and introduces additional skills needed to support collective training. Units continue individual training to improve and sustain individual task proficiency while training on collective tasks. Collective training requires interaction among individuals or organizations to perform tasks, actions, and activities that contribute to achieving mission-essential task proficiency. Collective training includes performing collective, individual, and leader tasks associated with each training objective, action, or activity. Unit training occurs at home station, maneuver CTCs, and mobilization training centers. It also takes place in joint training exercises and while operationally deployed. Unit training develops and sustains an organization's readiness by achieving and sustaining proficiency in performing mission-essential tasks. This training includes preparing to deploy and conduct operations across the spectrum of conflict. Installations ensure units have access to the training enablers needed to enhance readiness.

Major Training Events

3-42. Unit training is executed through training events. These events include situational training exercises, external evaluations, command post exercises, and deployment exercises. They create opportunities to train organizations and develop agile leaders.

3-43. Major training events help individuals, units, and their leaders improve and sustain their tactical and technical skills. Some units have not undergone a Battle Command Training Program or maneuver CTC experience recently. Commanders of these units use live, virtual, constructive, and gaming training enablers to provide combined arms and unified action training experiences. Major training events let commanders assess their unit's mission-essential task proficiency. These events also allow leaders to solve unfamiliar problems and hone their decisionmaking skills. Major training events provide opportunities for obtaining observations, insights, and lessons on units' use of tactics, techniques, and procedures.

3-44. In unified action exercises, leaders learn how to function as part of a diverse team and draw on the strengths of all team members. Actual representatives or role players should represent the joint, interagency, intergovernmental, or multinational participants in unified actions, as well as the wide variety of contracted support present during operations.

Operational Missions

3-45. Operational missions reinforce what individuals and organizations learn in the institutional and operational training domains. Deployments let individuals, staffs, and units develop confidence in the skills they developed during training. Individuals, staffs, and units also improve performance based on observations, insights, and lessons gained during operations.

3-46. Training continues during a deployment—whenever and wherever a commander can fit it in. This training minimizes degradation of key skills and refines and refreshes skills needed for current and future operations. Operational experience confirms or refutes what leaders and subordinates have learned from training in all three domains. Operational missions also require individuals and organizations to learn to adapt to ambiguous, changing situations. Adapting may include modifying tactics, techniques, and procedures based on operational experiences.

COMBAT TRAINING CENTER PROGRAM

3-47. CTCs support training and leader development in both the operational and institutional training domains; they are not a separate training domain but serve as a bridge between the domains. The three maneuver CTCs (the National Training Center, Joint Readiness Training Center, and Joint Multinational

Readiness Center) and the Battle Command Training Program comprise the Army's CTC program. The CTC program is not a place; it is a training concept that supports an expeditionary Army. The CTCs help commanders develop ready units and prepare agile leaders to conduct full spectrum operations in uncertain situations at any point along the spectrum of conflict. The CTCs are a critical element of transforming the Army. Doctrinally based, they help units and their leaders master the doctrine in FM 3-0. They drive the transformation of training for an expeditionary army. As they help the Army transform, the CTCs continue to transform themselves by focusing on the following imperatives:

- The CTC experience must be demanding—both physically and intellectually.
- The opposing forces and training environment must help drive the development of innovative leaders and organizations.
- Units must be prepared to fight upon arrival at a CTC—just as they would in operations.
- Full spectrum operations—offensive, defensive, and stability or civil support—conducted within the operational themes of major combat operations and irregular warfare—will be the norm during CTC exercises.
- Scenarios must challenge the intellect of leaders and test their skills in a unified action environment.
- The CTCs must leverage live, virtual, and constructive training enablers to integrate unified action partners and broaden the training experience.
- Observer-controller/trainers must have a solid breadth and depth of experience.
- Feedback must focus on output and not on process.
- Feedback must be timely so leaders can make corrections.
- Observer-controller/trainers must know and enforce standards. Restarting or repeating a mission develops leaders and units more than continuing to the next mission when the current mission was not executed to standard.
- CTCs must reflect threat trends and future capabilities.
- CTCs provide assistance to units at home station within existing resources and scheduling priorities.
- CTCs exist to help commanders increase unit readiness to deploy as they progress through each Army force generation (ARFORGEN) phase.

SELF-DEVELOPMENT TRAINING DOMAIN

3-48. Learning is continuous for professionals. Training and education in the institutional and operational training domains cannot meet every individual's needs in terms of knowledge, insights, intuition, experience, imagination, and judgment. Professionals need to pursue improvement in the self-development training domain as well. **The *self-development training domain* includes planned, goal-oriented learning that reinforces and expands the depth and breadth of an individual's knowledge base, self-awareness, and situational awareness; complements institutional and operational learning; enhances professional competence; and meets personal objectives.** Self-development enhances previously acquired knowledge, skills, behaviors, and experiences. Self-development focuses on maximizing individual strengths, minimizing weaknesses, and achieving individual development goals. Individuals establish self-development goals and identify ways to achieve them in their self-development plan.

3-49. Professionals at all levels continually study Army and joint doctrine, observations, insights, lessons, and best practices. They learn from military history and other disciplines as well. Soldiers start their self-development plans during initial military training. Army civilians begin their self-development plans when they are hired. Self-development plans provide commanders and other leaders a means to improve Soldiers' and Army civilians' tactical and technical skills. A self-development plan follows all individuals from position to position throughout their careers.

3-50. Successful self-development requires a team effort between leaders and individuals. Self-development begins with a self-assessment of one's strengths, weaknesses, potential, and developmental needs. Commanders and other leaders create an environment that encourages subordinates to establish personal and professional development goals. Refinement of those goals occurs through personal coaching or mentoring by commanders and leaders. Reachback, distributed learning, and other technologies support self-development programs.

163

Chapter 4

Army Training Management

This chapter describes Army training management—the process used by Army leaders to identify training requirements and subsequently plan, prepare, execute, and assess training. Army training management provides a systematic way of managing time and resources and of meeting training objectives through purposeful training activities. The chapter begins with an overview of Army force generation and training the modular force. It then discusses leader roles in training management and describes mission-essential task list development. The chapter concludes with a description of the Army's training management model.

SECTION I – TRAINING MANAGEMENT IN THE MODULAR FORCE

4-1.   Persistent conflict, full spectrum operations, and modular force organizations have altered the way Army leaders manage training. *Training management* **is the process used by Army leaders to identify training requirements and subsequently plan, prepare, execute, and assess training**. This section provides an overview of Army force generation (ARFORGEN) and discusses effects modular organizations are having on training management. It also addresses new training relationships the Army has developed to support ARFORGEN, including responsibilities related to Reserve Component units. The complementary roles of officers, noncommissioned officers (NCOs), and Army civilians in training management continue in the modular force.

ARMY FORCE GENERATION DRIVES TRAINING MANAGEMENT

4-2.   The Army supports national policy by organizing, training, equipping, and providing forces to the combatant commands. The force size and capabilities mix are driven by the *National Military Strategy*, the Joint Strategic Capabilities Plan and combatant commanders' requirements. The Army prepares and provides campaign capable, expeditionary forces through ARFORGEN. ARFORGEN applies to Regular Army and Reserve Component (Army National Guard and U.S. Army Reserve) units. It is a process that progressively builds unit readiness over time during predictable periods of availability to provide trained, ready, and cohesive units prepared for operational deployments. ARFORGEN takes each unit through a three-phased readiness cycle: reset, train/ready, and available.

4-3.   Units enter the *reset* phase when they redeploy from long-term operations or complete their planned deployment window in the available force pool. Units conduct individual and collective training on tasks that support their core or directed mission-essential task lists. (See paragraphs 4-41 and 4-55.) Because of personnel retention and historically strong affiliation with local units, Reserve Component units may see less personnel turbulence upon redeployment than Regular Army units.

4-4.   Units move to the *train/ready* phase when they are prepared to conduct higher level collective training and prepare for deployment. Units with a directed mission (see paragraph 4-29) progress as rapidly as possible to achieve directed mission capability. Prior to receiving a directed mission, units focus on developing their core capabilities. In addition to preparing for operational requirements, Reserve Component units train for homeland security and homeland defense missions. Army National Guard units train to meet state-established requirements as well. Combatant command requirements accelerate the process as needed and influence when units are manned, equipped, and trained.

4-5. Forces and headquarters deploying to an ongoing operation or available for immediate alert and deployment to a contingency are in the *available* phase. At the end of the available phase, units return to the reset phase, and the cycle begins again.

4-6. Both the generating force and the operational Army participate in and respond to ARFORGEN. The generating force supports operational Army training. Operational Army commanders develop plans for training mission-essential tasks. Commanders prioritize resource allocation based on the following factors: time available, training time required, resource availability, and the directed mission. The generating force adjusts level of support to meet operational Army requirements. (See FMI 3-0.1 for additional information on ARFORGEN.)

THE MODULAR FORCE'S EFFECT ON TRAINING MANAGEMENT

4-7. In 2003, the Army implemented a fundamental shift towards a brigade-based, modular force. This transformation, combined with implementing ARFORGEN, has resulted in changes to training relationships and responsibilities, especially with regard to Reserve Component organizations.

MODULAR FORCE ORGANIZATIONS

4-8. The Army's shift to modular organizations and the need to conduct full spectrum operations as part of unified action have changed the way the Army views training and readiness in units. Army formations are no longer based on large, fixed divisions. Brigade-sized, functional organizations—brigade combat teams (BCTs), modular support brigades, and functional brigades—have replaced the larger, hierarchical ones. (See FM 3-0, appendix C.)

4-9. Units are tailored through ARFORGEN to create force packages to meet specific mission requirements. Force packages often are composed of units from multiple commands and installations. Thus, modular brigades often deploy and work for headquarters other than the one exercising administrative control (ADCON) over them. Senior commanders are responsible for the training and readiness of these units until they are assigned or attached to a force package. As a result, both ADCON commanders and future force-package commanders can influence the development, resourcing, and execution of unit training plans and deployment preparation. However, unit commanders are ultimately responsible for the training, performance, and readiness of their units. (FM 3-0, paragraphs B-25 through B-27, discusses ADCON.)

4-10. Staffs at all levels must be well-trained in the operations process in order to integrate modular formations—or for their unit to be integrated into a force package. Staffs, therefore, require a high degree of understanding of the limitations and capabilities of the different types of units that may compose a force package. Commanders also train their staffs to control, or be integrated into, a force package capable of conducting operations as part of unified action. Staffs must be agile, capable of helping commanders exercise command and control. Through the command and control warfighting function commanders, assisted by their staffs, integrate all the warfighting functions and subordinate units to accomplish missions. (See FM 3-0, chapter 4.)

4-11. Staff training requires frequent training on digital command and control information systems. The staff is a weapon system. As with crews of any weapon system, staffs require training as often as necessary to maintain readiness and ensure their ability to integrate their information systems with other digital systems. Staff training cannot be an afterthought. It must be an integral part of the unit's training plans. Leaders' operational experience in staff functions and coordination can help focus staff training requirements.

4-12. Modular formations are more agile, expeditionary, and versatile than previous Army organizations. However, modular organizations require a higher degree of training and operational synchronization at the brigade level. Today's BCT commanders coordinate and synchronize the training and proficiency of the many functional units organic to the BCT. This is quite different from a maneuver brigade commander's responsibilities under the Army of Excellence structure. For example, under the Army of Excellence, the artillery battalion was organic to the division artillery and the support battalion to the division support command. The commanders of the division artillery and support command oversaw training for their organic battalions. This arrangement allowed maneuver brigade commanders to focus on training their maneuver battalions. In contrast, today's BCT commander is responsible for training the BCT's organic artillery and support battalions. BCT commanders and staffs may need to reach outside their organization for expertise to help them train the functional components of their modular unit. Similarly, functional and multifunctional support brigade commanders are responsible for ensuring their subordinates maintain training proficiency regardless of location. For example, an engineer brigade headquarters on one post with subordinate battalions on other posts is responsible for training all those battalions. Thus, successfully conducting combined arms training in modular units requires agile commanders and staffs. This agility is necessary to ensure that their training strategies result in all BCT units being proficient in their mission-essential tasks.

4-13. Modular division and corps commanders and staffs must be agile and proficient as well. Divisions coordinate the operations of multiple BCTs and employ support and functional brigades. Corps and divisions prepare to exercise command and control of large operations. With augmentation, modular division and corps headquarters can act as joint task force, joint force land component command, ARFOR, and multinational force headquarters. (See FMI 3-0.1.) Army Service component commands require trained and ready deployable command posts that can operate anywhere in the world. Thus, while it is brigade focused, today's expeditionary Army requires all echelons to prepare for full spectrum operations anywhere along the spectrum of conflict.

TRAINING RELATIONSHIPS

4-14. Commanders are ultimately responsible for the training, performance, and readiness of their Soldiers, Army civilians, and organizations. A commander is the unit's primary training manager and trainer, responsible for training organic and attached components. As an organizing principle, Army units are assigned or attached to a designated headquarters. (See FM 3-0, appendix B.) Although commanders are responsible for the training and readiness of subordinates, commanders cannot meet this responsibility without support from the installation. Installations and other generating force organizations support commanders, not only in training but also in all aspects of sustainment and administration. Training support is a shared responsibility between the higher headquarters and the installation. The higher headquarters establishes training priorities and provides resources, such as evaluators, equipment, and Soldiers. The senior commander, through the garrison staff, provides facilities, logistics, and other training services and support. Installation support to all units stationed on that installation continues when the higher headquarters deploys.

TRAINING RELATIONSHIPS FOR EXPEDITIONARY FORCE PACKAGES

4-15. A key ARFORGEN tenet is that home station training responsibilities remain more static than dynamic to minimize command and control turbulence before deployment. Commanders providing units retain training responsibility—even after a subordinate unit is mission-sourced into an expeditionary force package—until the unit is actually assigned or attached to the expeditionary force package. Force package commanders normally influence the training of units projected for assignment or attachment to the force package by exercising coordinating authority, once delegated, with the providing commander. (See FM 3-0, paragraph B-23.) Force package headquarters periodically provide a training and readiness summary on assigned and attached units to their postdeployment headquarters to facilitate training plans for reset.

RESERVE COMPONENT TRAINING RESPONSIBILITIES

4-16. Responsibility for training in the Reserve Components has changed little under ARFORGEN. The Reserve Components have the additional challenges of interstate coordination and balancing core mission-essential task list (CMETL) training with homeland security requirements. Command and control of Army National Guard units in a Title 32, U.S. Code, status is exercised by the state governor or adjutant general. U.S Army Reserve units are under Title 10, U.S. Code. U.S. Army Reserve units based in the continental United States are under ADCON of the U.S. Army Reserve Command.

4-17. Before mobilization, Reserve Component commanders are supported commanders, with support provided by available Army training assets and capabilities. When mobilized, Reserve Component units are attached to a gaining headquarters. Most ADCON responsibilities then shift to the gaining headquarters, which becomes the supported command for training.

LEADER ROLES IN TRAINING MANAGEMENT

4-18. Officers, NCOs, and Army civilians have complementary roles and responsibilities to plan, prepare, execute, and assess training and to ensure training is conducted professionally and to standard.

OFFICERS

4-19. Commanders and other officers are involved in all aspects of training, from planning and preparation to execution and assessment. Planning for training is centralized and coordinated to align training priorities and provide a consistent training focus throughout all unit echelons. In contrast, the execution of training is decentralized. Decentralization promotes bottom-up communication of mission-related strengths and weaknesses of each individual and organization. Decentralized execution promotes subordinates' initiative in training their organizations. However, senior leaders remain responsible for supervising training, developing leaders, and providing feedback.

4-20. Commanders do more than plan and oversee training; they also prepare and execute both individual and collective training, as appropriate. Officers personally observe and assess training to instill discipline and ensure units are meeting Army standards. The unit senior NCO plays a significant role in helping the commander supervise the unit's training program. Senior NCOs observe and assess the quality of training and adherence to standards down to the organization's lowest levels. Commanders check the adequacy of external training support during training visits and require prompt and effective corrections to resolve support deficiencies. Commanders make coordination of training support for subordinate units a priority for unit staffs. Senior NCOs at every level perform these same actions.

4-21. By personally visiting training in progress, commanders and senior NCOs communicate the paramount importance of training and leader development to subordinate organizations and leaders. They receive feedback from subordinate Soldiers and leaders during training visits. Feedback allows commanders and senior NCOs to identify and resolve systemic problems in areas such as the following: planning, leadership, leader development, management, and support. Based on their observations and other feedback, commanders provide guidance and direct changes to improve training and increase readiness. The most beneficial training visits by senior leaders occur unannounced or on short notice. Such visits prevent excessive preparation—a training distraction—by subordinate organizations.

4-22. Warrant officers must be technically and tactically focused and able to perform the primary duties of technical leader, advisor, and commander. Through progressive levels of expertise in assignments, training, and education, warrant officers perform these duties during all operations and at all levels of command. While their primary duties are those of a technical and tactical leader, warrant officers also provide training and leader development guidance, assistance, and supervision. Warrant officers provide leader development, mentorship, and counsel to other warrant officers, officers, NCOs, and Army civilians. Warrant officers lead and train functional sections, teams, or crews. Finally, they serve as critical advisors to commanders in conducting organizational training.

NONCOMMISSIONED OFFICERS

4-23. NCOs are responsible for the care and individual training of Soldiers. Command sergeants major, first sergeants, and other key NCOs select and train specific individual and small-unit tasks. They also help identify unit collective tasks. All these tasks support the organization's mission-essential tasks. Commanders approve the tasks selected and then supervise and evaluate training along with the organization's officers and NCOs.

4-24. NCOs focus on the skills and knowledge Soldiers need to develop their fundamental competencies. Mastery of tasks occurs through repetition. This foundation—which includes such skills as marksmanship, protection, military occupational specialty skills, and physical fitness—is essential to unit readiness. NCOs integrate newly assigned enlisted Soldiers into organizations and develop them professionally throughout their assignment. First-line leaders train Soldiers to conduct individual tasks in their squads, crews, teams, and equivalent small organizations. First-line leaders and senior NCOs emphasize standards-based, performance-oriented training to ensure Soldiers achieve the Army standard. NCOs cross-train their subordinates to reduce the effects of unit losses and develop future leaders. Command sergeants major, first sergeants, and other senior NCOs coach junior NCOs and junior officers to help them master a wide range of individual tasks.

4-25. Commanders allocate time during collective training for NCOs to conduct individual training. The time allocated allows for repetition of tasks. NCOs train individuals to standard and understand how individual task training relates to mission-essential tasks and supporting collective tasks. Commanders select individual, crew, and small-team tasks to be trained based on recommendations from NCOs. NCOs base recommendations on their evaluation of training deficiencies. NCOs recommend tasks for training at training meetings. (See paragraphs 4-155 through 4-157.) When the commander approves tasks for training, the tasks are incorporated into the unit's training plans and subsequent training schedules. NCOs plan and prepare the approved training, execute after action reviews (AARs) during training, and provide feedback on individual Soldier performance during training meetings. For efficiency, Soldiers assigned a low-density military occupational specialty may be trained together by a senior NCO.

ARMY CIVILIANS

4-26. The Army Civilian Corps provides stability and continuity for the Army. Army civilians generally serve in organizations longer than their military counterparts. They provide specialized skills and knowledge in day-to-day Army operations. Normally, Army civilians are assigned to the generating force; however, they are integral to manning, equipping, resourcing, and training both the generating force and operational Army. Army civilians both support and lead Army operations. Army civilian leaders plan, prepare, execute, and assess training of their subordinates and organizations. They follow the principles of training outlined in chapter 2 and use the tools of this chapter to focus the training of their organizations.

ARMY FORCES AND JOINT TRAINING

4-27. Joint training follows joint doctrine. Joint training facilitates understanding of the other Services and of interagency and multinational partners. The Army trains with those partners to better understand their capabilities, limitations, cultures, and ways of conducting operations. When assigned as joint force commanders, Army commanders establish joint training objectives; plan, prepare, execute, and assess joint training; and assess training proficiency.

SECTION II – MISSION-ESSENTIAL TASK LIST DEVELOPMENT

4-28. Because sufficient resources, especially time, are not available, units cannot train to standard on every task needed for all operations across the spectrum of conflict. Therefore, commanders focus training on the most important tasks—those that help units prepare to conduct operations. They do this through mission focus and their mission-essential task list (METL). **A *mission-essential task list* is a compilation of mission-essential tasks that an organization must perform successfully to accomplish its doctrinal or directed mission.** Unit leaders emphasize the priority of METL training but find opportunities to include non-mission-specific requirements in training plans where possible.

MISSION FOCUS

4-29. ***Mission focus* is the process used to derive training requirements from a unit's core capabilities as documented in its authorization document** (a table of organization and equipment [TOE] or table of distribution and allowance [TDA]) **or from a directed mission. A *directed mission* is a mission the unit is formally assigned to execute or prepare to execute.** Commanders normally assign a directed mission in an execute order, operation order, or operation plan.

4-30. Commanders ensure their unit members train as they will fight by using mission focus to guide the planning, preparation, execution, and assessment of their training program. Mission focus is achieved primarily through performing a mission analysis and focusing training on tasks essential for mission accomplishment. Mission focus is critical throughout the entire training process. Mission focus enables commanders and staffs at all echelons to develop structured training programs that focus on mission-essential training activities and address tasks specified for all Army units in AR 350-1.

4-31. Commanders use mission focus to allocate resources for training based on mission requirements. An organization cannot attain proficiency on every mission-essential task because of time or other resource constraints. Commanders build a successful training program by consciously focusing on those tasks most critical to mission accomplishment. They identify those tasks on the unit METL.

MISSION-ESSENTIAL TASK LISTS

4-32. **A *mission-essential task* is a collective task a unit must be able to perform successfully to accomplish its doctrinal or directed mission**. All mission-essential tasks are equally important. Since organizations must be capable of performing all elements of full spectrum operations, sometimes simultaneously, they cannot afford to train exclusively on one element at the expense of the others. Similarly, they cannot feasibly be proficient in all tasks at all points on the spectrum of conflict. Therefore, commanders use their METL to focus organizational training.

4-33. Commanders and staffs assess the unit's state of training in terms of the METL. They determine each task's training priority. Commanders consider two factors when assigning training priorities: their assessment of the unit's proficiency in each task, and the risk to future operations entailed by accepting a lower level of proficiency on that task. Commanders assign training priorities in coordination with the higher commander.

4-34. The METL provides the foundation for the unit's training strategy (see paragraph 4-93) and, subsequently, its training plans. Commanders develop training strategies to attain proficiency in mission-essential tasks. All mission-essential tasks are essential to mission readiness; therefore, mission-essential tasks are not prioritized. However, commanders focus efforts and resources on those tasks assessed as needing the most training.

4-35. Commanders exercise a modified form of battle command to manage training. (See figure 4-1.) They determine—

- Tasks requiring training.
- Priority of training effort.
- How to replicate the conditions of the operational theme or projected operational environment.
- Risk involved in not training certain tasks to standard.

4-36. *Understanding* the expected conditions is essential to deciding which tasks to train, the conditions to replicate, and which risks are prudent. Conditions can be either those described by an operational theme or those likely to be encountered in a directed mission. *Visualizing* the required state of readiness and how to achieve it leads to developing a training strategy that describes the ends, ways, and means of attaining mission readiness. Finally, the commander *describes* that strategy in a training plan and *directs* its accomplishment. By participating in and overseeing training, commanders can assess the state of readiness and the value of the training.

4-37. There are three types of mission-essential task list:

- Joint mission-essential task list (joint METL or JMETL), which is derived from the *Universal Joint Task List*.
- Core mission-essential task list (core METL or CMETL), which is standardized and based on doctrine and the organization's mission according to its authorization document.
- Directed mission-essential task list (directed METL or DMETL), which is developed by the commander upon receipt of a directed mission.

Units train on only one METL at a time.

Army Training Management

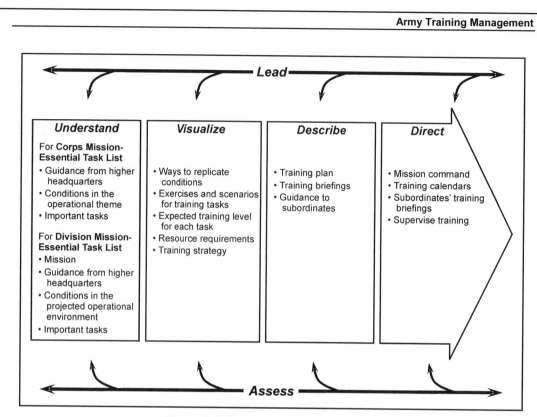

Figure 4-1. Battle command in training

JOINT MISSION-ESSENTIAL TASK LIST

4-38. A JMETL is a list of tasks that a joint force must be able to perform to accomplish a mission. JMETL tasks are described using the common language of the *Universal Joint Task List* (CJCSM 3500.04E). Joint force commanders select them to accomplish an assigned or anticipated mission. A JMETL includes conditions and standards as well as the tasks themselves. It requires identifying command-linked and supporting tasks. (CJCSM 3500.03B, enclosure C, describes JMETL development and linkage.)

4-39. Army organizations often provide forces to joint force commanders. A theater army, corps, or division headquarters may be designated as joint force headquarters. (See FMI 3-0.1.) This assignment requires the designated Army headquarters to develop a JMETL. The combatant commander or joint force commander who established the joint task force approves its JMETL. Commanders of Army forces assigned or attached to a joint force ensure their unit's DMETL nests with the joint force's JMETL.

4-40. CJCSI 3500.01E and CJCSM 3500.03B provide an overview of the Joint Training System. They address—

- Developing joint training requirements.
- Planning joint training.
- Executing joint training.
- Assessing joint proficiency.

CORE MISSION-ESSENTIAL TASK LIST

4-41. **A unit's *core mission-essential task list* is a list of a unit's corps capability mission-essential tasks and general mission-essential tasks**. Units train on CMETL tasks until the unit commander and next higher commander mutually decide to focus on training for a directed mission. Then units transition to a DMETL. (See paragraph 4-69.) A CMETL normally focuses unit training in the reset phase of

ARFORGEN; however, it can focus training in other ARFORGEN phases if the unit does not receive a directed mission. Units conduct CMETL training under the conditions found in a single operational theme and at an appropriate point on the spectrum of conflict (for example, midway between insurgency and general war) based on higher headquarters' guidance.

Standardization

4-42. In today's modular, expeditionary Army, commanders and leaders expect certain capabilities of organizations assigned to their force package. Standardized CMETLs and focused training conditions at brigade and above help meet these expectations in two ways: they enhance the Army's ability to rapidly assemble force packages, and they minimize the additional training needed for the most probable directed missions. Maintaining a CMETL training focus provides the Nation the strategic depth required for unforeseen contingencies. Headquarters, Department of the Army, adjusts training conditions periodically as it reassesses likely operational environments. Commanders cannot, and do not need to, train on all CMETL-related collective and individual tasks. (See paragraph 4-52.) Instead, they train on those tasks they deem most important. Commanders accept prudent risks on the others.

4-43. Proponents develop standard CMETLs for brigade-sized and higher level units based on unit authorization document mission statements, core capabilities, and doctrine. Headquarters, Department of the Army, approves—and updates, as needed—these CMETLs after Armywide staffing. CMETLs for corps, divisions, BCTs, functional brigades, and multifunctional support brigades are synchronized to ensure appropriate supporting-to-supported alignment of mission-essential tasks. Proponents ensure the appropriate CMETL is the basis for a unit's combined arms training strategy (CATS). (See paragraphs 4-94 through 4-95.)

4-44. Most brigade and higher level commanders can find their CMETL in their organization's CATS. Battalion and company commanders develop and align their CMETLs to support their higher organization's CMETL. Platoons and below plan and execute collective and individual tasks that support the company's CMETL. Staffs identify and train on task groups and supporting collective and individual tasks that support the headquarters company's CMETL—they do not have a "staff METL." Commanders of units for which a CMETL is not published develop a CMETL based on the unit's authorization document and doctrine. The next higher commander with ADCON approves this CMETL.

4-45. The CMETL for Reserve Component units is the same as that of Regular Army units with the same authorization document. State homeland security tasks for Army National Guard units are treated as a directed mission and require creating a DMETL. The Army National Guard command with ADCON approves the DMETL for Army National Guard units assigned a civil support mission.

CMETL Components

4-46. CMETLs include two types of tasks:
- A *core capability mission-essential task* **is a mission-essential task approved by Headquarters, Department of the Army, that is specific to a type of unit resourced according to its authorization document and doctrine.**
- A *general mission-essential task* **is a mission-essential task approved by Headquarters, Department of the Army, that all units, regardless of type, must be able to accomplish.**

CMETLs are supported by task groups, supporting collective tasks, and supporting individual tasks. (See figure 4-2 for an example of CMETL taxonomy.)

Task Groups and Supporting Collective Tasks

4-47. **A** *task group* **is a set of collective tasks necessary to accomplish a specific part of a mission-essential task.** For example, task groups for the mission-essential task "Conduct offensive operations," might be "Conduct an attack" and "Conduct a movement to contact." To accomplish a task group, a unit must be able to conduct the related supporting collective tasks.

171

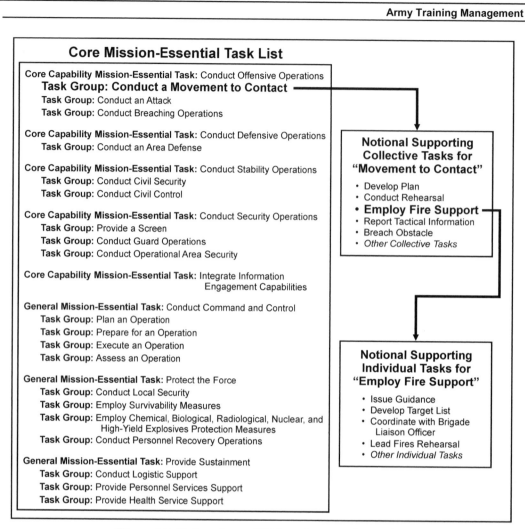

Figure 4-2. Notional core METL and supporting tasks

4-48. Supporting collective tasks are the tasks that make up a task group. The unit's CATS usually lists supporting collective tasks. Commanders assign training priorities to appropriate task groups based on their assessment of the unit's proficiency in each task group and the importance of the task group to potential missions. Then they identify specific supporting collective tasks to train. Identifying these important supporting collective tasks allows the commander to establish the tasks that—

- Integrate the warfighting functions.
- Receive the highest priority for resources such as ammunition, training areas, facilities (including live, virtual, constructive, and gaming training enablers), materiel, and funds.
- Receive emphasis during evaluations.
- Support the higher organization's METL.

Supporting Individual Tasks

4-49. Developing an effective training strategy requires crosswalking collective, leader, and individual tasks with each mission-essential task or task group. This crosswalk may involve subordinate commanders, staffs, command sergeants major, first sergeants, and other key officers, NCOs, and Army civilians. Senior NCOs understand the unit's METL; therefore, they are the best qualified to integrate individual tasks into mission-essential tasks during training.

4-50. After supporting collective tasks have been identified, the command sergeant major or first sergeant, with other key NCOs, develops a supporting individual task list for each collective task. Soldier training publications and CATSs are sources of appropriate individual tasks.

4-51. Some non-mission-specific requirements are critical to the health, welfare, individual readiness, and cohesiveness of a well-trained organization. Commanders select non-mission-specific requirements (for example, some of the mandatory training in AR 350-1) on which the organization needs to train. The command sergeant major or first sergeant usually helps the commander with this.

Identifying Tasks, Setting Prioirities, and Accepting Risk

4-52. Headquarters, Department of the Army, standardizes CMETL tasks and supporting task groups for echelons above battalion. However, commanders at all levels determine the collective and individual tasks to train, the training priority of each task, and the risk associated with not training other collective tasks. The intellectual process associated with METL development has not changed from the traditional process; however, now their CMETL provides commanders with a framework for training their units to perform all elements of full spectrum operations: offense, defense, stability, and civil support.

4-53. The supporting collective task lists for each task group can be extensive. Commanders react correctly by saying they cannot train on all the tasks listed. Instead of trying to train on too many tasks, commanders should consult with their higher commander and consider the conditions associated with the assigned operational theme. Lower commanders then focus training on the tasks most important to accomplishing the mission in that operational theme. The higher commander underwrites the subordinates' acceptance of the risk of not training on the other tasks. Tasks not trained are usually those peripheral to the mission or those the commander has assessed that the unit can perform without significant additional training. The higher and subordinate commanders' experiences affect their judgment of what to train and what not to train. As discussed in paragraphs 4-35 through 4-36, commanders can use the battle command framework to help focus their training efforts and develop training plans.

4-54. The assignment of an operational theme for CMETL training helps commanders identify the most important tasks. Given enough time, it may be possible to train sequentially on CMETL tasks under two different operational themes; however, training for more than one operational theme simultaneously is likely to be counterproductive. (Appropriate commanders assign an operational theme for training in the training and leader development guidance. See paragraph 4-60.)

DIRECTED MISSION-ESSENTIAL TASK LIST

4-55. **A *directed mission-essential task list* is a list of the mission-essential tasks a unit must perform to accomplish a directed mission.** When a unit is assigned a mission, the commander develops a DMETL by adjusting the unit's CMETL based on mission analysis and the higher commander's DMETL. Once the DMETL is established, it focuses the unit's training program until mission completion. Theater-assigned and theater-committed support units perform the same functions whether deployed or not deployed. Therefore, these types of units, as well as units in support of specific operation plans, train based on a DMETL.

Developing a Directed Mission-Essential Task List

4-56. The DMETL development technique helps commanders identify tasks in which an organization must be proficient to accomplish its directed mission. (See figure 4-3.) This technique can also be used by units to develop a CMETL, if none exists for the unit. The technique is a guide, not a fixed process. It melds the directed mission and the training and leader development guidance with other inputs filtered by commanders and subordinate leaders to help commanders determine directed mission-essential tasks. Commanders personally analyze the directed mission and involve subordinate commanders, staffs, and their command sergeant major or first sergeant in DMETL development. Subordinates help identify tasks essential to mission accomplishment. Their participation aids in developing a common understanding of the organization's critical mission requirements. This understanding allows DMETLs of subordinate organizations to support the higher headquarters' or supported organization's DMETL.

173

THE TRAINER

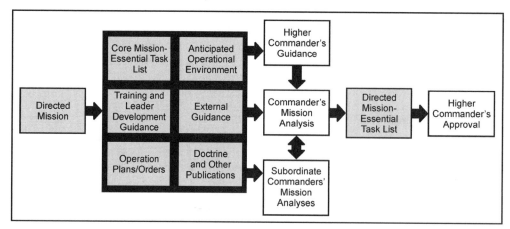

Figure 4-3. Commander's directed METL development technique

4-57. Applying the DMETL development technique—

- Focuses the organization's training on essential tasks.
- Provides a forum for professional discussion and leader development among senior, subordinate, and adjacent (peer) commanders and staffs concerning the links between mission and training.
- Enables subordinate commanders, staffs, and key NCOs to crosswalk collective, leader, and individual tasks to the mission.
- Leads to commitment of the organization's leaders to the organization's training plan.

Directed Mission-Essential Task List Development Fundamentals

4-58. The following fundamentals apply to DMETL development:

- A DMETL is derived from the commander's analysis of a directed mission.
- Directed mission-essential tasks apply to the entire unit. A DMETL does not include tasks assigned solely to subordinate organizations.
- Each organization's DMETL supports and complements the DMETL of the higher headquarters or the headquarters to which it provides support.
- Resource availability does not affect DMETL development. The DMETL is an unconstrained statement of tasks required to accomplish the unit's mission.
- Where directed mission-essential tasks involve emerging doctrine or nonstandard tasks, commanders establish tasks, conditions, and standards based on their professional judgment, guidance, and observations, insights, and lessons from similar operations. Higher commanders approve standards for these tasks as part of DMETL approval.

4-59. During DMETL development, commanders consider how they intend to integrate the warfighting functions through plans and orders to conduct combined arms operations. Commanders employ the warfighting functions to ensure that tasks necessary to build, sustain, and apply combat power are collectively directed toward accomplishing the mission. A *warfighting function* is a group of tasks and systems (people, organizations, information and processes) united by a common purpose that commanders use to accomplish missions and training objectives (FM 3-0). The warfighting functions are—

- Movement and maneuver.
- Intelligence.
- Fires.
- Sustainment.

- Command and control.
- Protection.

Commander's Mission Analysis

4-60. The starting point for DMETL development is the organization's directed mission. In some cases, higher commanders may want to identify an operational theme for the projected operation—major combat operations, irregular warfare, peace operations, limited intervention, or peacetime military engagement—to help focus Soldiers and leaders and create a mindset. (Normally they do this in their training and leader development guidance.) This provides the means to coordinate, link, and integrate a focused DMETL and appropriate supporting collective and individual tasks throughout the organization.

4-61. When time is limited, commanders may specify DMETL tasks for subordinate units. Commanders may need to be more prescriptive in their training and leader development guidance as well. When specifying DMETL tasks, commanders acknowledge a commensurate level of risk involved. Risk also occurs when there is not enough time to analyze all aspects of the mission. Those conditions may result in subordinate commanders and staffs failing to include a task on which the unit must train to prepare completely.

4-62. Commanders consider several factors during their mission analysis and subsequent DMETL development. These include the following:
- The unit's CMETL.
- Plans and orders.
- The anticipated operational environment.
- External guidance.
- Doctrine and other publications.

Unit CMETL

4-63. A CMETL can serve as a starting point for DMETL development, since some of the unit's core capabilities may be the capabilities needed to accomplish the directed mission. These core capabilities are derived from the unit's mission as documented in doctrine and paragraph 1 of the unit's authorization document—the fundamental reasons for the unit's existence.

Plans and Orders

4-64. Operation plans and orders provide missions and related information that are important in determining required tasks for training. Input for training plans may include—
- Deployment order.
- Execution of a contingency plan.

Anticipated Operational Environment

4-65. An operational environment is described in terms of the eight operational variables: political, military, economic, social, information, infrastructure, physical environment, and time (PMESII-PT). (See FM 3-0.) Each affects how Army forces conduct (plan, prepare, execute, and assess) military operations. Commanders tailor forces, employ diverse capabilities, and support different missions to succeed in today's complex operational environments. The operational variables form the basis for determining the conditions under which a unit will not only operate but also under which it will train. These conditions, when combined with the standards for the DMETL tasks, help commanders assess unit readiness for a mission.

External Guidance

4-66. External guidance serves as an additional source of tasks that relate to a unit's directed mission. Sources of external guidance include—
- Commander's training and leader development guidance.
- Higher headquarters' DMETL or the DMETL of the deployed or deploying supported force.

175

- Higher headquarters' or the receiving force's directives.
- Mobilization plans (for Reserve Component units).
- Force integration plans.

Doctrine and Other Publications

4-67. Doctrine and other sources can provide additional information relating to a directed mission. These include—

- FM 7-15, *The Army Universal Task List.*
- CJCSM 3500.04E, *The Universal Joint Task List.*
- AR 350-1, *Army Training and Leader Development.*
- CATSs and proponent-developed collective tasks and drills.
- Proponent-developed CMETLs approved by Headquarters, Department of the Army.

Directed Mission-Essential Task List Approval

4-68. DMETL approval resides with the next higher commander unless otherwise specified. Commanders of units projected to be assigned to, attached to, or under operational control of a deploying or deployed force coordinate with that force's commander during DMETL development. The higher commander with ADCON approves the DMETL and ensures that the unit's DMETL supports the deploying or deployed force's DMETL. This may involve consulting with the receiving force commander. When Reserve Component units are mobilized, DMETL approval shifts to First Army or the appropriate Army Service component command.

TRANSITIONING FROM A CORE METL TO A DIRECTED METL

4-69. At the time agreed to by the unit commander and the higher commander, the unit's training focus transitions from CMETL tasks and assumed conditions of an operational theme to DMETL tasks and conditions that portray the anticipated operational environment. (See figure 4-4.) Since a directed mission may be assigned during any ARFORGEN phase, commanders prepare to quickly adapt their training and training support systems from a CMETL to a DMETL focus. Organizations undergoing ARFORGEN are notified of an upcoming mission or deployment early enough for commanders to adjust their METL and training focus. A unit begins training on DMETL tasks upon achieving the CMETL proficiency agreed to by the unit commander and the next higher commander. Exceptions include units with insufficient time between operational deployments to train on CMETL tasks, and units assigned a mission significantly different from their doctrinal mission, capabilities, and equipment. Such units may begin training on DMETL tasks immediately upon learning of a new mission.

Figure 4-4. Transition from a core METL to a directed METL

Chapter 4

SECTION III – THE ARMY TRAINING MANAGEMENT MODEL

4-70. The foundation of Army training is the Army training management model. (See figure 4-5.) This model provides the framework commanders use to achieve proficiency in their unit's mission-essential tasks. This model mirrors the operations process described in FM 3-0. There are two primary differences between the two: First, while battle command drives the operations process, the METL drives training management. And second, the training management model includes bottom-up feedback to support commanders' assessments. While each of the model's activities is important, successful training largely results from thorough preparation.

Figure 4-5. The Army training management model

4-71. Automated training management helps commanders plan, prepare, execute, and assess unit training. The Digital Training Management System (DTMS) is an automated information system that helps commanders do this. It aids commanders in managing information and solving problems involving training and training management. It also provides links to individual and collective tasks through several sources, such as CATSs, *The Army Universal Task List*, and the *Universal Joint Task List*. DTMS provides commanders with snapshot statuses of unit training. It can also produce the following products:

- Long- and short-range planning calendars.
- Event training plans.
- Training schedules.
- Individual training records.
- METL assessment records.

TOP-DOWN/BOTTOM-UP APPROACH TO TRAINING

4-72. The top-down/bottom-up approach to training is a team effort that applies mission command to training. This approach requires senior leaders to provide training focus, direction, and resources. Subordinate leaders develop objectives and requirements specific to their organization's needs and provide feedback on training proficiency. They also identify specific organizational training needs and execute training to standard according to the training schedule or event training plan. This team effort maintains training focus, establishes training priorities, and enables effective communication among command echelons.

4-73. Guidance, based on mission and priorities, flows from the top down and results in subordinate unit identification of specific collective and individual tasks that support the higher headquarters' mission-essential tasks. Input from the bottom up is essential because it identifies training needed to achieve task proficiency. Leaders at all echelons communicate with each other on requirements and the planning, preparing, executing, and assessing of training.

PLAN

4-74. Conducting training to standard begins with planning. Units develop training plans that enable them to attain proficiency in the mission-essential tasks needed to conduct full spectrum operations under conditions in likely operational environments. Commanders determine a training strategy for the unit and prepare training plans. Developing these plans involves identifying and scheduling training events, allocating time and resources, and coordinating installation support. Commanders perform long-range, short-range, and near-term planning. They present a training briefing to their higher commander to obtain approval of their long- and short-range plans. Commanders also request approval of the commander-selected collective tasks that support the METL during this briefing.

4-75. Planning extends the mission-focus process that links the METL with the subsequent preparation, execution, and assessment of training. Centralized, coordinated planning develops mutually supporting, METL-based training at all unit echelons. Planning involves continuous coordination from long-range planning, through short-range and near-term planning, and ultimately leads to training execution.

4-76. Long-range, short-range, and near-term planning all follow the same process. Commanders at all levels assess training, provide guidance, and publish training plans. The only difference among echelons is the complexity of assessment, scope, scale, and form of the training and leader development guidance. Planning begins with two principal inputs: the METL (see paragraph 4-37) and training assessment (see paragraphs 4-186 through 4-210).

4-77. Training assessments provide focus and direction to planning by identifying training tasks that are new, where performance needs improvement, or where performance needs to be sustained. Training assessments provide commanders with a starting point for describing their training strategy. The training assessment compares the organization's current level of training proficiency with the desired level of proficiency based on Army standards. This results in training requirements that are necessary to achieve and sustain mission-essential task proficiency. The commander, assisted by key leaders, develops a training strategy that prepares the unit to meet each training requirement.

FUNDAMENTALS OF PLANNING FOR TRAINING

4-78. Adhering to the following fundamentals contributes to well-developed training plans:
- Maintain a consistent mission focus.
- Coordinate with habitually task-organized supporting organizations.
- Focus on the correct time frame.
- Focus on organizational building blocks.
- Focus on the unit's mission-essential and supporting tasks.
- Incorporate composite risk management (CRM) into all training plans.
- Lock in training plans.
- Make the most efficient use of resources.

Maintain a Consistent Mission Focus

4-79. Each headquarters involves its subordinate headquarters when developing training plans. Based on the higher headquarters' plans, subordinate commanders prepare plans with a consistent mission focus.

Coordinate with Habitually Task-Organized Supporting Organizations

4-80. Commanders of BCTs and battalion task forces plan for coordinated combined arms training that includes their habitually supporting organizations. Commanders of other units deploying with BCTs actively participate in developing their supported unit's training plans and develop complementary training plans. Commanders at all echelons require subordinates to integrate their training plans and monitor coordination efforts during planning.

Focus on the Correct Time Frame

4-81. Long-range training plans in the Regular Army and mobilized Reserve Component units extend out at least one year. They may cover an entire ARFORGEN cycle. Reserve Component long-range plans consider a minimum of two years or an entire ARFORGEN cycle. Short-range training plans in the Regular Army and mobilized Reserve Component units normally focus on an upcoming quarter; however, their focus may be dictated by a particular ARFORGEN cycle. Reserve Component short-range training plans typically use a one-year time frame. Near-term planning for the Regular Army and mobilized Reserve Component units starts six to eight weeks before the execution of training; Reserve Component near-term planning starts approximately four months prior. Time frames are flexible and determined between appropriate commanders.

Focus on Organizational Building Blocks

4-82. Organizational building blocks include the following:
- Individual and small-unit skills.
- Leader development.
- Battle rosters.
- Staff training.

Individual and Small-Unit Skills

4-83. The individual Soldier is the heart of any organization's ability to complete its mission. Soldiers first learn to perform individual or leader skills to standard in the institutional training base; however, effective, periodic repetition of tasks in the operational Army is necessary to hone and maintain them. Well-trained Soldiers—grounded in such basics as physical fitness, first aid skills, marksmanship, and small-unit drills—are essential to successful collective training. Commanders should emphasize collective training proficiency of small units—crews, teams, squads, sections, platoons—over company and higher level training. Small-unit proficiency provides the foundation for large-unit readiness.

Leader Development

4-84. Leaders spend much of their available training time supervising the training of subordinates. However, they themselves must also develop as leaders. Leaders do learn on the job during collective training. Nonetheless, commanders need to provide leader development opportunities and challenges for subordinates during training as well.

Battle Rosters

4-85. **A *battle roster* is a listing of individuals, crews, or elements that reflects capabilities, proficiencies in critical tasks, or other information concerning warfighting abilities.** Battle rosters track key crew training information on selected mission-essential systems (such as aircraft, tanks, howitzers, automated information systems, and forklifts). These rosters are maintained at battalion level and below. Commanders also track training data pertinent to readiness, such as crew stability, manning levels, and qualification status. Battle rosters designate qualified back-up operators or crewmembers assigned elsewhere in the unit. During the execution of training, crewmembers on the battle roster train with their assigned crews.

THE TRAINER

Staff Training

4-86. Staffs balance routine garrison duties with operational training. However, a staff is a weapon system. As with any weapon system, a staff requires training to function properly. Staffs provide commanders with the relevant information needed to make timely, correct decisions. Doing this well requires a commander and staff to operate as a cohesive team. Forming this team requires the staff and commander to train together—ideally using live, virtual, constructive, and gaming training enablers. This training helps a staff understand how the commander operates and thinks. Staff training objectives are derived from the collective tasks that support the unit METL. Only through frequent, challenging training on digital information systems can commanders and their staffs become proficient in the intuitive art of battle command.

Focus on the Unit's Mission-Essential and Supporting Tasks

4-87. Effective training plans focus on raising or sustaining unit proficiency on mission-essential tasks.

Incorporate Composite Risk Management into All Training Plans

4-88. Commanders train their units to tough standards under the most realistic conditions possible. Applying CRM does not detract from this training goal; rather, it enhances execution of highly effective, realistic training. CRM involves identifying, assessing, and controlling risks arising from operational factors and making decisions that balance risk costs with mission training benefits. (See FM 5-19.) Leaders and subordinates at all echelons use CRM to conserve combat power and resources. Leaders and staffs continuously identify hazards and assess risks. Then they develop and coordinate control measures to mitigate or eliminate hazards. CRM is continuous for each mission or training event. It is incorporated into all training plans and is a continuous part of preparation for training.

Lock In Training Plans

4-89. Unplanned or unanticipated changes disrupt training and frustrate subordinates. Planning allows organizations to anticipate and incorporate change in a coordinated manner. Stability and predictability can result from locking in training plans. This stability is crucial to training Reserve Component units, where a disruption or delay in training has a significant impact. For instance, a two-hour delay in the start of training during a weekend assembly represents a 12.5-percent loss in available training time. As much as possible, senior commanders protect subordinate organizations from unnecessary changes. Commanders decide the lock-in period for training plans. Nevertheless, change is a part of any operational environment; good organizations adapt to unavoidable changes.

Make the Most Efficient Use of Resources

4-90. Time and other training resources are always limited. When allocating them, commanders give priority to the training that contributes most to achieving and sustaining operational proficiency levels.

TRAINING OBJECTIVES

4-91. After mission-essential tasks are selected, commanders identify training objectives for each task. A *training objective* is a statement that describes the desired outcome of a training activity in the unit. It consists of the task, conditions, and standard:

- *Task*. **A clearly defined and measurable activity accomplished by individuals and organizations**.
- *Conditions*. Those variables of an operational environment or situation in which a unit, system, or individual is expected to operate and may affect performance (JP 1-02).
- *Standard*. **A quantitative or qualitative measure and criterion for specifying the levels of performance of a task**. A measure provides the basis for describing varying levels of task performance. A criterion is the minimum acceptable level of performance associated with a particular measure of task performance. For example, the measure when donning a protective mask is time, and the criterion is a certain number of seconds.

180

4-92. The conditions and standards for the majority of a unit's collective training tasks are identified in applicable training and evaluation outlines. A ***training and evaluation outline*** **is a summary document that provides information on collective training objectives, related individual training objectives, resource requirements, and applicable evaluation procedures for a type of organization.** CATSs contain training and evaluation outlines. These can be accessed through DTMS. The following resources can assist commanders and staffs in developing collective and individual training objectives:

- Combined arms training strategies.
- Soldier training publications.
- DA Pamphlet 350-38, *Standards in Training Commission.*
- Deployment or mobilization plans.
- FM 7-15, *The Army Universal Task List.*
- The Universal Joint Task List Portal (available as a link from the Joint Exercise and Training Division Web page on the Joint Doctrine, Education, and Training Electronic Information System [JDEIS] Web site, https://jdeis.js.mil/jdeis/index.jsp).

TRAINING STRATEGIES AND COMBINED ARMS TRAINING STRATEGIES

4-93. A training strategy describes the ways and means the commander intends to use to achieve and sustain training proficiency on mission-essential tasks. The strategy is based on the commander's assessment and discussions with the higher commander. Training strategies include the following:

- Tasks to be trained.
- Training audience.
- Training objectives.
- Order in which the tasks are to be trained, given limited time and other resources.
- Frequency at which tasks are trained.
- Types of events used to create conditions for training tasks.
- Conditions under which the tasks are to be trained.
- Resources required to execute the training strategy.
- Alternative ways of training tasks.

4-94. CATSs are publications that provide commanders with a template for task-based, event-driven organizational training. They can be adapted to the unit's requirements based on the commander's assessment. CATSs state the purpose, outcome, execution guidance, and resource requirements for training events. Commanders can modify these to meet unit training objectives. Each CATS describes how a particular unit type can train to and sustain the Army standard. CATSs identify and quantify training resources required to execute long- and short-range collective training.

4-95. There are two types of CATSs: those that are unique to a unit type (a unit CATS), and those that address a functional capability common to multiple units (a functional CATS). Unit CATSs are based on the core capabilities described in a unit's authorization document and doctrine. The unit CMETL is published in the CATS for that unit type. Functional CATSs are based on standard capabilities performed by most Army units, such as command and control, protection, and deployment.

4-96. Each CATS is a training management tool for commanders, leaders, and other unit trainers. CATSs identify and group the supporting collective tasks into task groups for each mission-essential task. The discussion of each task group includes guidance for training the task group, resource requirements, and training support requirements for each proposed training event.

4-97. CATS training events are iterative to compensate for personnel turbulence, turnover, and skill degradation. Each event's discussion includes instructions on applying the crawl-walk-run approach to it. (See paragraphs 4-180 through 4-184.) CATSs identify training objectives and suggest ways to conserve resources by using multiechelon training opportunities. Combined with live, virtual, constructive, and gaming training enablers, these strategies can help commanders efficiently achieve training proficiency.

TRAINING EVENTS

4-98. Commanders link training strategies to training plans by designing and scheduling training events. Training events are building blocks that support an integrated set of training requirements related to the METL. During long-range planning, commanders and staffs broadly assess the number, type, and duration of training events required to complete METL training. Included in long-range training plans, these events form the resource allocation framework. They also provide early planning guidance to subordinate commanders and staffs. In the subsequent development of short-range training plans, senior commanders describe training events in terms of METL-based training objectives, scenarios, resources, and coordinating instructions. Typical training events include joint training exercises, situational training exercises, live-fire exercises, and combat training center (CTC) exercises. (For a complete listing, see CATSs.)

4-99. Effective training events are well-coordinated and use mission-focused scenarios. They focus the entire organization on one or more mission-essential tasks or task groups. Leaders concentrate on supporting collective tasks and subordinate unit mission-essential tasks. Well-developed events incorporate conditions replicating the anticipated operational environment. As appropriate, they place Soldiers and leaders in ambiguous, uncertain, and rapidly changing conditions. Commanders can do this during the run and even in the walk phase. (See paragraphs 4-180 through 4-184.) Training should include events that require leaders and units to make quick transitions between offensive, defensive, and stability or civil support operations within the limits of the applicable METL.

4-100. Training events require training areas and facilities. Some events may require opposing forces (OPFORs), observer-controller/trainers, and role players. Other events may need training support system products and services, such as instrumentation and training aids, devices, simulators, and simulations (TADSS). Finally, a training event itself is only a tool to meet and sustain METL proficiency. All training events should be evaluated for their contribution to readiness.

4-101. As much as possible, commanders and leaders at all echelons make the training environment as close to the anticipated operational environment as possible. They include the appropriate level of combined arms, unified action capabilities, and special operations forces capabilities in all training events. A combination of live, virtual, constructive, and gaming training enablers can make the training environment approximate an actual operational environment. By complementing the live environment with virtual and constructive training enablers, commanders can increase the effective size of the training area, incorporate joint capabilities, and increase the realism of the training environment. CATSs can assist commanders in developing training events, including mission rehearsals.

4-102. Large-scale, multiechelon training events should be centrally planned so that senior commanders can exercise and integrate warfighting functions into coordinated combined arms training. For example, BCTs can integrate warfighting functions while their battalions exercise their core capabilities. Although events are centrally planned, training objectives and scenarios should be developed collaboratively by leaders of the levels to be trained. This collaboration helps all units meet their training objectives and focuses training on the right echelons. It also minimizes training overhead.

4-103. Externally supported events, including evaluations, allow units to focus on executing training. Higher headquarters usually provide the following support: scenarios derived from the unit's METL and commander-derived training objectives, an OPFOR, observer-controller/trainers, role players, and evaluation support. The maneuver CTCs and Battle Command Training Program are examples of externally supported training opportunities that provide combined arms, mission-focused training. Maneuver CTC and Battle Command Training Program events provide training events based on each participating unit's training objectives. These events are performed under realistic, stressful conditions.

4-104. Sequential training programs successively train each echelon from lower to higher. However, limited resources (such as time) often prevent using sequential training programs. Therefore, commanders structure each training event to take full advantage of multiechelon and concurrent training.

TRAINING RESOURCES

4-105.   Commanders use their assessments of mission-essential and critical collective tasks to set training resource priorities. Resources include, for example, time, facilities, ammunition, funds, and fuel. When possible, commanders confirm resources before publishing long- and short-range training plans. Other-wise, resource shortfalls may require deleting low-priority training requirements, substituting less-costly training alternatives, or reallocating resources to execute METL training not resourced.

4-106.   Commanders give resource priority to events that support training on mission-essential tasks. All tasks may not require equal training time or other resources. Commanders allocate training resources to sustain the METL proficiency based on their assessments of past performance and current proficiency in performing mission-essential tasks.

4-107.   When available resources limit the size or number of live training events (such as field training and live fire exercises), commanders can substitute a mix of virtual and constructive simulation exercises. Using these simulations helps commanders maintain training proficiency while staying within resource constraints. Commanders determine how these substitutions will affect attaining desired proficiency levels and provide this information to the next higher commander. The higher commander either provides addi-tional resources or approves the constrained resource plan.

4-108.   Higher commanders estimate resources required to support their training strategies by assessing subordinate units' fiscal resource projections. Higher commanders complete similar analyses to estimate ammunition, facilities, and other resource requirements. Based on these analyses, higher commanders allo-cate resources to subordinates. Higher and subordinate commanders discuss this resource allocation during the dialog preceding the training briefing. (See paragraphs 4-126 through 4-127.) Subordinate commanders include the events and associated resources allocated to them in the long-range training plan. Installation Management Command manages all ranges, training areas, and TADSS. Therefore, unit commanders work closely with installation and garrison commanders concerning training resource requirements.

Live, Virtual, and Constructive Training

4-109.   The Army relies on a creative mix of live, virtual, constructive, and gaming training enablers to provide realistic training. Live, virtual, and constructive training is a broad taxonomy that covers the de-gree to which a training event uses simulations. Units perform, for example, field training exercises, live fire exercises, deployment exercises, and battle drills under live conditions that replicate an actual opera-tional environment as closely as possible. This is especially true at the battalion level and below. Virtual, constructive, and gaming training enablers are used to supplement, enhance, and complement live training. They can help raise the entry level of proficiency for live training and reduce time needed to prepare train-ing. They can also provide a variety of training environments, allowing multiple scenarios to be replicated under different conditions. Based on training objectives and available resources—such as time, ammuni-tion, simulations, and range availability—commanders determine the right mix and frequency of live, vir-tual, and constructive training to ensure organizations use allocated resources efficiently.

Live Training

4-110.   Live training is training executed in field conditions using tactical equipment. It involves real people operating real systems. Live training may be enhanced by TADSS and tactical engagement simula-tion to simulate combat conditions.

Virtual Training

4-111.   Virtual training is training executed using computer-generated battlefields in simulators with the approximate characteristics of tactical weapon systems and vehicles. Virtual training is used to exercise motor control, decisionmaking, and communication skills. Sometimes called "human-in-the-loop training," it involves real people operating simulated systems. People being trained practice the skills needed to oper-ate actual equipment, for example, flying an aircraft.

183

Constructive Training

4-112.   Constructive training uses computer models and simulations to exercise command and staff functions. It involves simulated people operating simulated systems. Constructive training can be conducted by units from platoon through echelons above corps. A command post exercise is an example of constructive training.

Gaming

4-113.   **Gaming is the use of technology employing commercial or government off-the-shelf, multi-genre games in a realistic, semi-immersive environment to support education and training**. The military uses gaming technologies to create capabilities to help train individuals and organizations. Gaming can enable individual, collective, and multiechelon training. Gaming can operate in a stand-alone environment or be integrated with live, virtual, or constructive enablers. It can also be used for individual education. Employed in a realistic, semi-immersive environment, gaming can simulate operations and capabilities. Gaming can also be used with live, virtual, and constructive training enablers.

4-114.   Games are categorized according to their use. For example, a first-person shooter game is an action video game that involves an avatar, one or more ranged weapons, and a varying number of enemies. First-person shooter games can enhance such skills as individual and small-unit tactics, battle drills, mission planning and rehearsal, troop leading procedures, battlefield visualization, and team building. Another game category is the real-time strategy game. These games are played continuously without turns—players act simultaneously. As gaming tools are developed, they provide commanders with additional means to train for full spectrum operations in any operational theme.

Using Live, Virtual, Constructive, and Gaming Training Enablers

4-115.   Using a mix of live, virtual, constructive, and gaming training enablers enhances an organization's ability to train effectively and efficiently. These enablers let commanders simulate participation of large units, scarce resources, or high-cost equipment in training events. Using these enablers reduces the resources required (including maneuver space) to conduct training. For example, properly using these enablers lets commanders perform command and control tasks in a combat vehicle based on messages from higher headquarters, adjacent units, and subordinates without those elements participating in the training. The goal of using live, virtual, constructive, and gaming training enablers is to make the training event as realistic as possible at the lowest cost.

4-116.   Brigade-sized and larger units rely more on constructive training events to attain and sustain their proficiency.

4-117.   Battalion-sized and smaller units attain and sustain proficiency and develop warrior tasks primarily using live training. They use simulation and gaming capabilities to—

- Improve decisionmaking skills.
- Practice staff drills.
- Refine standing operating procedures.
- Rehearse and war-game plans.
- Practice maintaining situational awareness.
- Develop leaders.

4-118.   In general, commanders at battalion level and lower plan, prepare, execute, and assess training events using virtual, constructive, and gaming training enablers to—

- Prepare for live training.
- Rehearse unit collective tasks, and squad, team, and crew drills.
- Retrain on—
  - Selected organizational tasks.
  - Supporting squad, team, and crew critical tasks.
  - Leader and individual Soldier tasks evaluated as either "P" (needs practice) or "U" (untrained).

- Virtually expand the training area of operations without expanding the physical training area.
- Perform tasks repetitively under varying conditions to develop intuition on how to execute the tasks.
- Exercise all warfighting functions.
- Increase training realism.
- Allow geographically dispersed units to train as a team.

4-119. Virtual, constructive, and gaming training should be maximized during the reset phase of ARFORGEN. Units usually do not have all their equipment available for live training then. Units in reset should take every opportunity to sustain their digital individual and collective battle command proficiency. Installation battle command training centers (formerly battle simulation centers) are good resources for this. These facilities conduct digital, simulation-driven command and control exercises. Repetitive, simulation-driven exercises can, over time, help contribute to leader proficiency in the art, as well as the science, of battle command.

Training Support System

4-120. The Army's training support system provides resources to support commanders' training strategies on request. The training support system provides—

- Products—instrumentation and TADSS.
- Services—training support operations and manpower.
- Facilities—ranges, simulation centers, and training support centers.

4-121. Leaders use these products, services, and facilities to provide a training environment that replicates projected operational environments. The training support system provides tools to execute Soldier, leader, staff, and collective training at any location. The system also enables school programs of instruction and training strategies, such as CATSs and weapons training strategies. In addition, the system provides the operations staff for ranges, command and control training capabilities, training support centers, and training area management. These resources help leaders focus on the training rather than the training support requirements.

4-122. The Army is adapting installation training support system capabilities to enable CMETL and DMETL training. Range modernization supports new weapons systems, integrates command and control information systems, and allows units to conduct training using a variety of scenarios. Urban operations facilities and combined arms collective training facilities support training for urban operations. Battle command training centers support many types of training, among them, operator and leader training on command and control information systems, staff section training, command post exercises, and mission rehearsal exercises.

TIME MANAGEMENT

4-123. Installation commanders use time management cycles—such as red-green-amber and training-mission-support—to manage time requirements and resources. The purpose of establishing a time management cycle is to give subordinate commanders predictability when developing their training plans. These cycles establish the type of activity that receives priority during specific periods. Time management cycles identify and protect training periods and resources that support training so subordinate units can concentrate on METL training during those times. This predictability helps commanders meet and sustain technical and tactical competence, maintain training proficiency, and support the installation.

4-124. Time management periods are depicted on long-range planning calendars. Typically, cycles last anywhere from four to eight weeks. A common cycle consists of three periods, one focused on collective training, one on individual training, and one on installation support. However, specific cycles and their lengths vary among installations according to the local situation and requirements, such as ARFORGEN phases, unit deployment dates, and installation size and type.

4-125. No one solution for time management exists, since so many factors affect managing time and prioritizing resources. A system that works at one installation may not work at another. Different circums-

THE TRAINER

tances require different solutions. Therefore, installation commanders develop a system that best suits the installation. This may involve establishing priorities based on ARFORGEN cycles in coordination with force package commanders. Allocation of available training time is a significant resource consideration in Reserve Component planning for training. Limited training time requires Reserve Component commanders to prioritize training requirements carefully.

TRAINING BRIEFINGS

4-126. Commanders present a training briefing to their higher commander to obtain approval of their long- and short-range training plans. Creating a training briefing has two steps: first a dialog, and then the formal training briefing. The importance of this two-step collaboration cannot be overstated. Prior to the training briefing, a unit commander and the next higher commander conduct a dialog. The dialog focuses on either CMETL or DMETL training. The dialog's purpose is to determine the specific task groups and supporting collective tasks to be trained. This dialog helps commanders agree on the following:

- Commander's assessment of unit readiness in light of—
  - The operational theme (for CMETL training), or
  - The operational theme and projected operational environment (for DMETL training).
- The conditions under which the unit is to train.
- Key challenges to readiness.
- Any nonstandard or unavailable resources required to replicate those conditions.
- Risks involved with accepting a lower training level on selected tasks.

4-127. In the case of CMETL training, the dialog helps commanders estimate how long it will take to achieve CMETL proficiency before the unit begins training on its DMETL. The dialog saves both commanders' time during the training briefing. It also ensures that the training unit's plan is synchronized with the higher commander's vision and Department of the Army's focus.

4-128. The second step, the training briefing, results in an approved training plan and a resource contract between commanders. The higher commander determines the timing of the dialog and briefing. However, both should be held early enough to ensure that resources can be locked in for the training unit.

4-129. A training briefing focuses on two subjects: how the unit commander intends to achieve proficiency in the CMETL or DMETL tasks identified during the dialog, and the resources required to do so. While each unit's CMETL usually remains constant, the operational theme determines the training conditions, and the assessment determines the supporting collective tasks to be trained. Those training conditions and the unit's experience with the mission-essential tasks determine the priority of effort devoted to the supporting task groups and collective and individual tasks. For example, if the unit is to train under irregular warfare conditions, the commander may decide to focus more on collective tasks supporting the core mission-essential task "Conduct stability operations" than those supporting offensive or defensive operations. When a unit receives a directed mission, the two commanders determine the unit's DMETL and when the unit will transition from CMETL to DMETL training. The two commanders repeat the above process to develop an approved training plan and contract to achieve DMETL proficiency.

4-130. Training briefings produce "contracts," verbal or otherwise, between the higher commander and supporting and subordinate commanders. The contract is an agreement on the following:

- Tasks to be trained.
- Training conditions.
- Resources required to create those conditions.
- Risks associated with where the commanders are focusing training.
- When the unit will transition from CMETL to DMETL training (for CMETL training briefings).

In agreeing to the negotiated training plan, the higher commander agrees to provide the required resources, including time, and to minimize subordinate unit exposure to unscheduled taskings. The subordinate commander agrees to execute the approved training plan and conduct training to standard. This shared responsibility helps maintain priorities, achieve unity of effort, and synchronize actions to achieve quality training and efficient resourcing.

186

4-131. As discussed in paragraphs 4-35 through 4-36, commanders can apply a modified form of battle command to facilitate the dialog. *Understanding* the operational environment in terms of the operational variables (PMESII-PT) is essential to determining the tasks to train, conditions to replicate, and prudent risks to take. *Visualizing* where the unit needs to be with respect to training proficiency and readiness helps focus training. *Describing* the training plan (including the time required, training areas, facilities, ranges, and other resources) based on the visualization helps clarify the unit's resource requirements. Finally, based on the contract, the commander *directs* the execution of the plan and, as required, assigns responsibilities to each commander.

Example – Commanders' Dialog (CMETL)

The 3d Brigade Combat Team (BCT), Heavy, of the 52d Division is preparing to redeploy after a year of conducting irregular warfare operations in support of a counterinsurgency operation. The BCT commander, COL Smith, is planning his core mission-essential task list (CMETL) training at home station. His unit will be resetting equipment and personnel and will not have received orders for a directed mission.

To gain approval of his training plan, COL Smith and the division staff schedule a training briefing to the commanding general. Then COL Smith sets up a video teleconference dialog with the division commander to ensure the training plan is on track.

The purpose of the dialog between the commanders is as follows:

- For COL Smith to present his assessment of the unit's CMETL training ratings. Tasks on which the BCT is fully trained are rated T; those partially trained, P; and those untrained, U.

- To gain the commanding general's concurrence with COL Smith's proposed training focus. The focus includes task groups and supporting collective tasks on which the BCT will train to a T.

- To agree on the task groups and supporting collective tasks the BCT will not train at all (and why), and those they will not train to a T—and the associated risks.

- To identify reset issues, such as when unit equipment will be available for training.

- To identify the resources the BCT requires to replicate the operational theme in training events—especially those resources not available through the installation training support system or funded through unit operating tempo.

- To agree on the time COL Smith will receive to reach CMETL training objectives.

- To agree on the means COL Smith will use to assess CMETL readiness.

The dialog allows the commanders to prioritize the BCT's training efforts to achieve Army force generation (ARFORGEN) readiness requirements, given equipment, personnel, and time constraints.

To prepare for the dialog, COL Smith reviews the commanding general's training and leader development guidance. The guidance includes the operational theme under which the unit is to train. The theme describes the operating conditions that the BCT should replicate—the typical threats and operational environment of a point midway between general war and insurgency on the spectrum of conflict. Before beginning the dialog, COL Smith accesses the Digital Training Management System to review the supporting task groups and collective tasks for each CMETL task. Then, with his subordinate leaders, he assesses the BCT's ability to perform its CMETL tasks.

The commanders begin the dialog by talking about the challenges the BCT will face. They agree on how they expect the majority of the unit's leadership changing during reset to affect training. They also agree on the BCT's CMETL assessment—one based primarily on the unit's recent deployment. COL Smith rates the BCT's proficiency, given the operational theme conditions, as follows:

- Conduct offensive operations: P
- Conduct defensive operations: P
- Conduct security operations: P
- Conduct stability operations: T
- Conduct information engagement: T
- Conduct command and control: T
- Protect the force: T
- Provide sustainment: P

The assessment provides a common frame of reference and helps the commanding general understand the BCT commander's resource requests. COL Smith's position is that even though the 3d BCT operated successfully at company level and below, the irregular warfare theme requires BCT-level proficiency. Information engagement skills have matured significantly during the current operation. The commander is confident that the team can achieve BCT-level proficiency in command and control, protection, and stability tasks with little additional training. However, BCT- and battalion-level offensive, security, and sustainment operations have not been trained or evaluated in over a year. Further, the BCT and battalions have not trained on defensive operations for over a year and a half. However, the companies have conducted both offensive and defensive operations during the deployment.

The assessments lead COL Smith to recommend a focus on collective tasks that support the following CMETL tasks: "Conduct security operations," "Provide sustainment," and "Conduct offensive operations." He is confident that he can sustain a T in "Conduct command and control" through one or two BCT-level command post exercises. He believes he can allow "Conduct stability operations" to become a P, since recent operational experience will let him raise it to T very quickly. He also thinks he should maintain "Conduct defensive operations" at a P, since the operational theme does not indicate the likelihood of a threat with near-peer offensive capabilities. The obvious risk in this plan is that it will not prepare the BCT and its subordinate organizations to face an enemy with significant offensive capabilities.

The commanding general agrees with COL Smith's assessments and logic, and concurs that the risk entailed in not training for defensive operations is low. However, he tells COL Smith that the 3d BCT needs to be able to conduct a mobile defense at the P level.

Both commanders agree that there is not enough time available for the BCT to train on all eight mission-essential tasks (including 21 subordinate task groups), let alone the many supporting collective tasks associated with each task group. The commanders draw on their experience and exercise battle command to understand the situation, visualize the requirements, and decide on a suitable plan. They determine which task groups and supporting collective tasks are most critical to readiness and which ones need training. They also decide which tasks do not require training—either because they are already trained, can be trained quickly, or are a low risk.

After some give and take between the two commanders, they decide to assign the following task groups training priority in this order:

- Conduct an attack.
- Conduct a movement to contact.
- Conduct guard operations.
- Conduct logistic support.
- Conduct a mobile defense.

The division commander also identifies several prioritized supporting collective tasks for each task group. He reminds COL Smith that while mission-essential tasks are not prioritized, task groups and supporting collective tasks are prioritized since some mission-essential tasks require more effort and resources than others.

COL Smith then highlights his significant reset issues:

- The need for equipment for training as soon as possible after redeployment.
- The need to fill certain key positions early in the reset period.
- The rumored shortage of allocations for such schools as sniper, master gunner, and joint fires observer.
- The usual overscheduling of the virtual and constructive simulation facilities.
- When and how new equipment training is to occur.
- The need for mobile training teams to support collective training on digital command and control information systems as soon as possible after new equipment training ends.

The commanding general tasks his staff to provide solutions soon enough to influence the BCT commander's training briefing.

The commanding general's training and leader development guidance addresses how best to replicate the operational theme's conditions during training. For example, the commanding general expects units to be prepared to do the following:

- Face an active insurgency in urban areas.
- Deal with an unfriendly population able to support and generate organized guerrilla or insurgent activity during stability operations.
- Operate in an austere environment with few essential services to support the population.
- Coordinate with interagency and nongovernmental organizations.
- Face an organized company-to-battalion-sized mechanized force.

The commanding general expects these conditions to be replicated during collective training. He states that the division's 2d BCT can support the 3d BCT's training with role players, observers, and a battalion-level opposing force. He also suggests that the 3d BCT maximize the use of the simulation center to exercise large-scale staff operations, rather than use troops as training aids during field training exercises.

During the dialog, COL Smith identifies resources he needs that are not available at home station. These include an urban operations site located at another post and the use of a close combat tactical trainer suite, since his installation does not have an urban operations site and the installation's suite is under renovation.

Because his artillery battalion has operated as light infantry during the deployment, the BCT commander asks to exceed the Standards and Training Commission allowance for 155mm rounds. However, the commanding general says he will make that decision after the COL Smith describes his training plan and justifies the need in the training briefing.

COL Smith also recognizes that after so many months of focusing on counterinsurgency, he will need assistance from the fires brigade commander to train his field artillery battalion on delivery of fires and fire support tasks. The division commander concurs and says he will forward the request.

Finally, the leaders acknowledge that if the time allotted for training is cut short, the 3d BCT may not be able to train all the supporting collective tasks to the agreed on rating. That could result in training "Conduct offensive operations" to a "P" rating, thus diminishing the BCT's offensive capabilities. They agree that this risk is acceptable since BCT-level offensive operations are not anticipated in the projected operational environment.

COL Smith then states his estimate of the proficiency level he expects to achieve on each CMETL task before transitioning from the reset to the train/ready phase. He bases this estimate on the tasks, training conditions required for task proficiency, likely risks, and ARFORGEN requirements. The commanding general directs COL Smith to train his platoons and companies to at least a T on their supporting collective tasks and to train the brigade and battalion staffs to at least a P on their CMETL tasks as quickly as possible. Accomplishing those training objectives would place the BCT in the best possible readiness status should a contingency mission cut available training time short. The commanders agree that a sound assessment of the BCT's readiness to transition to training focused on the directed mission-essential task list (DMETL) requires a two-part evaluation: an externally evaluated command post exercise to assess the staff, and a BCT external evaluation. Both evaluations will occur at home station.

The two commanders have clarified the following:

- The BCT commander's CMETL assessment.
- Tasks the BCT will train and not train.
- The conditions under which the BCT will train.
- Estimates of resources and subject matter experts required.
- Reset and regeneration issues.
- Timelines to achieve CMETL readiness objectives.
- Associated risks to readiness and their potential implications.
- Means for measuring CMETL readiness.

The next step is developing the training plan to achieve the CMETL proficiency the two commanders have agreed to. When the plan is complete, COL Smith briefs the commanding general and his staff to obtain approval and finalize the contract between the two commanders. The commanding general agrees to provide the required resources and protect the BCT commander's training time. The BCT commander agrees to execute the approved training plan.

COL Smith knows that he will have to develop a DMETL training plan if he receives a directed mission. He would follow a process similar to the one used to develop the CMETL training plan. The major differences will be that he will have to develop and gain approval of the BCT's DMETL, determine when the BCT's training focus will transition from the CMETL to the DMETL, and determine how to replicate the conditions in the projected area of operations.

4-132. Division commanders receive a training briefing from all assigned or attached brigades for which they have responsibility and from the battalions subordinate to those brigades. Brigade commanders and command sergeants major personally present the overview of the brigade training plan; battalion commanders and command sergeants major brief battalion training plans. All habitually associated commanders participate in preparing and presenting training briefings. Brigade commanders follow a similar process internally with their battalions and separate companies.

4-133. Installation Management Command representatives should attend all training briefings. Coordination between commanders and the installation representatives is required to ensure installation training resources are available and properly allocated.

4-134. The training briefing is a highlight of a commander's leader development program. The briefing gives commanders an opportunity to coach and teach subordinates. In addition to discussing their philosophies and strategies for conducting training and full spectrum operations, commanders may also address doctrine, force integration, and leader development. This interaction enables subordinate commanders and senior NCOs to better understand how their training relates to the mission-focused training programs of their higher commanders and peers.

4-135. The higher commander specifies the format and content of training briefings. However, the briefing guidance should be flexible enough to allow subordinates latitude to highlight their initiatives and priorities. The command sergeant major normally provides an analysis of the unit's individual training proficiency and discusses planned individual training and education.

4-136. Units should not discuss readiness issues during training briefings unless the issues are training-related. Statistical, logistic, manning, or other management data are more appropriate to readiness review forums. They distract participants from the overall focus of the training briefing.

TRAINING PLANS

4-137. A training plan translates the commander's training and leader development guidance and training strategy into a series of interconnected requirements and events to achieve the commander's training objectives. Planning documents include the frequency and duration of each training event and the resources required. Required resources and events drive planning considerations. The three types of training plans are long-range, short-range, and near-term. (See table 4-1.)

Long-Range Planning

4-138. The long-range training plan starts the process of implementing the commander's training strategy. Long-range plans identify the major training events for the unit along with the resources required to execute the training events. A long-range plan normally covers 12 months for Regular Army and mobilized Reserve Component units. It covers two years to an entire ARFORGEN cycle for other Reserve Component units. However, commanders can adjust the time frame covered to meet their needs.

4-139. A long-range training plan consists of training and leader development guidance and the long-range planning calendar. Senior commanders publish training and leader development guidance early enough to give their units enough time to plan, both during operations and in peacetime. Guidance from senior command echelons is critical to developing and integrating subordinate Regular Army and Reserve Component long-range training plans. Therefore, long lead times, consistent with the ARFORGEN cycles, are normal. Each headquarters follows an established timeline so subordinates have time to prepare their plans. Higher headquarters should give subordinate units more planning time than they keep for themselves.

Long-Range Training and Leader Development Guidance

4-140. Training and leader development guidance includes the commander's training assessment. Commanders down to company level can develop this guidance. Commanders ensure their guidance aligns with their higher commander's guidance. Commanders prepare their subordinate leaders for the mission at hand and develop them for their next duty position. Unit training and leader development guidance is based on the Chief of Staff, Army's, training and leader development guidance.

4-141. Commanders refer to the higher commander's guidance when developing their own training and leader development guidance. The higher commander's training and leader development guidance forms the basis for the dialog that determines the mix of tasks to train, how much time to spend on training various tasks, and other resources needed.

Table 4-1. Comparison of long-range, short-range, and near-term training planning

Long-Range	Short-Range	Near-Term
Disseminate mission-essential task list and supporting collective tasks	Refine and expand on the appropriate portions of the long-range plan	Refine and expand on the short-range plan by holding training meetings
Conduct commander's assessment	Cross-reference each training event with specific training objectives	Publish event training plans or operation orders as needed
Establish training objectives for each mission-essential task	Identify and allocate short-lead-time resources, such as local training facilities	Determine best sequence for training
Schedule projected major training events	Coordinate the short-range calendar with all support agencies	Provide specific guidance for trainers
Identify long-lead-time resources and allocate major resources, such as major training area rotations	Publish the short-range training and leader development guidance and planning calendar	Allocate training support system products and services, including training aids, devices, simulators, simulations, and similar resources
Identify available training support system products and services; identify new requirements	Provide input to unit training meetings	Publish detailed training schedules
Coordinate long-range calendars with supporting agencies to eliminate training distracters		Provide the basis for executing and evaluating training
Publish long-range training and leader development guidance and planning calendar		
Provide a basis for the command operating budget		
Provide long-range training input to higher headquarters		

4-142. Subordinate commanders use their training and leader development guidance as a ready reference to perform training throughout the long-range time frame. Commanders determine the period the guidance covers based on the mission and situation. The time frame can span an entire ARFORGEN cycle or part of it. Alternatively, commanders can establish a time frame of a calendar year or more, again depending on mission and situation. Units of both the generating force and operational Army publish training and leader development guidance. Table 4-2 (page 4-30) lists topics this guidance often addresses.

Table 4-2. Training and leader development guidance topics

• Commander's training philosophy	• Major training events and exercises
• Commander's concept for training	• Organizational inspection program
• METL and supporting collective tasks to be trained	• Battle staff training
• Guidance for conducting major training events	• Individual training
• Resources for training	• Self-development training
• Guidance for leader development	• Standardization
• Training conditions	• Training evaluation and feedback
• Command priorities	• New equipment training and other force integration considerations
• Leader development program	• Resource allocation
• Combined arms training	• Time management cycles
• Unified action training, as applicable	• Composite risk management
• Long-range planning calendar	

Long-Range Planning Calendar

4-143. The long-range planning calendar depicts the schedule of events described in the training and leader development guidance. Major training events and deployments scheduled beyond the plan's time frame also appear on the long-range planning calendar. Upon approval by the higher commander (normally during a training briefing), long-range planning calendars are locked in. This provides planning stability for subordinate units. Only the approving commander can change a long-range planning calendar. The approving commander agrees to allocate and protect the required resources, including time. Subordinate commanders agree to conduct training to standard.

4-144. Reserve Component units require extended planning guidance. Therefore, Regular Army and Reserve Component planners forecast major events that require Reserve Component participation up to five years into the future. They include such major events as annual training periods and overseas training deployments. Both Regular Army and Reserve Component long-range planning calendars contain this information.

4-145. During long-range planning, commanders organize training time to support METL training and mitigate training distracters. (Time management cycles are one technique for doing this.) In addition to individual requirements, such as leave and medical appointments, units may have temporary duty details and other support functions at the installation level. Failure to consider these requirements early in planning can disrupt training.

Short-Range Planning

4-146. Short-range training plans consist of the short-range training and leader development guidance and a planning calendar. These plans refine the guidance contained in the long-range training and leader development guidance and planning calendar. They allocate resources to subordinate units and provide a common basis for near-term planning. When designing training events, planners allocate enough time to conduct the training to standard and time for retraining, if necessary.

Short-Range Training and Leader Development Guidance

4-147. Short-range training and leader development guidance enables commanders and key leaders to further prioritize and refine guidance contained in the long-range guidance. Commanders should publish the short-range guidance early enough for subordinate commanders to develop their short-range training plans. (See table 4-3.) This guidance should be synchronized with the appropriate ARFORGEN phases and should be provided to subordinate commands and installations before training starts. After receiving guidance from their higher headquarters, subordinate units down to company level publish their short-range training guidance.

Table 4-3. Example of a Regular Army short-range training cycle

Action	Publication Date	Time Frame
Division, or similar level command, publishes training and leader development guidance	3 months prior to start of training	3 months
Brigade publishes training and leader development guidance	2 months prior to start of training	3 months
Battalion, squadron, and separate company publish training and leader development guidance	6 weeks prior to start of training*	3 months
Conduct training briefing	At discretion of commanders; prior to start of training	3 + months

*To allow sufficient time for near-term planning at company level before the start of the training; must be synchronized with the Army force generation cycle, when appropriate.

4-148. Reserve Component commanders develop training and leader development guidance the same way as Regular Army commanders do except that Reserve Component timelines are normally longer than those of the Regular Army. Often Reserve Component unit commanders publish their short-range training and leader development guidance as annual training guidance. (See table 4-4.) Additionally, Reserve Component unit commanders develop a plan for postmobilization training. Commanders update this plan concurrently with the short-range training plan.

Table 4-4. Example of a Reserve Component short-range training cycle

Action	Date	Time Frame
Division, or similar level command, publishes training and leader development guidance	6 to 8 months prior to start of fiscal year	1 + years
Brigade and separate battalion publish training and leader development guidance	4 to 6 months prior to start of fiscal year	1 + years
Battalion, squadron, and separate company publish training and leader development guidance	3 to 4 months prior to start of fiscal year	1 + years
Conduct training briefing	At discretion of commanders; prior to start of training	1+ years

4-149. NCOs play an important role in short-range planning. The command sergeant major or first sergeant and other key NCOs provide planning recommendations on the unit's individual training program based on the commander's guidance. Their most important duty is identifying individual training tasks to integrate into mission-essential tasks during training execution. These tasks are included in the short range training plan.

Short-Range Planning Calendar

4-150. The short-range planning calendar refines the long-range planning calendar and provides the timelines necessary for small-unit leaders to prepare training schedules and event training plans.

4-151. In preparing a short-range calendar, leaders add details to further refine the major training events contained on the long-range planning calendar. Some examples of these details include—

- The principal daily activities of major training events.
- Home station training scheduled to prepare for major training events, evaluations, and deployments.
- Mandatory training that supports the METL, such as command inspections as part of the organizational inspection program, Army physical fitness tests, weapons qualification, and preventive maintenance checks and services.
- Significant nontraining events or activities, such as national holidays and installation support missions.

4-152. The short-range training calendar is coordinated with appropriate Installation Management Command and supporting agencies. This coordination creates a common training and support focus for supported and supporting units.

Near-Term Planning

4-153. Near-term planning is performed at battalion level and lower. It includes conducting training meetings and preparing training schedules and event training plans. Near-term planning is done to—

- Schedule and execute training events specified in the short-range training plan.
- Provide specific guidance to trainers.
- Make final coordination for allocating training resources.
- Complete final coordination with other organizations scheduled to participate in training as part of the task organization.
- Prepare detailed training schedules.

4-154. Near-term planning normally covers the six to eight weeks before the training for Regular Army units and four months before the training for Reserve Component units. In coordination with the higher headquarters, commanders determine which timeline works best for them and their subordinate units. Formal near-term planning culminates when the organization publishes its training schedule. Commanders assign responsibilities and subordinates make coordination for training events during training meetings. When necessary, they issue event training plans or operation orders for specific training events. (See paragraph 4-168.)

Training Meetings

4-155. The single most important company meeting is the training meeting. (See TC 25-30.) Training meetings create the bottom-up flow of information regarding the specific training needs of the small-unit, staff, and individual Soldier.

4-156. Normally platoons, companies, and battalions hold weekly training meetings. At company and platoon level, meetings directly concern the specifics of training preparation, execution, and preexecution checks. At battalion level, training meetings primarily cover training management issues.

4-157. Training meetings address only training. Appropriate representatives of subordinate and supporting units attend. Bottom-up feed of information and requirements is essential to the success of the meeting.

Training Schedules

4-158. Near-term planning results in a detailed training schedule. Senior commanders establish policies to minimize changes to training schedules. At a minimum, training schedules—

- Specify when training starts and where it takes place.
- Allocate adequate time to train all tasks to standard, including time to repeat training when standards are not met.
- Specify individual, leader, and collective tasks on which to train.

195

- Provide multiechelon and concurrent training topics to make maximum use of available training time.
- Specify who prepares, executes, and evaluates the training.
- Provide administrative information concerning uniform, weapons, equipment, references, and safety precautions.

4-159.   Command training schedule responsibilities consist of the following:

- Company commanders approve and sign their company's draft training schedule.
- Battalion commanders approve and sign the schedule and provide necessary administrative and logistic support. Training is considered locked in when the battalion commander signs the training schedule.
- The brigade commander reviews each training schedule published in the brigade.
- The brigade's higher headquarters reviews selected training schedules and the list of unitwide training highlights.

4-160.   Senior commanders provide feedback to subordinates on training schedule quality. Those commanders visit training to ensure that training objectives are met and tasks are trained to standard.

INSTALLATION AND GARRISON COMMAND TRAINING

4-161.   Garrison commanders' training plans incorporate the following requirements: mobilization, post-mobilization, deployment, redeployment, and demobilization. These commanders plan and schedule periodic mobilization exercises, emergency deployment readiness exercises, and other contingency plan exercises to sustain proficiency on relevant tasks. Garrison commanders coordinate their training plans with their supported corps, divisions, and tenant organizations. Garrisons routinely support scheduled unit training deployments. Garrisons also perform deployment tasks such as operating departure and arrival airfield control groups and seaports of embarkation and debarkation.

PREPARE

4-162.   Formal near-term planning for training culminates when the unit publishes its training schedule and written event training plans (when necessary). Informal planning, detailed coordination, and preparation for executing the training continue until the training is completed. Preparation is the heart of training management. Commanders and other trainers use training meetings to assign responsibility for preparing all scheduled training.

4-163.   Preparation includes the following:

- Training the trainers.
- Confirming training area availability.
- Site reconnaissance.
- Continuing CRM.
- Ensuring required TADSS availability.
- Issuing event training plans.
- Performing rehearsals and preexecution checks.
- Continuing to identify and eliminate potential training distracters to maximize training attendance.

4-164.   Identifying the responsibility for preexecution checks is a critical portion of any training meeting. Preexecution checks include the following:

- Identifying responsibility for training support tasks.
- Monitoring preparation activities.
- Assessing whether training can be executed to standard, given the training conditions.

4-165.   Subordinate leaders identify and select the collective, leader, and individual tasks necessary to support the identified training objectives. They do this based on as bottom-up feedback from internal training meetings. Commanders develop tentative plans, including requirements for preparatory training, multiechelon training, concurrent training, and training resources. Often these plans take the form of verbal guidance issued during training meetings. When necessary, commanders prepare a written event training plan. All training plans include time and other resources necessary for retraining.

SELECTING AND PREPARING TRAINERS

4-166.   Trainers include leaders, evaluators, observer-controller/trainers, OPFOR personnel, and role players. These people are identified, trained to standard, and rehearsed before training events begin. Executing challenging, doctrinally correct, and professional training requires preparing leaders and trainers beforehand. This involves coaching them on how to train, giving them time to prepare, and rehearsing them. Commanders ensure that trainers and evaluators are tactically and technically competent on their training tasks. Commanders also make sure these people understand how the training relates to the unit METL and training objectives. Properly prepared trainers, evaluators, and leaders project confidence and enthusiasm to those being trained.

4-167.   Training the trainers is a critical step in preparation for training. Leaders, evaluators, observer-controller/trainers, and OPFOR personnel involved in any training event must know, understand, and be proficient on the standard for each task. All leaders are trainers, but all trainers are not necessarily leaders. A junior Soldier or subject matter expert may be the best person to train a particular collective or individual task. Subordinate leaders may be the trainer as well as the leader of an element conducting collective training.

EVENT TRAINING PLANS

4-168.   A complex training event may require a formal event training plan. Commanders issue the event training plan as early as possible. They do this after completing a training site reconnaissance and identifying additional training support requirements with their subordinate leaders and trainers. This plan guides the organization in completing the training event. It identifies elements necessary for the unit to conduct the training to standard. It may be in the form of an operation order, or it may be oral guidance given in the weekly training meeting. Trainers coordinate to obtain the equipment, products, and ammunition needed to support training, based on the site reconnaissance and event training plan. Formal event training plans include the following:

- Confirmed training areas and locations.
- Training ammunition allocations.
- TADSS that have been coordinated for.
- Confirmed transportation resources.
- Soldier support items that have been coordinated.
- Risk management analysis.
- Designation of trainers.
- Final coordination requirements.

INSPECTIONS

4-169.   Preparing for training requires inspections to ensure the needed resources are available. Inspections can be as simple as pretraining checks for a training event. Alternatively, they can be as complex as an organizational inspection program that scrutinizes the unit's entire training program. Inspections also aim to ensure equipment is ready and serviceable, trainers are prepared, resources are available, and safety is a priority. Inspections help leaders ensure the following:

- Their organizations have what they need to conduct quality training.
- Their organizations conduct training to standard.
- Training time is optimized.
- Training is focused on the METL.
- Training objectives are achievable.
- Individual skills and knowledge are improved.

REHEARSALS

4-170.   Rehearsal is a critical element of preparation. Often called a "ROC (rehearsal of concept) drill," it allows leaders and subordinates involved in a training event to develop a mental picture of responsibilities and events. It helps the organization synchronize training with times, places, and resources. A simple walk-through or sand table exercise helps leaders visualize where individuals are supposed to be to perform a coordinated action at a certain time. Leaders see how training is supposed to unfold, what might go wrong, and how the training could change to adjust for intended and unintended events. Commanders and leaders also perform rehearsals to—

- Identify weak points in the event training plan.
- Teach and coach effective training techniques.
- Ensure training meets safety and environmental considerations.
- Ensure leaders and trainers understand training objectives.
- Determine how trainers intend to evaluate the performance of individuals or organizations.
- Assess subordinate trainer competencies and provide feedback to them.
- Give trainers confidence in the event training plan.

EXECUTE

4-171.   Training execution occurs at all echelons, from a unified action training exercise to a first-line leader conducting individual training. Ideally, leaders execute training using the crawl-walk-run approach—as appropriate and tailored to the individual's, team's, or unit's needs and capabilities—to build confidence over time and emphasize fundamentals and standards. Effective training execution, regardless of the specific collective, leader, and individual tasks being executed, requires adequate preparation, effective presentation and practice, and thorough evaluation. After training is executed, leaders ensure individuals recover from training and review successes and challenges to apply observations, insights, and lessons to future training and operations.

CHARACTERISTICS OF EFFECTIVE TRAINING

4-172.   Properly presented and executed training is realistic, safe, standards-based, well-structured, efficient, effective, and challenging.

Realistic

4-173.   Realistic training requires organizations to train the way they intend to operate in all dimensions of the projected operational environment. Realistic training includes all available elements of combined arms teams and, as appropriate, organizations or individuals normally involved in unified action. It optimizes the use of TADSS to replicate the stresses, sounds, and conditions of actual operations.

Safe

4-174.   Safe training is the predictable result of performing to established tactical and technical standards. Through CRM, leaders at all echelons ensure safety requirements are integral, not add-on, considerations to all aspects of planning, preparing for, executing, and assessing training.

Standards-Based

4-175.   Standards-based training complies with joint and Army doctrine and is technically correct. Adherence to standards should not stifle innovation and prudent risk taking. Field manuals, CATSs, and other training publications provide information to facilitate training, coach subordinate trainers, and evaluate training results. Training and evaluation outlines (contained in CATSs) provide information concerning collective training objectives. These outlines also include individual and leader training tasks that support collective training objectives.

Well-Structured

4-176. Well-structured training contains a mixture of initial, sustainment, and improvement training events. It also consists of a mix of individual and leader tasks incorporated into collective tasks. It organizes and sequences training events to allow units to meet their training objectives.

Efficient

4-177. Efficient training makes the best use of training resources. Efficiently executed training makes the best use of everyone's time.

Effective

4-178. Effective training builds proficiency, teamwork, confidence, and cohesiveness. Effective training allows commanders and their organizations to achieve their training objectives.

Challenging

4-179. Challenging training is competitive. Although individuals and organizations may sometimes compete against one another, they should always compete to achieve the prescribed standard. Once the standard has been achieved, trainers alter the conditions to make the task more challenging. If the standard is not achieved, trainers take corrective actions and repeat the training. They do this until the standard is met. Training is done to standard, not to available time.

CRAWL-WALK-RUN

4-180. The crawl-walk-run technique is an objective, incremental, standards-based approach to training. Tasks are initially trained at a very basic level (crawl), then become increasingly difficult (walk), and finally approach the level of realism expected in combat (run). Training starts at the basic level, beginning with the crawl stage. However, leaders first assess individual and unit training levels. Some individuals and organizations may be ready for the walk, or even the run stage, depending on their experience.

4-181. Crawl stage events are simple to perform and require minimal support. The crawl stage focuses on the basics of the task and proceeds as slowly as needed for individuals and the organization to understand task requirements. Walk stage training becomes incrementally more difficult. It requires more resources from the unit and home station and increases the level of realism and the pace. At the run stage, the level of difficulty for training intensifies. Run-stage training requires the resources needed to create the conditions expected in the projected operational environment. Progression from crawl to run for a particular task may occur during a one-day training exercise or may require a succession of training periods.

4-182. In crawl-walk-run training, tasks and standards remain the same; however, the conditions under which they are trained change. Live, virtual, constructive, and gaming training enablers help provide the variable conditions for supporting a crawl-walk-run training strategy. Ways to change conditions include the following:

- Increasing the difficulty of conditions under which tasks are being performed.
- Increasing the tempo of the training.
- Increasing the number of tasks being trained.
- Increasing or decreasing the number of personnel involved.

4-183. Trainers use the crawl-walk-run approach to determine the amount of detail to include in practice. If individuals or organizations are receiving initial training on a task, trainers emphasize basic conditions. If individuals are receiving sustainment training, trainers raise the level of detail and realism until conditions replicate an actual operational environment as closely as possible. Trainers challenge those with considerable experience to perform multiple training tasks under stressful conditions.

4-184. Trainers conduct training using the combination of demonstrations, conferences, discussions, and practice appropriate to the experience of those being trained. They inform individuals of the training objectives (tasks, conditions, and standards) and applicable evaluation procedures. Trainers immediately follow presentations with practice to convert information into usable individual and collective skills.

RECOVERY FROM TRAINING

4-185.   Recovery is an extension of training. A training event is not ended until recovery is complete. Recovery ends when the organization is again prepared to conduct operations. At a minimum, recovery includes the following:

- Performing maintenance training.
- Cleaning and accounting for equipment and components.
- Turning in training support items and ammunition.
- Performing final AARs.
- Performing final inspections.

ASSESS

4-186.   **In the training context, *assessment* is the leader's judgment of the organization's ability to perform its mission-essential tasks and, ultimately, its ability to accomplish its doctrinal or directed mission**. Training assessments address a wide variety of areas, including training support, force integration, logistics, and personnel availability. These assessments form the basis for determining the organization's training ratings for readiness reporting. Commanders consider the following when making assessments:

- Their own observations and those of subordinate leaders.
- Feedback from AARs.
- Results of unit evaluations, where performance is measured against standards to arrive at the assessment.

4-187.   Battalion and higher echelon commanders are concerned with overall unit readiness. Accordingly, they perform organizational assessments that aggregate numerous evaluations. These commanders establish an organizational assessment program that—

- Fixes responsibility within the staff and subordinate organizations for gathering and analyzing evaluation data and preparing recommendations.
- Concentrates on the effectiveness of leader and unit training.
- Uses command sergeants major and other senior NCOs to gather feedback on the individual, crew, team, and section training.
- Allows the senior commander to monitor outcomes and act to reshape priorities, policies, or plans to overcome weaknesses and sustain strengths.

4-188.   ***Feedback* is the transmission of verbal or written evaluative or corrective information about a process or task to individuals and organizations**. It provides the basis for assessments. Sources of feedback include—

- Personal observations.
- Reports from higher headquarters.
- Staff assistance visits.
- External evaluations, including CTC take-home packages.
- Readiness reports.
- Organized inspections.
- DTMS reports.

4-189.   CTC take-home packages provide excellent information for the commander's assessment of readiness. These packages may include video and written AARs, a report of unit strengths and weaknesses, and recommendations for future home station training.

EVALUATIONS

4-190. **In the training context, *evaluation* is the process used to measure the demonstrated ability of individuals and units to accomplish specified training objectives.** Evaluations are one form of feedback. Commanders evaluate subordinate units two echelons below their unit. Training evaluations provide commanders with feedback on the demonstrated proficiency of individuals, staffs, and organizations against a standard. Training conducted without evaluation is a waste of time and resources. Evaluations can be informal, formal, internal, external, or any combination of them.

Informal Evaluations

4-191. Informal evaluations occur when leaders evaluate their unit's training against established standards. Leaders follow an informal evaluation with either an AAR or a critique, depending on the nature of the feedback to be provided. An example is a squad leader providing verbal feedback on a fire team leader's ability to control the team during a movement to contact. Another example is a leader visiting ongoing training and discussing his or her observations of individual and unit performance with subordinate leaders. In all cases, leaders evaluate training against the standard. This type of evaluation provides real-time feedback on the training environment and the proficiency resulting from training.

Formal Evaluations

4-192. Formal evaluations involve dedicated evaluators and are scheduled in training plans. Normally, formal evaluations are highlighted during short-range training briefings. As much as possible, headquarters two echelons higher perform formal external evaluations. Division commanders evaluate battalions, brigade commanders evaluate companies, and battalion commanders evaluate platoons. Feedback usually takes the form of an AAR followed by a written report.

4-193. During and after formal evaluations, evaluators prepare their findings and recommendations. They provide these evaluations to the evaluated unit commander and higher commanders as required by the headquarters directing the evaluations. Evaluation documentation can range from an annotated training and evaluation outline for an internal training evaluation to a comprehensive report for an external evaluation.

Internal Evaluations

4-194. Internal evaluations are planned, resourced, and performed by the organization undergoing the evaluation. Unit-conducted situational training exercises are an example.

External Evaluations

4-195. External evaluations are planned, resourced, and performed by a higher headquarters or a headquarters outside the chain of command. The exercise director is normally two echelons above the evaluated organization.

4-196. External sources should evaluate training whenever possible to objectively measure performance in terms of Army and joint standards. However, self-evaluation of individual and organization performance is just as, if not more, important as that from external evaluators. Effective commanders establish a climate that encourages open and candid feedback.

Training and Readiness

4-197. Training evaluations are a critical component of measuring readiness. Evaluation measures the demonstrated ability of individuals, leaders, staffs, and units to perform against the Army or joint standard.

4-198. Senior commanders and leaders focus on unit readiness by requiring evaluations of specific mission-essential and critical collective subtasks. They also use evaluation results to determine which observations, insights, and lessons constitute lessons learned. Lessons learned are distributed throughout their commands and used in planning future training. (See FM 6-01.1, paragraphs 3-52 through 3-55.)

4-199.   Evaluation of individual and small-unit training normally includes every individual involved in the training. For large-scale training events, evaluators usually base their evaluation on the performance of a sample of individual and subordinate organizations.

4-200.   An evaluation of training is not a test. Evaluations are not used to find reasons to punish leaders and subordinates. Leaders use evaluations as opportunities to coach and develop subordinates. Evaluations tell organizations and individuals whether they achieved the standard and help them determine the overall effectiveness of their training plans.

4-201.   Results of evaluations can strongly affect the command climate of an organization. Senior commanders should underwrite honest mistakes and create a positive learning environment so the same mistakes do not reoccur.

AFTER ACTION REVIEWS

4-202.   **The *after action review* is a method of providing feedback to organizations by involving participants in the training diagnostic process in order to increase and reinforce learning.** Leaders use formal or informal AARs to provide feedback on training. The AAR provides a forum for structured review and information sharing. AARs allow participating individuals, leaders, staffs, and units to discover for themselves what happened during the training, why it happened, and how to execute tasks or operations better. The AAR is a professional discussion requiring active participation by those being trained. AARs—

- Are two-way discussions, rather than one-way critiques, of the performance of an individual or organization.
- Increase the likelihood of learning and foster the development of a learning organization by actively involving participants.
- Use "leading questions" to encourage key participants to self-discover important observations, insights, and lessons from the training event.
- Emphasize corrective action rather than dwelling on what went wrong.
- Focus directly on attainment of training objectives derived from the METL.
- Emphasize meeting Army or joint standards rather than pronouncing judgment of success or failure.

4-203.   AARs are often "tiered" to develop leaders at multiple echelons. For example, feedback from squad or section AARs should be brought into platoon AARs. Feedback from platoon AARs should feed discussion in company AARs. After completing an AAR with all participants, senior trainers may continue the professional discussion with selected leaders. These discussions usually address specific leader contributions to the training. Using this process links training and leader development.

4-204.   Some AARs are formal gatherings of unit key leaders. Others are simply one-on-one discussions between a commander and an observer-controller/trainer over a vehicle hood.

4-205.   Unit leaders must be trained to complete informal, internal evaluations as well. They must be able to plan, prepare, and execute AARs effectively whenever and wherever needed. Taking too much time between an event and the AAR can cause a loss of learning. This means leaders remain—

- Familiar with their unit's METL and how it supports their higher headquarters' METL.
- Tactically and technically proficient in the evaluated tasks.

4-206.   AARs should be conducted during training as well as at the end of training events or during recovery. Leader feedback to subordinates during training allows subordinates to take corrective action immediately. Frequently providing feedback gives organizations opportunities to correct deficiencies before a training event ends. If leaders only conduct end-of-exercise AARs, valuable lessons may be lost.

4-207.   AARs with leaders focus on tactical judgment. These AARs contribute to leader learning and provide opportunities for leader development. Including evaluator, observer-controller/trainer, and OPFOR performance in AARs provides additional leader development opportunities. These AARs contribute to the commander's overall evaluation of training effectiveness and assessment of unit proficiency.

4-208. AARs performed during recovery focus on the planning, preparation, and execution of the training just completed. Organizational AARs focus on individual and collective task performance. They identify shortcomings and the training required to correct them.

RETRAINING

4-209. Leaders understand that not all tasks will be performed to standard on the first attempt. Thus, they allocate time and other resources for retraining in their training plans. Retraining allows participants to implement corrective action. Retraining should be completed at the earliest opportunity, if not immediately, to translate observations and evaluations into tasks trained to standard. Training is incomplete until the organization achieves the Army standard. Commanders do not allow an organization to end training believing that a substandard performance was acceptable. In some cases, a "restart" or "redo" of an event may be necessary before moving to the next training event.

EVALUATORS

4-210. Commanders ensure evaluators are trained as facilitators to perform AARs that elicit maximum participation from those being trained. External evaluators are trained in tasks they are evaluating and normally do not participate in the training being executed. In addition to being able to plan, prepare, and execute AARs, effective evaluators also—

- Are familiar with the evaluated organization's METL and training objectives.
- Are tactically and technically proficient and rehearsed in the evaluated tasks.
- Know the evaluation standards.
- Know the evaluated organization's tactical and field standing operating procedures.
- Consider such characteristics as the evaluated organization's missions, personnel turbulence, leader fill, and equipment status.

Not only do individuals and units receiving the training learn from the evaluator; evaluators also learn while observing the evaluated organization.

Glossary

The glossary lists acronyms and terms with Army or joint definitions, and other selected terms. Where Army and joint definitions are different, (Army) follows the term. Terms for which FM 7-0 is the proponent manual (the authority) are marked with an asterisk (*). The proponent manual for other terms is listed in parentheses after the definition.

SECTION I – ACRONYMS AND ABBREVIATIONS

AAR	after action review
ADCON	administrative control
AR	Army regulation
ARFORGEN	Army force generation
BCT	brigade combat team
CATS	combined arms training strategy
CJCSI	chairman of the joint chiefs of staff instruction
CJCSM	chairman of the joint chiefs of staff manual
CMETL	core mission-essential task list
COL	colonel
CRM	composite risk management
CTC	combat training center
DA	Department of the Army
DMETL	directed mission-essential task list
DTMS	Digital Training Management System
FM	field manual
FMI	field manual–interim
JP	joint publication
METL	mission-essential task list
NCO	noncommissioned officer
OPFOR	opposing force
PMESII-PT	political, military, economic, social, infrastructure, information, physical environment, and time
TADSS	training aids, devices, simulators, and simulations
TC	training circular
U.S.	United States

SECTION II – TERMS

administrative control

(joint) Direction or exercise of authority over subordinate or other organizations in respect to administration and support, including organization of Service forces, control of resources and equipment, personnel management, unit logistics, individual and unit training, readiness, mobilization, demobilization, discipline, and other matters not included in the operational missions of the subordinate or other organizations. (JP 1)

*after action review

A method of providing feedback to organizations by involving participants in the training diagnostic process in order to increase and reinforce learning.

ARFOR

The Army Service component headquarters for a joint task force or a joint and multinational force. (FM 3-0)

Army Service component command

(joint) Command responsible for recommendations to the joint force commander on the allocation and employment of Army forces within a combatant command. (JP 3-31)

*assessment

In the training context, the leader's judgment of the organization's ability to perform its mission-essential tasks and, ultimately, its ability to accomplish its doctrinal or directed mission.

battle command

The art and science of understanding, visualizing, describing, directing, leading, and assessing forces to impose the commander's will on a hostile, thinking, and adaptive enemy. Battle command applies leadership to translate decisions into actions—by synchronizing forces and warfighting functions in time, space, and purpose—to accomplish missions. (FM 3-0)

*battle roster

A listing of individuals, crews, or elements that reflects capabilities, proficiencies in critical tasks, or other information concerning warfighting abilities.

composite risk management

The decisionmaking process for identifying and assessing hazards, developing and implementing risk mitigation actions to control risk across the full spectrum of Army missions, functions, operations, and activities. (FM 5-19)

condition

(joint) Those variables of an operational environment or situation in which a unit, system, or individual is expected to operate and may affect performance. (JP 1-02)

*core capability mission-essential task

A mission-essential task approved by Headquarters, Department of the Army, that is specific to the a type of unit resourced according to its authorization document and doctrine.

*core mission-essential task list

A list of a unit's core capability mission-essential tasks and general mission-essential tasks.

*directed mission

A mission a unit is formally tasked to execute or prepare to execute.

*directed mission-essential task list

A list of mission-essential tasks that must be performed to accomplish a directed mission.

205

*evaluation

In the training context, the process used to measure the demonstrated ability of individuals and units to accomplish specified training objectives.

*feedback

The transmission of verbal or written evaluative or corrective information about a process or task to individuals and organizations.

*gaming

The use of technology employing commercial or government off-the-shelf, multigenre games in a realistic, semi-immersive environment to support education and training.

*general mission-essential task

A mission-essential task approved by Headquarters, Department of the Army, that all units, regardless of type, must be able to accomplish.

generating force

Those Army organizations whose primary mission is to generate and sustain the operational Army's capabilities for employment by joint force commanders. (FM 1-01)

*institutional training domain

The Army's institutional training and education system, which primarily includes training base centers and schools that provide initial training and subsequent professional military education for Soldiers, military leaders, and Army civilians.

measure of effectiveness

(joint) A criterion used to assess changes in system behavior, capacity, or operational environment that is tied to measuring the attainment of an end state, achievement of an objective, or creation of an effect. (JP 3-0)

mission

(joint) 1. The task, together with the purpose, that clearly indicates the action to be taken and the reason therefor. 2. In common usage, especially when applied to lower military organizations, a duty assigned to an individual or organization; a task. (JP 1-02)

mission command

The conduct of military operations through decentralized execution based on mission orders. Successful mission command demands that subordinate leaders at all echelons exercise disciplined initiative, acting aggressively and independently to accomplish the mission within the commander's intent. (FM 3-0)

*mission-essential task

A collective task a unit must be able to perform successfully in order to accomplish its doctrinal or directed mission.

*mission-essential task list

A compilation of mission-essential tasks that an organization must perform successfully to accomplish its doctrinal or directed missions.

*mission focus

The process used to derive training requirements from a unit's core capabilities as documented in its authorization document or from a directed mission.

mission orders

A technique for developing orders that emphasizes to subordinates the results to be attained, not how they are to achieve them. It provides maximum freedom of action in determining how to best accomplish assigned missions. (FM 3-0)

*multiechelon training

A training technique that allows for the simultaneous training of more than one echelon on different or complementary tasks.

operational Army

Those Army organizations whose primary purpose is to participate in full spectrum operations as part of the joint force. (FM 1-01)

operational environment

(joint) A composite of the conditions, circumstances, and influences that affect the employment of capabilities and bear on the decisions of the commander. (JP 3-0)

operational theme

The character of the dominant major operation being conducted at any time within a land force commander's area of operations. The operational theme helps convey the nature of the major operation to the force to facilitate common understanding of how the commander broadly intends to operate. (FM 3-0)

*operational training domain

The training activities organizations undertake while at home station, at maneuver combat training centers, during joint exercises, at mobilization centers, and while operationally deployed.

*self-development training domain

Planned, goal-oriented learning that reinforces and expands the depth and breadth of an individual's knowledge base, self-awareness, and situational awareness; complements institutional and operational learning; enhances professional competence; and meets personal objectives.

*standard

A quantitative or qualitative measure and criterion for specifying the levels of performance of a task.

*task

A clearly defined and measurable activity accomplished by individuals and organizations.

*task group

A set of collective tasks necessary to accomplish a specific part of a mission-essential task.

*training and evaluation outline

A summary document that provides information on collective training objectives, related individual training objectives, resource requirements, and applicable evaluation procedures for a type of organization.

*training management

The process used by Army leaders to identify training requirements and subsequently plan, prepare, execute, and assess training.

*training objective

A statement that describes the desired outcome of a training activity in the unit. It consists of the task, conditions, and standard.

unified action

(joint) The synchronization, coordination, and/or integration of the activities of governmental and nongovernmental entities with military operations to achieve unity of effort. (JP 1)

warfighting function

A group of tasks and systems (people, organizations, information, and processes) united by a common purpose that commanders use to accomplish missions and training objectives. (FM 3-0)

References

Field manuals and selected joint publications are listed by new number followed by old number.

REQUIRED PUBLICATIONS

These documents must be available to intended users of this publication.

FM 1-02 (101-5-1). *Operational Terms and Graphics*. 21 September 2004. (Available online: https://akocomm.us.army.mil/usapa/doctrine/index.html.)

JP 1-02. *Department of Defense Dictionary of Military and Associated Terms*. 12 April 2001.

RELATED PUBLICATIONS

These documents contain relevant supplemental information.

JOINT AND DEPARTMENT OF DEFENSE PUBLICATIONS

Most joint publications are available online: http://www.dtic.mil/doctrine/jpcapstonepubs.htm.

CJCSI 3500.01E. *Joint Training Policy and Guidance for the Armed Forces of the United States*. 31 May 2008. (https://jdeis.js.mil/jdeis/jel/training/cjcsi3500_01e.pdf. [Accessed 12 November 2008.])

CJCSM 3500.03B. *Joint Training Manual for the Armed Forces of the United States*. 31 August 2007.

CJCSM 3500.04E. *Universal Joint Task Manual*. 25 August 2008. (The Universal Joint Task List is available at the Universal Joint Task List Portal, which can be accessed via a link from the Joint Exercise and Training Division Web page on the Joint Doctrine, Education, and Training Electronic Information System [JDEIS] Web site, https://jdeis.js.mil/jdeis/index.jsp [accessed 12 November 2008].)

JP 1. *Doctrine for the Armed Forces of the United States*. 14 May 2007.

JP 3-0. *Joint Operations*. 17 September 2006.

JP 3-31. *Command and Control for Joint Land Operations*. 23 March 2004.

ARMY PUBLICATIONS

Most Army doctrinal publications are available online: https://akocomm.us.army.mil/usapa/doctrine/Active_FM.html. Army regulations are produced only in electronic media. Most are available online: http://www.army.mil/usapa/epubs/index.html.

AR 350-1. *Army Training and Leader Development*. 3 August 2007.

DA Pam 350-38. *Standards in Training Commission*. 24 July 2008.

FM 1-01. *Generating Force Support for Operations*. 2 April 2008.

FM 3-0. *Operations*. 27 February 2008.

FM 5-19 (100-14). *Composite Risk Management*. 21 August 2006.

FM 6-0. *Mission Command: Command and Control of Army Forces*. 11 August 2003.

FM 6-01.1. *Knowledge Management Section*. 29 August 2008.

FM 6-22 (22-100). *Army Leadership*. 12 October 2006.

FM 7-15. *The Army Universal Task List*. 31 August 2003.

FMI 3-0.1. *The Modular Force.* 28 January 2008.

TC 25-30. *A Leader's Guide to Company Training Meetings.* 27 April 1994.

OTHER PUBLICATIONS

The National Military Strategy of the United States of America. Washington, DC: U.S. Government Printing Office, 2004. (http://www.dtic.mil/doctrine/jel/other_pubs/nms_2004.pdf. [Accessed 12 November 2008.])

WEB SITES

Universal Joint Task List Portal. (Available as a link from the Joint Exercise and Training Division Web page on the Joint Doctrine, Education, and Training Electronic Information System [JDEIS] Web site, https://jdeis.js.mil/jdeis/index.jsp [accessed 12 November 2008]).

PRESCRIBED FORMS

None

REFERENCED FORMS

None

SOURCES USED

Tsouras, Peter G. ed. *The Greenhill Dictionary of Military Quotations.* London: Greenhill, 2000. (Field Marshal Rommel's observation cited in paragraph 1-22 is taken from page 186b.)

Index

Entries are by paragraph number unless specified otherwise.

Entries are by paragraph number unless otherwise specified.

Entries are by paragraph number unless specified otherwise.

Entries are by paragraph number unless otherwise specified.

Entries are by paragraph number unless specified otherwise.

215

Entries are by paragraph number unless specified otherwise.

OTHER PRODUCTS

Books

THE MENTOR: *Everything You Need To Know About Leadership And Counseling*

THE TRAINER: *A Training Guide For All Ranks (This book)*

THE EVALUATOR: *A Comprehensive Guide for Preparing NCOER Evaluation Reports*

THE WRITER: *A Comprehensive Guide for Writing Awards*

Wear It Right! ARMY UNIFORM Book: *Answer Your Army Uniform Questions Instantly*

Wear It Right! AIR-FORCE UNIFORM Book: *Answer Your Air Force Uniform Questions Instantly*

THE MILITARY SPOUSE: *Useful tools and information for military spouses and family members*

Digital Products

Award Quick: *Helps you quickly and accurately write the awards your soldiers deserve. Includes citations, achievement statements, forms, and much more.*

The Complete Digital Reference of US Army Field Manuals: *This DVD Contains every Army Field Manual that is authorized for public release. A valid AKO login will allow users access to all other manuals.*

Counsel Quick: *Innovative software that includes all the forms, examples, and references you will need to quickly compose and manage US Army counseling statements.*

- *Counsel Quick Vol. 1: Places special emphasis on counseling typically conducted by first line leaders.*

- *Counsel Quick Vol. 2: Places special emphasis on counseling typically conducted by senior leaders.*

- *Counsel Quick Vol. 3: Even more counseling templates and references! Available July 2009.*

Rater Quick: *Contains the latest forms, examples, and references you will need to quickly compose and manage professional looking Evaluation Reports all in one easy to use program. We offer both OER and NCOER versions of this software.*

Library of Air-Force Publications: *Contains over 2,280 Air Force Departmental Publications categorized by title and series. Includes AFIs, Airman Handbook, DoD Supplements, Tongue and Quill (AFH33-337), and Career Field Education and Training Plans (CFETPs).*

These products are available at your local AAFES MCSS and online at: http://www.GiPubs.com